THE POWER OF PUBLIC IDEAS

THE POWER OF PUBLIC IDEAS

Edited by
Robert B. Reich

BALLINGER PUBLISHING COMPANY
Cambridge, Massachusetts
A Subsidiary of Harper & Row, Publishers, Inc.

International Standard Book Number: 0-88730-128-2

Library of Congress Catalog Card Number: 87-1371

Printed in the United States of America

Library of Congress Cataloging in Publication Data

The Power of public ideas.

  Includes index.
  1. Political participation—United States. 2. Public
interest—United States. 3. Public policy (Law)—United
States. 4. United States—Politics and government.
5. Policy sciences—Philosophy. I. Reich, Robert B.
JK1764.P68 1987   323'.042'0973   87-1371
ISBN 0-88730-128-2

Contents

Introduction

Robert B. Reich

This book is about the philosophy of policy making in America. Beneath the daily activities of elected officials, administrators, and their advisers and critics, and beneath the public's tacit decision to accord legitimacy to specific policy decisions, exist a set of first principles that suggest what good policy making is all about. They comprise a view of human nature, of how people behave as citizens. They also reflect a view of social improvement, of why we think that society is better in one state than another. And they offer a view of the appropriate role of government in society—given human nature, our aspirations for social improvement, and our means of defining and solving public problems.

These principles are often implicit in policy making. They may be invoked to justify a particular policy, but the ground from which these principles spring is usually taken for granted. To state them is to end the conversation, because there seems to be nothing left to say. Nevertheless, they draw on ideas that have been debated for centuries; later in this introduction I will briefly place them in their historical context. The current incarnation of these principles is intimately related to America's present political culture. As it evolves, so will they.

Our task in this book is to examine these principles critically and suggest a revised view of what policy making is and should be.

The Prevailing View

To understand the task we have set for ourselves in this volume, it is useful to consider the prevailing philosophy of policy making, with which we take issue. At the risk of considerable simplification, its core principles can be summarized as follows: people are essentially self-interested rather than altruistic and behave much the same way whether they are choosing a new washing machine or voting on a new board of education. These personal preferences are not significantly affected by politics, social norms, or previous policy decisions. The public good, or "public interest," is thus best understood as the sum of these individual preferences. Society is improved whenever some people's preferences can be satisfied without making other people worse off. Most of the time, private market exchanges suffice for improving society in this way; public policies are appropriate only when—and to the extent that—they can make such improvements more efficiently than the market can. Thus the central responsibility of public officials, administrators, and policy analysts is to determine whether public intervention is warranted and, if so, to choose the policy that leads to the greatest improvements.

These principles are familiar, not because they describe how public policies are actually made in modern America but because they shape the way public policies are typically justified and criticized. They suggest what is and is not legitimate for government to do, how policy makers should act, how they and those who advise them should think about public problems. Importantly, these principles also sound a cautionary theme: the supposed tendency for individuals to use public policies to get what they want for themselves creates a danger that those who have the greatest stake in a given matter will collude against the rest of us, whose individual interests in any particular policy are apt to be small. This danger can be overcome if policy makers carefully ensure that everyone's preferences are objectively weighed, alternatives are fully considered, and net benefits are maximized.[1]

The ubiquity and robustness of these principles in contemporary America is quite remarkable. They undergird the position papers that stream out of policy institutes and assorted think-tanks. They serve as the basis for memoranda of policy analysts in government and academe, editorials in prominent newspapers and magazines, learned treatises on public policy, court opinions crafted by judges schooled in "law and economics," lobbyists' pleadings, and administrative hearings. You hear them even when politicians or administrators talk candidly about what they think they ought (but may not be able) to do. Whenever people who deal in public policy want to be (or to sound) objective and technically rigorous in discussing solutions to public problems, they tend to employ these assumptions—sometimes tacitly, often without further explanation or rationale.

Such assumptions—about human nature, about social improvement, and about the proper role of government—have proven useful in several respects. First, they are appropriate to a heterogeneous society comprising a multiplicity of values and viewpoints, all of which need to be considered in making policy. Rather than assume a single, unifying "public interest," it is often more accurate—and safer—to assume that interests collide and thus tradeoffs are inevitable. Second, these premises direct policy making to practical, answerable questions: who wants this policy and why? how do we know? how much do they want it? who will lose by it, and how much would it cost to compensate the losers? why can't the market take care of this? what are the advantages and disadvantages of each alternative way of accomplishing the objective?

The prevailing assumptions also suggest ready means of answering the questions and reaching solutions. It is a matter of measuring what people want and analyzing the most efficient way of satisfying these wants, or of engineering compromises among competing groups purporting to speak for the self-interests of their members. Finally, the assumptions are sufficiently neutral and commonsensical that policies derived from them can gain broad assent, thus avoiding conflicts based solely on ideology or personal rancor. Compromises can readily be reached. For all these reasons, these principles together comprise what is taken for the policy-making ideal in present-day America. They offer a model for what politics *should* accomplish—*would* accomplish—if it were less corrupted by special pleadings, money, ideology, and bias.

A Revised View

For all its virtues, the prevailing view of policy making ignores other important values.[2] In particular, it disregards the role of ideas about what is good for society and the importance of debating the relative merits of such ideas. It thus tends to overlook the ways such normative visions shape what people want and expect from their government, their fellow citizens, and themselves. And it disregards the importance of democratic deliberation for refining and altering such visions over time and for mobilizing public action around them.

We look on this book as an effort to redress the balance. In our revised philosophy of policy making, ideas about what is good for society occupy a more prominent position. The core responsibility of those who deal in public policy—elected officials, administrators, policy analysts—is not simply to discover as objectively as possible what people want for themselves and then to determine and implement the best means of satisfying these wants. It is also to provide the public with alternative visions of what is desirable and possible, to stimulate deliberation about them, provoke a reexamination of premises and values, and thus to broaden the range of potential responses and deepen society's understanding of itself.

Our interest in the power of public ideas arises from several sources. First, many of the most important policy initiatives of the last two decades cannot be explained by the prevailing assumptions about human nature or social improvement. Consider the civil rights laws and regulations of the 1960s; the subsequent wave of laws and rules governing health, safety, and the environment; and the reform of the tax code in 1986. These policies have not been motivated principally or even substantially by individuals seeking to satisfy selfish interests. To the contrary, they have been broadly understood as matters of public, rather than private, interest. And this perception has given them their unique authority. People have supported these initiatives largely because they were thought to be good for *society*.[3] Nor have public preferences with regard to these policies been stable and preordained. Public support has grown and changed as people have come to understand and engage with the ideas underlying them. The official acts of policy making—enacting the laws, promulgating the rules, issuing the court opinions—have been embedded within social movements and understandings that have shaped them and propelled them forward. To disregard these motivating ideas is to miss the essential story.

Second, there is evidence that the most accomplished government leaders—those who have achieved significant things while in office or at least set the direction of the public action—have explicitly and purposively crafted public visions of what is desirable and possible for society to do. These ideas have been essential to their leadership, serving both to focus public attention and to mobilize talent and resources within government. Ronald Reagan has been perhaps the clearest example of this approach to policy making. His speeches, interviews, and press statements have not been simply devices to muster public support behind a particular initiative or to glorify the accomplishments of his administration. They have been means of educating the public in an approach to governance, creating a coherent framework through which the public would come to support a wide variety of initiatives and to understand public issues. They have also served to direct and mobilize a vastly decentralized and often recalcitrant government behind him.

Third, we have been struck by how much the initial definition of problems and choices influences the subsequent design and execution of public policies. The act of raising the salient public question—how to overcome welfare dependency or Soviet aggression, how to improve American competitiveness or reduce the budget deficit—is often the key step, because it subsumes the value judgments that declare something to be a problem, focuses public attention on the issue, and frames the ensuing public debate. When questions "catch on" in this way, it is not because those who pose them are especially talented at manipulating public opinion or linking preconceived preferences to attractive agendas. The phenomenon is more interactive than that, and preferences are less defined, more fluid. Even before the question is asked, the public (or a significant portion of the public) seems already to be searching for ways to pose it—to give shape and coherence to events that seem random and unsettling—and thus to gain some measure of control. Rather than responding to pre-existing public wants, the art of policy making has lain primarily in giving voice to these half-articulated fears and hopes, and embodying them in convincing stories about their sources and the choices they represent.[4]

These observations have led us to a somewhat different conception of the role of government in a free society. The prevailing ideal casts government as problem solver, intervening when it can satisfy pre-existing preferences more efficiently than the market can. Democratic processes, in this view, are primarily means for alerting policy makers to what people want for themselves. But if we are correct in seeing policy making, inevitably, as a process of posing questions, presenting problems, offering explanations, and suggesting choices, then the prevailing view seriously understates the responsibilities of policy makers, policy analysts, and citizens.

It is not difficult to tally preferences in this era of instantaneous electronic polling and of sophisticated marketing techniques for discovering what people want and how much they want it.[5] It is a considerable challenge, however, to engage the public in rethinking how certain problems are defined, alternative solutions envisioned, and responsibilities for action allocated.

To the extent that deliberation and reflection yield a broader repertoire of such possibilities, society is better equipped to cope with change and to learn from its past. The thoughtless adherence to outmoded formulations of problems, choices, and responsibilities can threaten a society's survival. Policy making should be more than and different from the discovery of what people want; it should entail the creation of contexts in which people can critically evaluate and revise what they believe.[6]

This suggests a different role for policy makers and policy analysts than that of the prevailing ideal. The responsibility of government leaders is not only to make and implement decisions responsive to public wants. A greater challenge is to engage the public in an ongoing dialogue over what problems should be addressed, what is at stake in such decisions, and how to strengthen the public's capacities to deal with similar problems in the future. Such an explicative process, properly managed, can build on itself: as society defines and evaluates its collective goals, it examines its norms and beliefs; in defining its purposes, it becomes better able to mobilize its resources and achieve its goals.

By the same token the responsibility of policy analysts is not only to choose the best means of achieving a given objective. It is also to offer alternative ways of understanding public problems and possible solutions, and thus to expose underlying norms to critical examination. The analyst can provoke such examination in several ways: by juxtaposing widely accepted but morally or politically inconsistent assumptions about certain public problems and their solutions, by questioning the conventional metaphors and analogies used to justify and explain policies and offering new ones in their place, by providing plausible but novel interpretations of large events, by revealing underlying similarities and patterns in the public's approach to seemingly unconnected situations, and by advancing alternative future scenarios premised on how society might cope with certain problems.

Policy makers and analysts will not spend all their time in such explicative activities; there may be relatively few opportunities for effectively redefining and evaluating social norms. But these responsibilities should be understood as critically important to these jobs. Our concern with public ideas, rather than with pre-existing selfish preferences, is one of degree and emphasis. The prevailing philosophy comprises a useful set of precepts for guiding much policy making, particularly where there is wide and enduring consensus about the nature of the problems to be solved, the range of possible solutions, and appropriate allocations of responsibility for solving them; and where solving the problems *as understood* is more useful than understanding them differently. The prevailing philosophy is less helpful—indeed, may forestall social learning—where these conditions are not met. Our suspicion—difficult to document, hopeless to prove conclusively—is that many public issues, perhaps most of those considered important enough to be discussed in the newspaper or everyday conversation, fall in the second category, in which definitions, constraints, and responsibilities are centrally at issue.

The Debate in Context

In a sense, these differences of degree and emphasis are aspects of a broader debate that has raged for centuries over human nature and the purposes and methods of governance. Do we as citizens dare entrust our collective fates to a government reflecting the demands of self-interested individuals? If not, what is the alternative?

The modern debate had its origins in the Renaissance, in the first stirrings of humanist thought and the beginnings of the bureaucratic state. By the sixteenth century, the monarchs of Europe had evolved administrative machinery capable of organizing finance, waging war, and issuing laws and regulations. These bureaucracies were populated by men who owed their positions to specialized training and administrative competence, not to feudal right. They were uniquely skilled in using organization to accomplish complex tasks efficiently. Bureaucratic absolutism was elaborated and refined in the seventeenth century by Louis XIV of France, whose specialized, hierarchical system provided a model for Prussia, Spain, Austria, and Russia. By the eighteenth century, "enlightened despots" were firmly entrenched on the continent, having subjugated the few institutions—the Riksdag in Sweden, the Dutch Republic—that could be called democratic. The rise of bureaucracy was thus a central event in the political modernization of Europe.[7] Even with the advent of modern parliaments in the nineteenth and twentieth centuries, the instruments of central authority and bureaucratic control continued to dominate the core functions of government in continental Europe. As Max Weber described it, "the bureaucratic type of organization . . . is, from the purely technical point of view, capable of attaining the highest degree of efficiency and is in this sense formally the most rational known means for carrying out imperative control over human beings."[8]

The rise of this new, rationally authoritarian form of government paralleled a growing concern about the governability of the masses. By the seventeenth century many thinkers had concluded that moral exhortation and the threat of damnation could no longer be trusted to restrain man's destructive passions. Niccolo Machiavelli, for example, warned that men are "ungrateful, voluble, dissemblers, anxious to avoid danger, and covetous of gain."[9] Thomas Hobbes foresaw the fragility of an order based on human passion and had concluded that the only alternative was a strong central government—a leviathan.

England, however, was evolving another alternative—*deliberative* government. Victory over the Stuarts had forestalled the kind of bureaucratic absolutism taking root across the Channel. In its place, the House of Commons was elaborating what Edmund Burke would call a "deliberative assembly," guided by "the general reason of the whole."[10] It was through deliberation that common interests and attachments could be discovered and developed, and passions thus be restrained. Burke recoiled from the egoistic philosophy animating the French Revolution, whereby

laws are supported only by their own terrors, and by the concern which each individual may find in them from his own private speculations, or can spare to them from his own interests. In the groves of *their* academy, at the end of every vista, you see nothing but the gallows. Nothing is left which engages the affections of the commonwealth. On the principles of this mechanic philosophy our institutions can never be embodied, if I may use the expression, in persons; so as to create in us love, veneration, admiration, or attachment. But that sort of reason which banishes the affections is incapable of filling their place. These public affections, combined with manners, are required sometimes as supplements, sometimes as correctives, always as aids to law.[11]

The notion that democratic deliberation would inspire ideas about what was good for society, and thus instill common attachments and constrain selfish passions, was widely discussed in England and America during the late eighteenth and nineteenth centuries. John Stuart Mill saw in democracy a means of developing moral and intellectual capacities "by the utmost possible publicity and discussion, whereby not merely a few individuals in succession, but the whole public, are made, to a certain extent, participants in the government."[12] American Federalists and Antifederalists both worried about the instability of a society based on selfish passion and spoke of the need for citizens' "attachment" to institutions and "affection" toward one another.[13] After touring America, Alexis de Tocqueville mused that "the most powerful and perhaps the only means that we still possess of interesting men in the welfare of their country is to make them partakers in the government . . . civic zeal seems to me to be inseparable from the exercise of political rights."[14] And by 1872 Walter Bagehot could conclude that "no State can be first-rate which has not a government by discussion. . . ."[15]

A third alternative for dealing with the passions of a more worldly populace was also being advanced at about the same time. Rather than rely on bureaucratic absolutism to subjugate the passions or on deliberative government to civilize them, this alternative relied on calculated self-interest to constrain them. This third view emerged from the musings of eighteenth century political economists of the "Scottish Enlightenment," like Adam Smith, Adam Ferguson, and Sir James Steuart, who regarded the discipline of the marketplace as the key to social stability.[16] Steuart argued that a population governed by rational self-interest would be more stable than one susceptible to appeals to general interest, which were likely to ignite the passions. "[W]ere a people to become quite disinterested: there would be no possibility of governing them. Everyone might consider the interest of his country in a different light, and many might join in the ruin of it, by endeavoring to promote its advantages."[17] The British utilitarians— Jeremy Bentham and his progeny—and the economists and sociologists who followed in their wake, shared many of these assumptions. Although, in their view, "every agent is activitated only by self interest," egoistic behavior was entirely compatible with the general good.[18] Indeed, they argued, each individual's rational pursuit of his own self-interest would yield the highest utility overall. Government was necessary only as a last resort, a night watchman to guard against encroachments on trade and the freedom to pursue self-interest. Its purpose was entirely instrumental—to help maximize individual utility.

The reigning American philosophy of policy making has drawn on these three currents of thought—bureaucratic expertise, democratic deliberation, and utilitarianism—but in unequal parts. Especially in this century, beginning with the Progressives' efforts to insulate policy making from politics and continuing through the modern judiciary's oversight of policy making, there has been a tendency to subordinate democratic deliberation to the other themes. As the "administrative state" has grown, its legitimacy has increasingly rested on notions of neutral competence and procedural regularity.[19] The "public interest" has been defined as what individual members of the public want for themselves—as such wants are expressed through opinion surveys, data on the public's willingness to pay for certain goods, and the pleadings of interest groups. The ideal of public policy has thus become almost entirely instrumental—designed to maximize individual satisfactions.

The tradition of democratic deliberation, with its emphasis upon what is good for *society* and its concern for citizenship education and social understanding, has been subordinated in part, I think, because of our culture's understandable fear of demagoguery and intolerance. Particularly since the 1930s, we have had ample evidence of the dangers of totalitarianism—of moral absolutism and social engineering toward some monolithic view of the public interest. It seems far safer to assume that people *are* motivated primarily by selfish desires, that social improvement *does* require tradeoffs and compromises among such goals, and that the purpose of government *is* instrumental—to accomplish such tradeoffs and compromises, particularly when private transactions do not suffice. The great virtue of the American form of government has appeared to lie precisely in its pluralism and ethical relativism, its *lack* of any overarching public ideas about what is good for society.[20]

But there may be greater dangers in failing to appreciate the power of public ideas and the importance of deliberation about them. In an era like the present one—when overall public purposes are less clear than during wars or depressions; when the ways public problems are defined, choices posed, and responsibilities tacitly allocated can make all the difference; when many issues are so technically complex that values are easily hidden within expert judgments; and when "great communicators" can hold center stage on national media geared to visionary appeals—our strongest bulwark against demagoguery is the habit of critical discussion about and self-conscious awareness of the public ideas that envelop us.

Our Project

Thus our challenge, and yours. These are questions and concerns that we have shared for several years, as teachers, scholars, and practitioners of public policy making. This volume will not end our inquiry, for the conclusions reached in the following pages are at best tentative. The book should be regarded as a kind of work in progress, our present contribution to a continuing process of deliberation about the place of public ideas in the formulation of public policy. Nor, for that matter, do we speak in one voice. Our own deliberations in the preparation of this book occasioned sharp disputes, even as they refined our sense of what we were trying to accomplish together. Readers will detect differences in our approaches, divergences in our conclusions.

Ideally, however, you will be drawn along on the same intellectual journey we have traveled, exploring the same questions, becoming captivated by the same puzzles and dilemmas. In Chapter One, Gary Orren confronts the prevailing assumption, basic to the reigning philosophy of policy making, that self-interest explains most of people's behavior when they act as citizens. Next, Steven Kelman presents evidence supporting the contrary proposition that people are motivated to act in ways they think they *should* act and are thus highly responsive to normative conceptions about what is good for society. In Chapter Three, Mark Moore explores why certain of such normative ideas are particularly powerful for organizing how people think about public problems and for mobilizing them to take action.

Our discussion then turns to the implictions for a democratic society. Philip Heymann argues in Chapter Four that government inevitably expresses powerful normative ideas about what is expected of citizens and what society is for, that citizens want government to undertake this function, but that this role also presents significant problems and dangers for democracy. In Chapter Five, Michael Sandel examines the explicit devices American society has evolved for constraining and legitimating government activity—a system of individual rights and procedural regularity—and asks whether that system can foster the kinds of common commitments and mutual obligations on which society depends. One means of resolving the dilemma, as I suggest in Chapter Six, is to affirm that, at least on occasion, policy makers' primary responsibility should be to foster public deliberation about where the public interest lies and what our common obligations are, rather than simply to render decisions.

The three remaining chapters examine the possibilities and limits of such deliberation in modern America. In Chapter Seven, Giandomenico Majone argues that policy analysts should think of themselves less as neutral technicians in the policy making process, more as advocates who advance alternative means of defining and solving problems. Ronald Heifetz and Riley Sinder suggest in Chapter Eight that political leaders can help citizens learn to take responsibility for defining and solving problems, by carefully pacing and structuring deliberative processes. Finally, in Chapter Nine, Martin Linsky explores the role of the media in public deliberation and concludes that they too can and should play a crucial role.

Several words of acknowledgement are in order. All of us profited greatly from the continued interest, encouragement, and critical judgment of our colleagues and students. In particular, John Montgomery, Raymond Vernon, Andrew Nevin, and John Donahue debated our theses and offered useful suggestions. Hale Champion, Bill Hogan, Herman Leonard, Richard Neustadt, Michael O'Hare, Dennis Thompson, and Richard Zeckhauser commented on several of these chapters. And Glen Tobin provided exceptional research support.

CHAPTER 1

Beyond Self-Interest

Gary R. Orren

The scene is familiar. Commuters driving to work discover that an accident has occurred ahead. Most decide to slow down a bit in order to inspect the wreckage. Before long, traffic slows to a frustrating crawl. Each driver gets only a ten-second glance at the accident's aftermath, but ends up spending an extra ten minutes caught in traffic. Had the drivers reflected on the cumulative consequences of slowing down or had they made a decision as a group, they probably would have forgone the look and avoided the delay.

In *Micromotives and Macrobehavior*, Thomas Schelling examines just such phenomena, analyzing the process by which the pursuit of individual self-interest is translated into aggregate social patterns, often in striking and unexpected ways.[1] This chapter takes more or less the reverse position, arguing that collectively held values—macromotives, if you will—are powerful determinants of individual action, or microbehavior.

People do not act simply on the basis of their perceived self-interest, without regard to the aggregate consequences of their actions. They are also motivated by values, purposes, ideas, goals, and commitments that transcend self-interest or group interest. The Senate's rejection of the proposed Family Assistance Plan provides an illustration. By any accounting of individual or regional economic self-interest, Southerners would have been the major beneficiaries of the legislation, which would have provided a guaranteed income to poor families. Yet Southerners, both blacks and whites, were the group most strongly opposed to the program. The explanation for this seeming paradox lies in the widely shared attitudes of the region: whites opposed income redistribution and feared racial equality; blacks distrusted any proposal sponsored by the Nixon White House.[2] At times, in effect, people act as they feel they *should* act.

This is particularly true in the realm of policy making. David Hume exaggerated only slightly when he said that government is founded "on opinion only." Widely held ideas, broadly shared values, and intensely felt opinions are the most powerful forces in political life. The success of virtually every public action depends on the strength of shared judgments behind it. "With public sentiment on its side," said Abraham Lincoln, "everything succeeds; with public sentiment against it, nothing succeeds."

Hume and Lincoln were not simply mouthing the tenets of democracy. Rather, they recognized the power of shared purposes. Although they might have shuddered at the term, they realized that policies have macromotives derived from the climate of ideas, the "general will," or the Zeitgeist. These motives are at least as important in understanding public policy as are bureaucratic politics and economic efficiency. Indeed, analysts who emphasize the "inside game" to the exclusion of national moods or prevailing ideas are making a mistake akin to attributing the *Titanic* disaster to the behavior of the crew. Unfortunately, macromotives play only a limited role in the economic and political science models we use to analyze public policy, the conceptual lenses through which we interpret the political world.

In economics, the dominant model is neoclassical microeconomics, which envisions a world inhabited by rational, utility-maximizing individuals and profit-maximizing firms. In political science, the dominant model—at least in the United States—has been pluralism, a less precise but still mechanistic vision of competition among groups, each seeking to advance its own interests. The main alternative to these two models, Marxist theory, also grants little importance to ideas and shared values. These models have contributed enormously to the understanding of political and economic phenomena. But as their most distinguished expositors confess, often they cannot fully explain or reliably predict how individuals behave, how individual preferences are translated into social outcomes, and how society decides when to intervene to modify those outcomes. As practical tools, then, these models are far from adequate. I believe this is because none of them admits a central role for shared values.

Economics

"The first principle of Economics is that every agent is actuated by self-interest."[3] The standard neoclassical economic model treats ideas, beliefs, and values as "exogenous" elements beyond analysis. They are acknowledged only to the extent that they determine the initial desires of individuals. Each person has a set of preferences, or a "utility function," which is predetermined and wholly external to the economic model. The issue is how people who happen to have such preferences behave. Individuals are assumed to maximize their utility as rational actors who calculate the costs and benefits of every option.[4]

On this foundation economic theory builds a surprisingly simple and mathematically elegant construct: the price-auction model, in which goods and labor are priced and allocated. Sellers bring their goods to a market, consumers buy them. Prices are shaped by the relation between supply of the commodity and demand for it. The price of each good shifts until it reaches an equilibrium point where supply is equal to demand and the market "clears" since no one has an incentive for additional exchange. The markets for labor and for capital are assumed to work in precisely the same manner as those for physical commodities. Buyers (usually firms) and sellers (laborers or owners of capital) interact to generate equilibrium prices for labor and capital.

Like any model, this one tends to oversimplify complex reality. Nevertheless, much of economic and social behavior can be understood reasonably well in terms of this simple model of individuals pursuing self-interest without external coordination. The invisible hand posited by Adam Smith has been surprisingly effective in harmonizing this self-interested behavior. The model is so attractive, in fact, that Smith and his heirs have upheld it not only as a description of what actually happens but also as a prescription for what should happen.

On at least three levels, however, the neoclassical model yields an incomplete and often misleading picture of social affairs.[5] At the level of individual preferences, where the model should be strongest, it leaves out much that would help us explain human behavior. At the level of societal convention, the simplest version of the model ignores the widely shared beliefs and institutions that shape and constrain the very forces with which it is most concerned. Finally, at the level of public policy, where values and ideology determine the nature and extent of public intervention in the economy, neoclassical economics is largely silent.

With regard to individual preferences and behavior, the market model slights values in two important ways. First, it does not allow tastes to re-enter the calculus after their initial role in determining consumption patterns. Second, it distorts the role of values by treating them as a sort of consumption choice.

The model concedes that consumers may have all manner of

unusual tastes, but insists that they stick to rationally and predictably maximizing their utility, given these tastes. Evidence of the mutability and irrationality of consumer preferences abounds, however.[6] Producers are even more constrained by the market model, deprived of all personal discretion and forced to employ workers entirely according to the price of labor and its marginal product. Most of what real business managers do—decide whom to hire, what and how to produce, set prices, determine quantities, and take risks—is excluded from the simplest version of the microeconomic model. Yet clearly, there is more to employer behavior than market demand. Since the consumer does not care who makes his widget, the persistence of phenomena such as racism and sexism cannot be explained without introducing employers' values into the calculations.

Economic theory also ignores the tangle of motivation behind the sale of labor. Yet that motivation should be critical to the neoclassical theory, for as motivation varies, so presumably does the marginal product of labor. Collectively held beliefs about what constitutes a fair wage surely influence the distribution of wages, since employers have an incentive to establish wage structures that employees deem fair.

The second broad objection to the treatment of values in the market model—that they are reduced to a consumable good—is aptly illustrated by Milton Friedman's characterization of racial prejudice:

The man who exercises discrimination pays a price for doing so. He is, as it were, "buying" what he regards as a "product." It is hard to see that discrimination can have any meaning other than a "taste" of others that one does not share. We do not regard it as discrimination—or at least not in the invidious sense—if an individual is willing to pay a higher price to listen to one singer than another, although we do if he is willing to pay a higher price to have services rendered to him by a person of one color than by a person of another.[7]

According to this view, an individual who supports a charitable organization is simply gathering utility from the consumption of the good known as charity. It is traded off against the utility of spending the same amount of money to purchase a book or any other consumer good. But such a definition of utility maximization renders the concept all but meaningless. It is "just a fancy way of saying that individuals do whatever individuals do," says Lester Thurow. "By definition, there is no such thing as an individual who does not maximize his utility."[8] The great English essayist and historian Thomas Macaulay was one of the first to make this criticism, in his 1829 review of James Mill's *Essay on Government*:

When we see the actions of a man, we know with certainty what he thinks his interest to be. But it is impossible to reason with certainty from what *we* take to be his interest to his actions. One man goes without a dinner, that he may add a shilling to a hundred thousand pounds: another runs in debt to give balls and masquerades. One man cuts his father's throat to get possession of his old clothes: another hazards his own life to save that of an enemy. One man volunteers on a forlorn hope: another is drummed out of a regiment for cowardice. Each of these men has, no doubt, acted from self-interest. But we gain nothing by knowing this, except the pleasure, if it be one, of multiplying useless words. In fact, this principle is just as recondite, and just as important, as the great truth that whatever is, is. . . . And it is . . . idle to attribute any importance to a proposition which, when interpreted, means only that a man had rather do what he had rather do.⁹

This tautology leads economists to beg what are often the most interesting questions: why and how preferences change or resist pressure to change. To move beyond qualitatively useful but quantitatively imprecise predictions, the models must go further, attempting to explain how values are formed and how *interdependent* utility functions— *shared* values—affect social and economic equilibria.

In addition to shaping individual behavior, values also play a societal role, defining how the economic game will be played and what outcomes are acceptable. For example, the market's allocation of resources indisputably depends on initial claims and ongoing adjustment of property rights; and it is values that create and preserve the very idea of property rights. Rights to employment, or to free education, or to free health care, or to a minimum standard of living are not determined by economics, yet all these ideas are critical to the shape of economic outcomes. Shared values and ideology also determine the extent to which property owners may engage in self-interested maximization. Although owners of buildings may ordinarily charge whatever rent they desire, we often limit that right by controlling rents. Similarly, shop owners may charge what the market will bear in normal times, but in an emergency we regard it as unethical to double bread prices. These property rights are absolute only within limits set by shared values. Individuals may behave in self-interested ways, but only within the limits acceptable to society. General beliefs define, broadly, what can, what cannot, and what *must* be done, without written rules or government fiat. Process matters as well as results.

Shared values play a third role in the economic realm: shaping public policies that affect economic outcomes. Such policies are generally not reflected in the workings of the microeconomic model. As originally conceived, the model imagines no role for government, except establishing and enforcing rules like property rights, contracts, and law and order, which keep the free market running smoothly. In a perfectly competitive market, welfare is to be pursued in the private sector, not the public arena, with each individual maximizing on his or her own behalf.

Nowadays, however, microeconomics has much to say about public policy. Two of its offshoots—welfare economics and the theory of market failure—provide frameworks for probing the ends and means of government action.

Welfare economics builds on the premises of the neoclassical model: individuals are the best judges of their own welfare, social welfare consists of the sum total of individual welfares, people try to maximize their preferences, individual preferences are best revealed in the choices they make in competitive markets, and exchanges in such markets will yield economically optimum results (i.e., it will be impossible to improve one person's lot without hurting the welfare of another). Followed to its logical conclusion, this line of reasoning furnishes a way to judge the costs and benefits of public as well as private action. The claim is that the observed market prices of goods and services (or inferences about what individuals would be willing to pay for them) provide a rough approximation of the social value that citizens assign to them. By extension, these prices can be related to the effects of particular public policies in order to calculate the policies' social value. The policies that maximize net social benefits are deemed the most desirable.[10]

Economists are well aware that the many restrictive assumptions of microeconomics—including the welfare economics model—are rarely met in the real world. An accepted part of modern economic discourse, therefore, is the theory of "market failure": government intervention is justified to correct the shortcomings of imperfectly functioning markets.[11] Market imperfections include such things as unequal access to information among consumers or producers, impediments to market entry or mobility, inadequately competitive markets (monopoly or oligopoly), economic externalities (situations where some costs or benefits accrue to bystanders not directly involved in economic transactions), or public goods (commodities almost all of whose benefits or costs are shared by everyone). Even the most devoted free market advocates accept some government intervention to correct market failures and thus improve economic efficiency.

The principles of welfare economics and the theory of market failure provide convenient guidelines for analysts and practitioners of public policy. They offer criteria for deciding what goals government should set and for judging the consequences of policy action. In each case, however, the emphasis on maximizing individual preferences leaves little room for the role of broadly shared values.

The utilitarian criteria of welfare economics provide no clear-cut method for comparing the social welfare of one policy with that of another, or for weighing the satisfactions of some individuals against the satisfactions of others.[12] The reason is that such comparisons inevitably turn on widely shared values, collective purposes, public moods, and ethical norms—phenomena that are notably absent from the microeconomic model.

In his subtle and elegant critique of welfare economics, the philosopher I.M.D. Little argues that economists miss the point when they ignore or downplay the importance of values and norms:

Welfare economics and ethics cannot . . . be separated. They are inseparable because the welfare terminology is a value terminology. It may be suggested that welfare economics could be purged by the strict use of a technical terminology, which, in ordinary speech, had no value implications. The answer is that it could be, but it would no longer be welfare economics. It would then consist of an uninterpreted system of logical deductions, which would not be about anything at all, let alone welfare. As soon as such a system was held to be about anything, for example, welfare or happiness, it would once again be emotive and ethical. Getting rid of value judgements would be throwing the baby away with the bathwater. The subject is one about which nothing interesting can be said without value judgements, for the reason that we take a moral interest in welfare and happiness.[13]

Yet in practice, the language of values and ethics—the language of rights, obligations, and equity so prominent in public policy—is alien to welfare economics. That model rests squarely on the principles of individual self-interest, not collective ideas and purposes.

Nor can the theory of market failure rescue the microeconomic model as it applies to public policy. It falls short as a prescription for government policy making. On the one hand, government initiatives are necessary for reasons other than seeking greater economic efficiency through market corrections. For example, governments legitimately intervene in society in order to foster a more desirable (possibly more equitable) distribution of resources, to guarantee important rights of citizenship, to require or encourage citizens to perform certain civic duties, and to pursue vital social goals (such as promoting education and health). On the other hand, market failure alone is not a sufficient condition for government action, since governments may perform even worse than the malfunctioning market.[14]

Politics

In the realm of politics the reigning model is pluralism. Like microecoomics, pluralism is both a descriptive model of how the world works and, for some, a blueprint of how it ought to work. It has contributed much to our understanding of social affairs. But like the microeconomic model, pluralism has generally neglected the role of shared values.[15]

Pluralism is a less precise model than microeconomics, with many idiosyncratic variations that make it difficult to reduce the concept to its essential elements.[16] The generic pluralist analysis begins by asserting that political power and resources, while perhaps not evenly distributed, are widely dispersed. It then notes the tendency of individuals with similar interests to form groups. Whereas microeconomics shines the spotlight on the individual, pluralism takes the group as its prime unit of analysis. In a manner reminiscent of microeconomic competition, a multiplicity of groups seek to advance their interests by using their resources to maximum advantage. The outcome, a parallelogram of forces, is determined in a kind of political market through the pushing and pulling among the groups.

Though uncoordinated, such a system rests on certain underlying conditions. For example, several pluralist writers have emphasized the stabilizing effect of "overlapping memberships"; each American is attached to more than one group and thus tends to have multiple loyalties. Overlapping memberships moderate political passions, since almost everyone has more than one perspective on political questions. Moreover, just as microeconomics assumes that contracts will be honored, pluralism assumes that consensus on basic democratic

norms—due process, free speech, and other political rights—is necessary to control conflict and permit harmonious resolution of differences. Nevertheless, the model gives scant attention to the role of
values that cut across groups in defining "interests," creating and
maintaining groups, and motivating the political behavior of groups
and individuals. Like tastes in the microeconomic model, interests are
taken as given. They are generally equated with the "self-interest" of
the group. Even the formation of groups themselves is treated
essentially as an exogenous process, since the existence of groups
depends on the existence of shared interests. As a result, pluralism
cannot satisfactorily explain either the political changes that occur
without apparent shifts in economic or demographic patterns or the
persistence of the status quo when changes seem to demand political
shifts.

The pluralist interpretation of American politics has a long
tradition. In *The Federalist*, James Madison described a pluralist political
system, one with dispersed and shared power. Alexis de Tocqueville
chronicled a pluralist American society, distinguished by widespread
participation and a tendency to form groups. In subsequent years, a
rich literature has arisen to probe both the political and sociological
strands of pluralism. Since World War II, political scientists like David
Truman, Robert Dahl, and Charles Lindbloom have established the
pre-eminence of pluralism as a description of American politics and
celebrated it as an ideal toward which to strive.

Thus, like neoclassical economics, pluralism slides from description
to prescription. Pluralist political systems are applauded as fair and
desirable. Like the market, they are thought to be benignly self-
regulating: an invisible hand in the political market connects group
interests and renders once again a socially optimal result. Bargaining
and accommodation among a wide variety of groups mitigate conflict
and promote social harmony. As one American government textbook
put it: "in the pluralist conception, what begins as conflict between
selfish and parochial interests ends up promoting the general welfare."[17]

In politics as in economics, however, values set the boundaries of
the acceptable for the public agenda, the terms of the public debate, and
the ultimate shape of public policy. In the United States, for example,
certain redistributive policies are considered illegitimate because they
conflict with core values (such as ideas about property rights and the
proper role of the state). If we focus only on the debate within the

narrow confines of acceptability, without attending to the values that define that range, we may explain only a fragment of what actually shapes public policy and our predictions may be erroneous. A pluralistic perspective may direct our attention to battles over epiphenomena and peripheral concerns.

Shortcomings of the Models

The dominant models in economics and political science share many limitations because they rest on similar premises. Both are driven by the engine of self-interest, with individual preferences (in microeconomics) and group interests (in pluralism) taken as given. The calculus proceeds from personal pleasure and pain to aggregate social behavior. Advocates of both models often claim that these processes produce socially desirable outcomes.

The two models have something else in common: each in its own sphere is the major alternative to and critique of Marxist class analysis. Yet there are some important commonalities between the Marxist model and its competitors. Each slights the role of shared ideas. Marx denied that broad-based ideas exerted an independent force in history, arguing instead that cultural values and ideology were a reflection of objective economic class interests. "The ruling ideas," he wrote, "are nothing more than the ideal expression of the dominant material relationships." Ideologies were seen as mere camouflage, a superstructure of ideas generated by the bourgeoisie to serve its own ends.[18]

The microeconomic, pluralist, and Marxist models share two other views that are relevant to collective action and public policy: each pays little attention to the role of leaders and each takes a minimalist view of government.

A central idea in business education is that of the entrepreneur. Yet this figure is largely missing from the standard economic model, with its static conceptions of consumer preferences and producer competition. In a world in which consumer preferences are fixed, producers have no preferences, and labor works at a constant rate, there can be little room for leadership. In reality, of course, consumers face a constantly shifting menu of choices as new products and services are introduced. Indeed, according to Joseph Schumpeter, new product formation was the essential wellspring of capitalism.[19] And it is largely entrepreneurs who spur product development, not only by identifying demand but by creating it.

Furthermore, the dominant economic model assumes that producers compete solely on price. But in the real world of business there are many important dimensions to competition, including quality, service, and product innovation. Entrepreneurs have considerable discretion in choosing among them. These leaders can also evoke more or less productivity from labor; recent studies of America's most successful businesses have observed that their managers create a corporate culture that motivates workers and encourages innovation.[20]

In politics, the pluralist conception of leadership is at best fuzzy. One of the chapters in Robert Dahl's *Who Governs* is appropriately titled "The Ambiguity of Leadership." Dahl, espousing the pluralist point of view, concedes that leaders can be important, but views them mostly as led and constrained by the groups they purport to lead.[21] Like many other important elements, leaders simply appear exogenously in this model.

The limited role played by leaders in the pluralist scheme helped to inspire the power-elite critique.[22] That interpretation holds that power is much more concentrated and elites play a significantly greater role than the pluralist model assumes. In this view, leaders act largely as obstacles to change by defining public opinion, setting the public agenda, and controlling elections so as to keep themselves in power.

But sometimes leaders promote change. Groups rise and fall faster than group-based preferences would dictate, because leaders are central to group formation, transformation, and survival. Like economic entrepreneurs, political entrepreneurs not only respond to the interests of their constituents but also actively mold those interests. By framing issues in terms of fundamental values and by appealing to the sense of group identification, a political entrepreneur teaches group members what their interests are, or appear to be.[23]

Leadership is not a significant factor in Marx's theory either, for Marx believed that the iron laws of capitalism would lead inevitably to the development of true revolutionary consciousness. Indeed, Lenin's major contribution to Marxist thought was adding a role for leaders. Lenin believed that class consciousness would not emerge automatically out of class struggle, as in Marx's original formulation, but that a vanguard of professional elites would reveal to workers their true interests.[24]

Finally, all three models conceive of a minimal role for government. In the microeconomic market model, government acts only to enforce the rules of private property, ensure free competition, and correct for market failures. Pluralism regards government either as an arbiter of group conflict or as merely another interest group, albeit one with substantial clout. In the Marxist vision the state is an instrument of the ruling class and will ultimately wither away. Collective values pertaining to the proper role of government and the nature of government process—beliefs so central in a democracy that they often are the crux of political conflicts—do not figure prominently in microeconomics, pluralism, or Marxism.

Toward a New Vision

Although the microeconomic, pluralist, and Marxist models invite a variety of interpretations, they share a common deficiency: each underestimates the role of shared ideas in economic and political behavior. Political research over the last thirty years suggests that personal self-interest, group identifications, and ideological goals all influence thought and action significantly. Most public opinion surveys probe for all three factors: some questions aim to reveal people's personal interests (attitude questions and questions eliciting demographic data on age, income, occupation, and so on); others explore the nature and depth of the respondents' allegiances, associations, and loyalties; and still others seek respondents' views on broader policy issues.

With slight variations, these three general categories appear over and over in the social science literature. Analysts continually debate the relative weights of these factors in determining voters' choices, for example. Similarly, in examining what motivates people to join voluntary organizations, James Q. Wilson engages the same three categories, which he calls material, solidary, and purposive incentives.[25]

Of these three influences, self-interest plays the predominant role in our economic and political models. Yet the single most compelling and counterintuitive discovery of research on political attitudes and behavior over the last thirty years is how weak an influence self-interest actually exerts. Evidence has steadily accumulated that ideas and values are autonomous and do not merely rationalize action in accordance with self-interest. Often values arise quite independently of an individual's life experiences and exert an independent influence on political behavior.[26]

Common sense might suggest that people support policies that promote their self-interests and oppose those that do not. For all its plausibility, however, the empirical evidence for this argument is thin. For example, attitudes toward the war in Vietnam were found to depend much less on an individual's own experience with the war—such as personal or family involvement in military service—than on general views on foreign policy. Similarly, attitudes on busing to achieve integration had little to do with individuals' own experiences with busing in their communities. What counted was their beliefs and values about busing. And business people's attitudes toward foreign and defense policy depended on their general liberal or conservative outlook rather than on how closely their business was related to defense.[27]

The most consistent evidence for this disjunction between life experiences and politics is found in the economic sphere. Personal economic distress is only weakly related to political action. Being unemployed, for example, apparently has less effect on an individual's political values and behavior than does his or her attitude toward unemployment. Perceptions of the unemployment rate or beliefs about unemployment policies affect individuals' votes more than do their actual experiences in the job market. Certainly unemployment influences attitudes and behavior; it can be traumatic, significantly shaping what people do and how they view their lives. But the effects tend to be confined within the personal sphere; values and beliefs about public affairs occupy a separate realm.

The findings in relation to unemployment are echoed in other economic areas. For example, people's own financial troubles affect their voting choices much less than do their views on the state of the national economy. This undoubtedly reflects the commanding importance of individualism in American values: most people believe that they alone are responsible for their financial successes and that they, not the government, should shoulder the blame for their hardships. In short, pocketbook politics takes a back seat to macroeconomic politics.[28]

If ideas play an autonomous role among the public at large, one would expect them to have special potency in the attitudes of American leaders, who are better educated, more involved in political matters, and more articulate about them. And in fact, leaders' political values by no means reflect narrow self-interest. Their attitudes toward equality, for example, have far less to do with their demographic characteristics than with their leadership positions and general ideology. Though Democratic and Republican leaders differ widely in their views on equality, their social and economic positions, and by implication their objective interests, are much less divergent. Income, surprisingly, has no apparent influence on leaders' attitudes toward economic redistribution. Their views are shaped instead by their general values toward equality.[29]

Efforts to explain U.S. voting patterns in terms of economic self-interest have also failed consistently. "Solidary" factors (group psychological identifications, especially partisanship) and "purposive" goals (policy issues) are far more influential, analysts have found.[30] This is also true for political action in general. Although analysis may reveal that it is irrational for self-interested individuals to volunteer for any large-scale group endeavor (including voting), collective action is ubiquitous. This suggests that people pursue goals other than their material self-interest, including solidary and purposive urges.[31] Empirical evidence does not support the plausible notion, frequently advanced, that political interest and participation spring mainly from individuals' calculations of the tangible costs and benefits to them. Neither personal economic distress nor good fortune seems to enhance political participation. As one review of the literature on this subject concludes, "Political action may indeed be provoked when politics impinges upon cherished values, but these values may be largely independent of the material interests of private life."[32]

No one can deny that self-interest is a potent human impulse. Western society has gradually evolved—some would say inexorably marched—toward individualism. The rise of commerce and industry in the seventeenth and eighteenth centuries legitimized the previously heretical notion that the pursuit of private, material interests was preferable to other motives. The modern nation-state became the home of bourgeois society, with possessive individualism its hallmark, as people carefully attended to their personal welfare. Individualism, as Tocqueville observed with a mixture of admiration and anxiety, found a particularly friendly home in America. Indeed, individualism achieved its ultimate triumph in the United States with the development of an ideology that celebrates self-interested behavior, justifying the pursuit of happiness as something of a social duty. Though both scholarly and popular books bemoan the ever-growing commercialization and privatization of contemporary life, it is hardly surprising that self-interest has become the linchpin of academic models of politics and economics.[33]

This atomistic vision quickly evaporates when one looks closely at political thought and action, however. The longer one studies politics or participates in public affairs, the less it seems that our understanding of human behavior is advanced by the economic model of individual consumers competing fiercely for possessions and profit or the pluralist conception of political life as a clash of irreconcilable interests. The impoverished language and premises of self-interest can neither articulate nor explain powerful human sentiments like compassion, loyalty, affection, and duty. In most activities that really matter, what shapes people's views, moves them to action, and sustains their involvement is a collection of deep commitments and feelings reflecting social connections and attachments.

Beliefs appear to be rooted in two fundamental motivations. The first is the human desire for solidarity, for belonging, for attachment, for approval. Political ideas are "badges of social membership" that reflect complex social allegiances and antipathies.[34] People have few, if any, preconceived preferences divorced from their social relationships. Beliefs also reflect people's concern for general issues and larger purposes that transcend their own immediate situation. Few people have much appetite for abstract principles or coherent ideologies, but many cling to a set of core values and have strong feelings toward general politics.[35] The links between self-interest and belief are often simply overwhelmed by these enduring emotional claims.

From this perspective, politics has more in common with religion than with economics. Those wedded to the microeconomic framework can describe these broader values that transcend self-interest in the terms of consumption theory. Economists infer a person's preferences from his or her observed choices. But perhaps such first-order desires are governed by what some have called second-order desires or a meta-ranking of preferences.[36] These desires about desires are basic to human nature. They are the guideposts we commonly call conscience, morals, fundamental values—or macromotives. They typically originate in experiences unrelated to consumption, such as the lessons we learn in childhood.

The combination of these two vital sources of motivation—solidarity, on the one hand, and values or purposes on the other—creates shared values or shared purposes. This is the distinguishing characteristic of the political world: the acceptance of ideas and of commitments to goals by large numbers of people. In a democracy this mixture of values and solidarity is the richest source of political power. Commitment to ideas and purposes creates "will," and widespread agreement produces legitimacy. The combination is legitimate will. And with that, as Lincoln said, everything succeeds.

The power of shared values is felt throughout the political system.

At the societal level, it is reflected in the institutional arrangements we adopt to govern ourselves. As Don Price has eloquently argued, the United States' electoral and administrative machinery and procedures stem primarily from an "unwritten constitution" of collectively inherited political ideas—our antipathy toward established authority and our reverence for the specialized knowledge of experts. These strongly held beliefs have fostered a reformist and legalistic ethos that thwarts any effort to strengthen political authority and makes it difficult for us to develop coherent policies and manage consistent programs.[37]

Shared values are the main currency of electoral politics. Candidates compete with each other to articulate campaign themes that resonate with the hopes or fears of the largest number of voters. Office seekers call for peace with prosperity; getting the country moving again; law and order; respect for family, patriotism, work, and neighborhood; or getting the government off our backs. In their search for effective themes, they sometimes come up empty-handed and are reduced to tapping ephemeral issues. Occasionally, they hit upon deep-seated aspirations and anxieties of the electorate.

Widely shared values are the engine behind successful social movements and crusades—for abolition, women's suffrage, prohibition, consumer and environmental protection, and civil rights; against communism, drunk driving, and smoking. And as any veteran legislative insider will acknowledge, widely shared ideas and values are the driving force behind successful major legislation. The passage of the Voting Rights Act was impossible in 1962. Two years later it seemed inevitable. In that short span, equality of opportunity had become an idea so powerful as to sweep away the organizational inertia and political opposition that had obstructed it. In 1985 few people in Washington thought that a tax reform bill would be passed by Congress. In May 1986 tax reform legislation was unanimously reported out of the Senate Finance Committee, and in June all but three senators voted for it on the floor. As Senator Bill Bradley explained, "It shows the power of an idea [lower rates and fewer deductions] when persistently advanced can overcome the special interests."[38] John Maynard Keynes made much the same point: "The ideas of economists and political philosophers, both when they are right and when they are wrong, are more powerful than is commonly understood. Indeed, the world is ruled by little else. . . . I am sure that the power of vested interests is vastly exaggerated compared with the gradual encroachment of ideas."[39]

Yet shared ideas and values remain outside, or at least peripheral to, the main conceptualizations that scholars and policy analysts use to understand politics and economics. Though eminent and unconventional analysts have offered amendments to the prevailing models, the paradigms have not been toppled or replaced. Variants of models based on self-interest continue to be dominant.

The problem is not simplification itself. We will make little progress toward understanding politics unless we allow ourselves to invent abstractions for confronting the world. But we must always question how well the central principles and underlying assumptions of those abstractions approximate reality.

We should not expect scholars to ask this question readily or to abandon their paradigms without a struggle, even if the paradigms are inadequate descriptions of reality. After all, as Robert Klitgaard has observed, such models serve purposes beyond illuminating complicated subjects. The microeconomic, pluralist, and Marxist paradigms all spare their proponents the time-consuming task of gathering details or learning about other insights. In addition, they cause the initiated to feel frustrated with those who do not grasp the insight, and they degenerate easily into articles of faith.[40]

Understanding shared ideas and values is an enormous challenge. It amounts to unlocking the mysteries of human nature and human motivation. V.O. Key once wrote that "to speak with precision of public opinion is a task not unlike coming to grips with the Holy Ghost."[41] How much easier it would be to stick with the primitive notions that underlie our current models! Writing in 1767, the economist Sir James Steuart asserted that the "principle of self-interest" is the "only motive which a statesman should make use of, to engage a free people to concur in the plans which he lays down for their government." Otherwise, he explained, "the statesman would be bewildered," for "everyone might consider the interest of his country in a different light."[42]

For too long theorists have sought refuge in the principle of self-interest, ignoring those questions that might lead to truly useful models: where do values come from? how are they shared? how do they shape political and economic behavior? At the risk of bewildering a few statesmen, it's time we sought answers, and went after the Holy Ghost.

CHAPTER 2

Why Public Ideas Matter

Steven Kelman

As Gary Orren has shown in Chapter One, the conventional wisdom—enshrined both in Washington journalism and in the writings of political scientists and economists—is that public policy in the United States is driven primarily by the efforts of partisans to advance their private interests through government action. To some, like the pluralists of the 1950s, this purported character of the policy-making process seems desirable. They argue that self-interest protects citizens against fanaticism or that the competition of self-interested groups produces good public policy by an invisible hand that weights the features of policies according to the number and intensity of their advocates. Others, in the tradition of *The Federalist*, regard self-interested partisanship as inevitable and seek only to design institutions that pit ambition against ambition, thus "supplying, by opposite and rival interest, the defect of better motives."[1] Still others, from Common Cause members to "public choice" economists, deplore the implications of the domination of self-interest for the results of the political process.

At the risk of being considered hopelessly naive (despite some practical experience in government), I wish to argue for a different point of view. I believe that the level of public spirit in the policy-making process is reasonably high and that the presence of public spirit is important in understanding the results of policy making in the United States. By "public spirit," I mean the wish to choose good public policy, evaluating options against a standard of general ideas about right and wrong. Public-spirited behavior shows concern for others, not just oneself.[2]

"Public Choice" Scholarship and the Self-Interest View

Over the past thirty years the view that political behavior is dominated by self-interest gained strength in academic discussions as the assumptions of microeconomic theory were incorporated into the analysis of the political process. Assuming that people's choices are motivated by self-interested maximization—the effort to get as much as one can of the things one wants for oneself—economics has developed a remarkable body of theoretical propositions about the production and exchange of goods in the marketplace. These propositions have been powerful enough and (not unimportantly for scholars) often counterintuitive enough to earn economics the title of "queen of the social sciences"—and to generate a powerful urge among economists to apply their tools to the analysis of institutions outside the marketplace, from the family to the political process. Thus was born the field known as "public choice," drawing converts from the ranks of political scientists, and with a cachet of respectability in a world where not very many people have very much bad to say about people who have very little good to say about the way the political process works.

Writing in 1957, Anthony Downs posited "the self-interest axiom," that is, the view that political behavior is "directed primarily toward selfish ends." Politicians, in Down's view, "act solely in order to attain the income, prestige, and power which come from being in office . . . [They] never seek office as a means of carrying out particular policies; their only goal is to reap the rewards of holding office *per se*. They treat policies purely as a means to the attainment of their private ends." In fact, Downs acknowledged, people "are not always selfish, even in politics." But he justified his supposition of self-interest by noting that "general theories of social action always rely heavily on the self-interest axiom," adding that "practically all economic theory, for example, is based on this premise."[3] Five years later James Buchanan and Gordon Tullock made the same behavioral assumptions. "The average individual," they wrote, "acts on the basis of the same over-all value scale when he participates in market activity and in political activity."[4] Or, as Tullock put it in a later book, "Voters and customers are essentially the same people. Mr. Smith buys and votes; he is the same man in the supermarket and in the voting booth."[5]

Common to all public choice writing is the conclusion that, while pursuit of self-interest in the marketplace maximizes social welfare, pursuit of self-interest in the political process creates catastrophe. Scholars arrive at this view in different ways, however. Buchanan and Tullock, for example, argue that problems arise from simple majority rule. Other observers emphasize instead the baleful effect of interest groups.

Many of the arguments about interest groups can be seen as outgrowths of Mancur Olson's 1965 *Logic of Collective Action*.[6] Among political scientists, the most common criticism of the pluralists had been that the wealthy gain disproportionate power in the political system by their ability to give money to political campaigns or to hire lobbyists, as well as by their high social status and prestige. The poor could not wield power proportionate to their numbers because of their lack of money and education, and the overwhelming pressures of their everyday lives, which left little psychic energy for politics. Olson made the novel argument that *any* sort of organization for collective goals, whether by the wealthy or the poor, was problematic.

For Olson, the problem is that the benefits to be gained from group action are a "public good," to use the economist's term. If they come about, they are shared by all, regardless of the individual's contribution toward their realization. (If a law providing higher welfare payments is passed, it will benefit all recipients, not just those who worked to get the legislation enacted.) Therefore, it is irrational for self-interested individuals to organize in support of a government program that might benefit them. Each individual would do better to let the others organize and get a free ride from their efforts. Of course, if everyone takes that attitude, nobody will organize—and that was Olson's general expectation. He argued that the failure of the poor to organize need not result from any special lack of education or psychic energy: inaction would be rational behavior for everyone. Developing Olson's argument, economist George Stigler suggested that the propensity to organize depends on both the benefit each member has at stake and the size of the group.[7] Producer interests will generally be better organized than the far larger group of consumers, since government policies aiding producers may impose only a tiny cost on each individual consumer while offering enormous benefits to each producer. A benefit of $100,000 a year to a producer, if borne by 100,000 consumers, will cost each one only a dollar. Although a minority, the well organized will thus win out in the political process over the poorly organized.

This public choice analysis, based on the benefits and costs of organization, points to the danger that the relatively diffuse interests of citizens or consumers can be overwhelmed by special interests of any kind, not just the particular case of the wealthy. Auto workers may win restrictions on foreign cars; rifle enthusiasts may defeat gun control efforts. In each case, the political process will tend to subsidize the organized by imposing individually small (but cumulatively large) costs on the unorganized. (Economists often call this "rent-seeking" behavior.)

Public choice scholars have also applied the self-interest assumption to the behavior of government bureaucrats. Because they are monopoly suppliers of public services that people want, and because they know much more than their legislative overseers about the true costs of supplying those services, bureaucrats are able to demand larger budgets than they actually need, it has been argued. Since they act as "budget maximizers," the result is that "all bureaus are too large."[8] Others have argued that the growth of government is due to the right of government officials to vote. Government grows, writes Tullock," to a very large extent because the factor suppliers"—that is, agency officials—"are permitted to vote." They are a constituency for larger government and will inevitably elect a government larger than the median nonbureaucrat citizen would want.[9]

The growing influence of the public choice approach in studies of the political process was marked in the mid-1970s by the publication of two widely praised and influential political science books: David Mayhew's *Congress: The Electoral Connection* and Morris Fiorina's *Congress: Keystone of the Washington Establishment.*

Mayhew begins with the view that members of Congress are "single-minded seekers of re-election."[10] Because the connection between the behavior of individual representatives and final legislative results is difficult to pin down, and because voters generally know little about their representatives' actions in any case, the single-minded concern with re-election produces two kinds of behavior: "credit claiming" ("acting so as to generate a belief" among voters that "one is personally responsible for causing the government" to do something they like) and "position taking" ("the public enunciation of a judgmental statement" on issues voters care about).[11]

Both these behaviors have harmful consequences. It is easier to take credit for obtaining particular benefits for one's district, such as a new federal building, than for such vast achievements as, say, beating back inflation. Moreover, as long as representatives are clearly identified as publicly supporting the legislation their constituents favor, they suffer little disadvantage electorally if the bill fails to pass. The result is a government that is not necessarily too big or too small, but ill proportioned. There is too much particularized legislation of the pork barrel variety, and too little legislation dealing with general problems. And representatives put more effort into making impassioned statements, to show that they "care" about issues important to constituents, than in actually accomplishing anything. ("On legislation bereft of particularized benefits, "Mayhew writes, "the members' intrinsic interest in winning vanishes.")[12]

Fiorina's portrait of politicians is even more pessimistic. To the assumption that representatives will favor pork barrel legislation as a means to their primary goal, re-election, he adds the disturbing observation that they benefit from their constituents' problems with the bureaucracy.[13] Members of Congress have increased their ability to win re-election, Fiorina argues, by enacting new government programs that create bureaucratic nightmares and then helping constituents deal with those problems! This analysis suggests that government will inevitably be too large, for an activist government is required to generate the citizen complaints from which representatives can derive re-election advantages.

Writing in 1962, Buchanan and Tullock virtually apologized for their application of the self-interest assumption to the political process. Earlier theorists, they note, had generally assumed that the average political participant "seeks not to maximize his own utility, but to find the 'public interest' or 'common good.'"[14] By the late 1970s, however, Tullock could note that "the traditional view of government has always been that it sought something called 'the public interest'" but that, "with public choice, all of this has changed." (Tullock adds, with a bit of contempt, that "the public interest point of view still informs many statements by public figures and the more old-fashioned students of politics."[15]) The public choice perspective, which might once have been seen as conspiratorial speculation, had become a highly acclaimed insight of respectable scholarship. Times, and academic fashions, have changed.

Political Behavior and the Possibility of Altruism
Clearly self-interest plays an enormous role in motivating people. From the theory of evolution, one can argue that self-interest prevails over the long run because creatures who do not take a healthy interest

in their own survival and prosperity simply fail to survive and reproduce as well as those who do.

At the same time, it would take an observer not only cynical but also blind to fail to see that concern for others also can motivate behavior. In a sense this observation goes back as far as Aristotle's statement in *The Politics* that human beings are social animals who live in a community. People depend on others for the satisfaction of both material and psychological needs. There is a division of labor in production even in the most primitive societies. People gain approval, respect, and love from others. It would be surprising if the close webs of connection among people did not make individuals empathetic toward the situation of others.

Indeed, there is ample evidence that people experience empathy— and feel distress—when faced with the suffering of others. Laboratory experiments confirm such reactions, with measurable physiological changes, in people witnessing a staged mishap in which, for example, an experimenter falls off a ladder. In a dramatic experiment, soldiers' responses to highly realistic combat simulations were measured. Reactions to a simulation that led subjects to "believe that they were in some way responsible for the injury of a fellow soldier in an explosion" were compared with reactions to simulations of personal threats. The simulation of responsibility for another's injury produced the highest level of stress, researchers found, and "a level of deterioration in complex motor performance that was second only to being potentially under artillery fire."[16] Such empathy seems to be largely involuntary. One researcher observed, "It is hard for people to avoid empathizing with someone in pain or distress unless they engage in certain perceptual or cognitive strategies such as looking away from the victim or trying hard to think about other things."[17] And if distress is extreme and the time to react is short, many people will engage in "impulsive helping," behavior that occurs so quickly it could hardly have been preceded by an extensive decision process. Thus, for example, when a person with a cane collapsed in a subway car in a staged experiment, 90 percent of the subjects went to the victim's assistance in less than 10 seconds.[18] Furthermore, these reactions appear early in infancy: research shows that infants two to three days old cry in reaction to hearing others cry.[19]

The seemingly involuntary nature and early appearance of empathy in human beings suggests that altruism may have a genetic, evolutionary base, just as self-interest does. Individuals who cooperate to ward off predators (or to hunt or forage) increase the fitness of the cooperating group and promote development of "genes" for concern for others.[20] Even altruistic behavior that lowers the chances of individual survival can be selected in evolution, it has been hypothesized, if it allows others sharing similar genes to survive. The "gene" for altruism would be passed on through those who were benefited and shared a similar gene pool.[21]

Ethics cannot be reduced to biology. That some behavior has a genetic base does not mean that it is ethically right. (Homocide may have a genetic base as well.) It would be more appropriate to argue that genes, not only those that hardwire us for altruism but also those that allow us to reason, make it possible for us to think about ethical truths that it otherwise would be impossible for us to conceive. (There are almost certainly many truths that the human mind is simply incapable of understanding.)

In an effort simply to define altruism out of existence, some have suggested that showing concern for others is merely a special case of behavior chosen because it provides more rewards than costs. Satisfaction at having done the right thing is counted as a reward. Given that the behavior satisfied a cost-benefit calculation, continues the argument, it was selfish and not altruistic.

What is one to make of this argument, beyond any wonderment over the apparent eagerness to read altruistic motivation out of the human personality? It certainly is true, and an important insight, that the view that concern for others is part of ourselves suggests a fuller view of the self and its nature—a view that our satisfactions can be tied to those of others. Empathetic distress establishes a link between concern for oneself and concern for others since, as social psychologist Martin Hoffman puts it, "it has the property of transforming another person's misfortune into one's own distress."[22] Most people who display concern for others, and feel good because they do so, do not try to distinguish whether their "real" motivation is to help others or to feel better themselves, since they accomplish both goals at the same time. As political philosopher Joseph Carens puts it, people do not normally "regard the good to others and the good to themselves as distinct and independent motives."[23] The fact that this linkage exists does not mean that one type of behavior is "really" another. Furthermore, altruistic behavior sometimes provides few rewards. "I wanted to go to the movies tonight, but I visited my sick grandmother because I believed I had an obligation to" is a sentence that expresses thoughts that should be perfectly plain to most of us. Ethical behavior can result from values that we have reasoned toward, not simply emotions that assault us.

It would be a mistake to exaggerate the force of the inclination to show concern for others. Even utopian settlements have had a very hard time motivating members consistently to sacrifice themselves for the group. "Rather than proving that people will automatically choose the benefits of an affective, communal form of life if only they have the opportunity to experience them, the record of most nineteenth-century communes seems to indicate otherwise," notes political scientist William Kelso.[24] Despite the possibility of altruism, self-interest certainly plays an overwhelming role in human affairs.

How can people deal with these conflicting desires? One strategy is to weight altruism against self-interest in any decision where both are relevant and make the choice that optimizes one's total utility. Thus, the Boy Scout who can help an elderly person cross the street at little cost to himself will behave altruistically. If he would need to go to the ends of the earth to bring his friend a candy bar, he will behave selfishly.

An alternative strategy involves sequential attention to goals. Rather than weighing conflicting objectives in each individual decision, one may use different decisions to give expression to the different goals. One can try to reserve pride of place to altruism in certain decisions, while emphasizing self-interest in others.

Psychologically, such a strategy spares people the pain of choosing between desired, but conflicting, goals in each decision. Moreover, people may wish to make concern for others pre-eminent in some spheres of decisions as a way of demonstrating that ethics is important. One way to show something is important is to insist on treating it separately from ordinary things with which it might otherwise be confounded. This is, as Emile Durkheim noted long ago, the essence of sacredness.[25] Thus people may display self-interest in certain forums, altruism in others. They would seek forums to display an altruism that does not get expressed often enough in their everyday lives in the marketplace. Just as there is a time to be born and a time to die, there may be a time to care about oneself and a time to care about others as well.

Such choices would not be random. We dance at parties, not in the classroom; we contemplate art in museums, not in garbage dumps; we make love in our homes, not on the street—so too, can there be fitting forums for self-interested and for ethical behavior.

In arguing that political behavior is motivated by self-interest, James Buchanan notes that otherwise "man must be assumed to shift his psychological and moral gears when he moves from the realm of organized market activity to that of organized political activity." One would have to show "something in the nature of market organization, as such, that brings out the selfish motives in man, and something in the political organization, as such, which in turn, suppresses these motives and brings out the more 'noble' ones. . . . "26

But this may be true. There may well be features of public life that make it an appropriate forum for public spirit. In this alternative view, self-interest does not disappear from political life—it is far too powerful a motivating force in human behavior for that. But public spirit has a pride of place that translates into an important role in the political process.

Public Spirit and Political Behavior: The Evidence

The best operational test of the importance of public spirit in the political process is the ability of ideas to overcome interests in determining political choices. If self-interested behavior, whether of popular majorities or of interest groups, would dictate one outcome and general ideas about good public policy another, then the extent to which political choices reflect the ideas rather than the interests will constitute a strong test of the importance of public spirit.

Certainly, many political choices are crucially determined by participants furthering quite narrow selfish interests. Everyone has a favorite story of a highway built because a powerful member of Congress wanted it in his district or of a tax loophole sneaked through Congress by an interest group. As a general rule, however, self-interest becomes a less powerful influence as the importance of a policy choice increases. Self-interest may explain the location of a new federal building in Missoula, but it fails with regard to the major policy upheavals of the past decades.

How can self-interest account for the vast increases in spending for the poor that occurred in the 1960s and early 1970s? The poor were not an electoral majority, nor were they well organized into interest groups. (Public choice theorists sometimes point to the power of interest groups representing those who provide services to the poor. But it is hard to take seriously the notion of an invincible lobby of social workers overwhelming a defenseless political system.) What about the growth of health, safety, and environmental regulation during the same period? These programs were adopted against the wishes of well-organized producers, to benefit poorly organized consumers and environmentalists. (The organization of environmentalists into interest groups generally *followed* environmental legislation, rather than preceded it.)

In addition, the *growth* of government in the 1960s and 1970s does not seem to be explained by any biases in the political process that public choice advocates believe produce a government that is too big. Those biases are not new, and should have already produced larger government in the earlier period.[27] Furthermore, the big increases in government spending since the 1950s have not been in grants to localities, which provide particularized constituency benefits, but in various general transfer programs that do not allow representatives to demonstrate they have gotten something special for their district.[28]

Nor can the self-interest model of politics account for rollbacks in government programs since the mid-1970s. In the late 1970s, the greatest victories for industry deregulation were won in exactly those industries, such as trucking and airlines, where well-organized producers benefited from regulation and the consumers who would benefit from deregulation were largely unorganized. By contrast, little occurred in areas, such as environmental policy, where well-organized producers supported deregulation.[29] In other words, the pattern of deregulation was exactly the opposite of that predicted by the self-interest model.

It is also hard to see any simple correspondence between the economic difficulties of the United States during the 1970s and the response of reduced government intervention. Economic difficulties in the 1930s had been met with an expanded government role in managing the economy, not a rollback. Furthermore, well-entrenched interest groups fought to retain each government program President Reagan sought to cut. Often, only the diffuse interest of taxpayers in general stood on the other side. What made government grow or shrink, it seems, was not economic distress itself but the force of ideas linking the problems everyone perceived with solutions that government could adopt.

The stories of government growth in the 1960s and of its limitation in the 1980s, then, are both illustrations of the power of ideas. They reinforce quite powerfully the message that persuasiveness is the most underrated political resource.

Besides failing to explain policy decisions, self-interest theories give a misleading picture of the political process. To be sure, that process is hardly a model of deliberation and learning, with all participants open to reasoned persuasion based on a shared standard of seeking good public policy. But the view of the process that grows out of the self-interest model is a parody.

To public choice theorists, people's willingness to go to the polls is a paradox. The chance that an individual will affect an election outcome is so minute that the expected value of his vote is likely to be considerably less than the cost of deciding whom to vote for and getting himself to the polls.[30] Yet in the real world most people vote.[31]

Confronted with this embarrassing fact, exponents of the public choice perspective seem a bit like the economist who, as Walter Heller put it, sees that something works in practice and wonders whether it will also work in theory. It has been suggested that voting is rational because citizens receive rewards from "compliance with the ethic of voting" or "affirming allegiance to the political system."[32] These "rewards," however, are given for behaving in ways inconsistent with the model of self-interested behavior. If people thought the way public choice advocates believe they do, their expectations about how close an election will be should predict their likelihood of voting. Yet it has been shown that scores on a "citizen duty" scale are far better predictors.[33] The solution to the "paradox" of voting is public spirit.

Self-interest theories also do a poor job of explaining how the process functions in the institutions of government. They do not capture the importance of skill in making a good argument, of having the facts on one's side, of presenting an appealing public vision, or of having a reputation for seriousness and commitment. Yet close observers of the process identify these elements as critical to political success.[34]

And what about the influence of the media? At first glance that might seem consistent with the view that people in government seek only adulation and/or re-election, since one's treatment by the media certainly influences one's prospects for achieving those goals. But what generates good (or bad) attention in the media is generally whether an official has sought to do the right thing or acted selfishly. If no one thought it was important to try to do the right thing in politics, media criticism would not trouble its intended victims. The great influence of the media suggests that failure to show public spirit indeed *can* hurt elected officials, in their own eyes and in others'. The media's choice of topics for coverage also testifies to the strength of the public spirit ideal.

In a political system where self-interest was considered the acceptable norm, there would be no reason to "expose" instances of bias or corruption.

Congress is generally thought to be the political institution most closely resembling the vision of political process embodied in the self-interest literature. Yet it has been significantly misrepresented there. Mayhew argues that "the congressmen's lack of interest in impact has as a corollary a lack of interest in research. To assign committee staffs or the Congressional Research Service to do research on the nonparticularistic effects of legislation . . . would be to misallocate resources. Hence, generally speaking, congressmen do not so assign them."[35] But in fact reams of policy research are produced by the General Accounting Office, Congressional Budget Office, Office of Technology Assessment, Congressional Research Service, and the staffs of every major committee, not to mention studies advocates prepare for members of Congress. Mayhew's conclusion about lack of interest in research follows logically from his earlier statement that representatives do not care about accomplishing anything for which they cannot claim individual credit. That statement in turn followed logically from his starting assumption of a single-minded interest in re-election. It is the starting point that must be questioned. Regarding Fiorina's contention that Congressmen pass legislation to create bureaucratic problems they can then solve for their constituents it may simply be noted that he provides no empirical evidence for his view.[36]

Moving down from the level of the system as a whole, how important are self-interest and public spirit in the behavior of individual citizens and government professionals? Consider voting behavior first. The classic view of early empirical studies emphasized the influence of self-interest. During the 1970s this view was developed in works on the link between economic conditions and election results. The modern techniques of social science were used to confirm what every politician knew intuitively: incumbents do well in times of economic prosperity and badly during economic distress.[37]

In what has probably been the most interesting body of empirical political science research of the last decade extensive evidence has now been assembled to question this view.[38] The connection between overall economic conditions and electoral results remains very clear. But when individual economic conditions and voting decisions are compared, the results are surprising. If self-interest rules, one would expect voters to favor or reject the incumbents on the basis of the change in their personal economic circumstances. But surveys have shown there is no statistically significant correlation between voting behavior and respondents' answers to a question about changes in their economic situations over the previous year. But there are substantial correlations between voting behavior and a voter's view of economic conditions in society *as a whole*. This relationship holds even after controlling for the possible effects of personal economic situation on judgments of overall economic conditions. The observed connection between economic performance and the electoral success of incumbents does not result from voters' self-interest, but from their judgments about whether the economy *as a whole* is doing well, independent of how they are doing *personally*.[39]

Other researchers have investigated how well personal self-interest accounts for attitudes on political issues.[40] The findings are dramatic. An individual's views regarding U.S. policy in Vietnam, for example, were far less influenced by having a relative or close friend fighting there than by the respondent's self-anchoring on a liberal-conservative scale or his attitudes toward communism. Multiple regression analysis showed that a respondent's views on government national health insurance or guaranteed jobs programs were better predicted by his liberal or conservative ideology than by his own health insurance or employment status. In other words, conservatives who themselves had no health insurance protection were less likely to favor national health insurance than liberals who had coverage of their own. Similarly, corporate executives' views on foreign policy issues were more closely related to their attitudes on domestic liberal-conservative issues such as civil rights than to the extent of their company's defense contracts or investment overseas. In fact, the connection between the self-interest economic variables and foreign policy views was quite small.[41]

These data suggest that general ideas about what kinds of policies are right have an important influence on individual citizens' attitudes on many political issues. These ideas may also form a context that shapes one's interpretation and evaluation of personal experience. For example, having a relative fighting in Vietnam might reinforce attitudes on U.S. policy there given a context of general ideas that made that personal involvement a source of pride or dissatisfaction.[42]

One might interpret these data to mean that most people find it easy to display public spirit in their political attitudes because politics is not very important to them. On issues that really are important to people, including political issues, one might expect self-interest to hold sway.

Clearly most people are far less than obsessively interested in politics. Many citizens have weakly held opinions, or no opinions at all, on many political issues. People are not self-denying saints. Indeed, having political opinions based on general views about what public policies would be right may be a low-cost form of altruism. (There may be a real cost in taxes, however, at least for those whose views lead them to support expensive government programs.) Nor are most people philosophers or professional policy analysts. But views can be based on general conceptions of right and wrong without being particularly sophisticated. The point is that, in a world of many political issues and an overall modest level of interest in politics, one can expect a strong reservoir of political input based on general ideas of what policy would be right. Such input is likely to be an important factor in the policy-making process.

An individual's beliefs about what constitutes good public policy will often be influenced by his upbringing, social class, and religious, ethnic, or regional identity. That does not mean public spirit is absent: such a person may sincerely believe that the face of the issue he sees is the one that embodies good public policy. But self-interest is also involved, both because one's perspective is strongly biased by one's personal experience and because, in general, the policy one advocates will end up helping one's own group, class, or organization.

Where people have substantial personal interests at stake—interests that can be perceived fairly clearly without the interpretation that general ideas of right and wrong provide—and where some clear government policy will affect those interests, self-interest is likely to have a greater influence on the political behavior of individuals. Examples include tax policy and decisions regarding particularized government-provided benefits, as in public works construction. Thus, defense contractors were far more likely than executives in general to favor high levels of defense spending although their overall foreign policy views were not distinctive.[43] Behavior is also more likely to be self-interested when a policy alternative under consideration will make a person demonstrably worse off than he is now.

People in a situation promoting self-interest are more likely to organize into interest groups because of their strong concern with a certain issue. Groups such as the Synthetic Organic Chemicals Manufacturing Association, the National Association of Dredging

Contractors, the Society of American Travel Writers, or the National Association of Scissors and Shears Manufacturers, which are everywhere in Washington, would hardly seem to have been brought into existence by public spirit. Their behavior can be held in check by public-spirited norms in the system, which affect the way interest groups present their demands and the nature of the demands they can make on the political system. As interest group members and representatives participate in the political process, these norms may even influence their attitudes, so that they are no longer motivated simply by self-interest. But certainly the political behavior of many interest groups constitutes the most important exception to the conclusion that public spirit is important in accounting for the stands that citizens take in the political process.

What of professional participants in government? Elected officials, officials of government agencies, and judges receive rewards and bear costs far more significant than those of individual citizens participating casually in politics. Politicians see their names in the newspapers and their faces on television. They may be the objects of deference and adulation. And those with formal political authority experience the feeling of power that comes from the ability to establish public policies with the force of law. But politicians also work very long hours, spending long periods away from their families, for salaries that are low in relation to their responsibilities. Given the diversity of rewards and punishments, the motivations of professional participants in government are doubtless more complex than either showing public spirit or advancing personal economic interests. Furthermore, of course, motivations vary. Harold Lasswell probably got the study of politicians' . . . . motivations off to a poor start when he argued that they sought power above all.[44] Other approaches, based on typologies of politicians with different predominant motivations, are more promising.[45]

In the past, politics could be a fairly conventional job for professional participants. Studies have found that politicians tend to come from families of politically active people—just as the children of plumbers tend to become plumbers.[46] However, as the distinctive features of professional participation in government have become more marked, particularly for elected officials, and as the demands of the job and the opportunities for public attention have increased, politics has become a more distinctive occupation.

What advantages might draw people to government? The lust for power, in a general sense, is not a *distinctive* advantage of a career in government. Business leaders doubtless exercise greater power within their own firms, with fewer checks against its exercise, than do participants in the political process of a democratic society. "The search for the jugular of power," notes political scientist Robert Lane, "may very likely lead to the world of finance, journalism, or industry instead of politics."[47] It is unlikely that the power-hungry will go into politics in disproportionate numbers.

Two motivations seem relatively distinctive to government. One is the desire for attention and adulation. Media attention is tremendously important to many politicians, particularly elected officials. The entertainment world offers similar opportunities for attention, but, despite the example of President Reagan, few politicians have the aptitudes to make that a realistic career alternative. A second motivation is the desire to participate in formulation of the right public policies. Only participation in the public sector can provide this opportunity. People who go into politics for this reason may be "seeking power," but of a special sort—influence over public choices.

The sparse literature on why people choose careers in government is not very enlightening. It relies too much on self-reports of respondents, and many authors have an unhelpful bias toward psychoanalyzing their subjects. But the literature suggests that public spirit may play an important role. A study of Connecticut legislators, for example, found that most are significantly motivated by the satisfaction of producing good legislation.[48] In explaining why they went into government, top federal appointed officials emphasize the unique opportunity to help make the world a better place.[49] When senior civil service managers in the federal government were asked about their reasons for remaining in government, only 18 percent said salary was a strong reason for staying (or more of a reason to stay than to leave), and only 10 percent cited opportunities for promotion. Fully 76 percent noted "opportunity to have an impact on public affairs" as a reason to stay.[50] Another study concludes that the importance of pay as a motivator for managers is greatest in industrial organizations, less in government agencies, and least in hospitals and social service organizations.[51] Efforts to recruit people to serve as assistant secretaries in federal departments, which would often involve considerable financial sacrifice, rely heavily on arguments about serving one's country. Similarly, those who accept such positions often say that a major reason for their decision was the opportunity to influence policy in the direction of their own views.[52]

Some interesting insights come from vocational guidance tests used to help young people choose careers suited to their interests and inclinations. The most widely used test does not list politician as a possible occupation, but it does include public administrator. Significantly, public administration is included in a cluster of occupations, based on similar responses to the battery of questions, that also includes rehabilitation counselor, YMCA general secretary, social worker, and minister.[53]

The desire for adulation and attention can reinforce public spirit. People driven by self-interest will not be highly esteemed by others. Indeed, people who seek public admiration are by nature unusually dependent on others, and thus particularly likely to realize that others are important.

Public Spirit and Good Public Policy

I believe that high levels of public spirit are necessary if the policy-making process is to produce good public policy. This is, however, a minority view. More often it is argued that U.S. institutions have been designed so that the system can work well even though people seek primarily power, domination, and selfish economic advantage through government. This notion underlies two related but somewhat different perspectives, which might be called the Madisonian and pluralist views of the policy-making process.

By Madisonianism I mean the doctrine of American constitutionalism as presented in *The Federalist Papers*, which argued that political institutions should be designed to fragment power. With power divided, ambition can be made to counteract ambition. Selfish political actors will check each other, preventing any one from dominating the system. Policies can then be adopted only when there is wide agreement among these actors—and hence when the interests of the community as a whole are being served.

The Madisonian argument represents a political counterpart to Adam Smith's contemporary argument for the free market. With market institutions that allow free establishment of business firms, Smith held, competition for consumer favor would lead self-interested producers to serve the interests of the public. Altruism was not needed, because market institutions created an invisible hand that promoted such a result. Madison argued that our constitutional institutions would create a similar invisible hand, "supplying, by opposite and rival interest, the defect of better motives."[54]

The doctrine of pluralism, a product in its full-blown form of American political science in the 1950s, was partly a development, partly a modification, of Madisonian themes. Pluralists argued that it was important not only to spread power among the institutions of government, but among interest groups that pressure government. The major new contribution of pluralism was the view that interest groups helped assure that interests held with greater intensity received greater representation in political decisions. In this sense, pluralists saw interest groups as something that complemented majority rule. The interests of the greatest number are served by the democratic principle of one person, one vote. Interest groups provide an extra voice, beyond the vote, for people unusually concerned about an issue.[55] If a city plans to build a superhighway, the population at large has a relatively minor interest in securing somewhat more convenient transportation. They will be represented through majority rule. But residents of the area through which the highway will pass can organize an interest group to protest construction.

With pluralist institutions, public spirit seems unnecessary to achieve good public policy. If each individual votes his self-interest and groups are organized around intensely important self-interests, then the pressures on the political system will be a weighted sum of extent and intensity of interest that will automatically register, like an accurate scale, what constitutes the greatest good for the greatest number. (This criterion is different from "what is good for the greatest number," a simple expression of majority rule that takes no account of intensity of interest.)

These arguments trouble me, for several reasons. The connection between public spirit and good public policy is a straightforward one: if political discourse asks explicitly what would be a good public policy in a given situation, then the competition of ideas will be reasonably likely to lead to good policy decisions. The argument that a certain institutional design, whether Madisonian or pluralist, will achieve good public policy is much more circuitous. It does not require—indeed, its very point is not to require—that any participant in the system actually intend to achieve good policy. The argument proceeds indirectly by establishing institutional mechanisms that will tend to produce *policies with certain features*, not policies that are chosen because they are good. With Madisonian institutions, government will be able to act only where there is wide consensus—consensus sufficient to overcome the fragmentation of power in the system. With pluralist institutions, adopted policies will weight number and intensity so as to produce the greatest good for the greatest number. But will policies with these features indeed turn out to be good policies?

The Madisonian model is a good one for protecting certain kinds of rights against *interference* by an overbearing majority—for example, rights to freedom of speech, of religion, of assembly, and of liberty of action. But if one believes that individuals also enjoy certain rights to social *action*—such as a right to life that encompasses positive social actions to save lives that otherwise would be lost, or a right to a minimum standard of living—then the protection of rights encouraged by the Madisonian model is incomplete.

The Madisonian model makes government action difficult, inhibiting undue interference with minority interests, but also impeding positive support of minorities. Thus, for example, Madisonian institutions would help prevent construction of a superhighway without efforts to locate its path so as to minimize disruption. But they would not help residents of a community near an airport who need government action to change airline flight patterns that are drowning their lives in noise. And they can make it more difficult to satisfy the legitimate interests of the majority (when, for example, the majority is sufficiently large that the sum of its interests, though individually modest, outweighs even the intense interests of the minority). In short, Madisonian institutions cast far too wide a net. To protect the rights or the intense interests of minorities against government interference, they make it more difficult to produce government action of *any* sort. Without public spirit, I believe, Madisonian institutions therefore cannot be trusted to produce good public policy.

Pluralist institutions also fail the test, though for different reasons. A pure pluralist system, without Madisonian features, will not be biased against government action, but will create two other problems. One is the failure to protect rights when the vulnerable group is not large or intense enough to overcome majority opposition. Thus, for example, pluralism gives little protection to a small group of unpopular people whom the majority would enjoy persecuting. The second problem is that in practice interest-group formation is unlikely to reflect intensity of interest with perfect accuracy. In particular, differences in wealth can confound differences in intensity of view. A poor person whose life is at stake may not be able to influence the system as much as a wealthy one with only moderate interest in the results.[56]

In short, policies with the features encouraged by either Madisonian or pluralist institutional design will not necessarily be good policies. There are other problems as well with the institutional design approach. For example, how could the decision to adopt the required Madisonian or pluralist institutions be made and sustained in a world where public behavior is simply driven by self-interest?

To establish procedures most likely to produce good public policy, proposed alternatives—whether Madisonian constitutionalism, pluralism, or some other option—need to be evaluated in terms of their ability to encourage good choices. In theory, one could have a system in which some self-interested participants articulate their interests and others disinterestedly establish procedures for mutual adjustment among the partisans. But it is hard to see how such a division of labor could be sustained in practice. If politics is generally seen as an arena for articulation of one's own interests alone, where could the public-spirited participants be found? And how could candidates be selected to establish procedures for the process? It is hardly safe to assume that self-interested parties will share an interest in choosing disinterested procedures. Because different procedures bestow different advantages, advocates will disagree about what procedures they want. Without public spirit, arguments about procedures will tend to be resolved by the law of the jungle.

Furthermore, the constitutional design of institutions for policy making leaves undetermined many details of how the system will work. Choices must continually be made, on a level of detail far less cosmic than the Constitution of the United States, about procedures for making political choices. Should a certain bill be sent to the finance committee or the commerce committee of the Senate? Should the White House be able to stop a regulatory agency from establishing a certain government regulation? Even apparently small procedural choices often have a large influence on whether good policies are ultimately chosen. Yet such procedural choices must be made all the time, and in a world without public spirit they could badly distort a grand constitutional design.

The final problem with relying on institutional design to check self-interest is that it can generate a self-fulfilling prophecy. The controls signal to people that they are expected to behave badly. At a minimum, this removes any sense of responsibility from people already inclined to behave selfishly. They are told they can leave it to "the system" to correct their depredations. At worst, the signal may lead people to behave selfishly, as expected, when they might not have done so otherwise. Design your institutions to assume self-interest, then, and you may get more self-interest. And the more self-interest you get, the more draconian the institutions must become to prevent the generation of bad policies—draconian in the sense that ever-increasing restraints are placed on government action, lest the action be wrong.

There is still good reason to design institutions so as to restrain the self-interested. I would interpret such institutions as efforts to create room for public spirit by preventing the rapacious from exploiting those who are not out simply for themselves. Even if many participants in the political process try initially to do the right thing, such a situation is unstable if others behave selfishly. If others will not respect my interests or my rights, and if my public spirit leads me to regard my own interest or rights as only one consideration among many, then my own legitimate demands for myself are likely to be slighted. The public spirited will eventually conclude they have been chumps and should abandon ethical behavior.[57] Institutions that make it more difficult for the selfish to get their way may thus be seen as bulwarks against the collapse of public spirit. By decreasing the rewards for greed, they create a space where concern for others may flourish. They act as a sort of fallback or redundant protection for the system.

My own conclusion is that institutions designed to foster good public policy even in a world dominated by self-interested behavior are helpful, but they are not enough. Madison himself asked, "Is there no virtue among us? If there be not, no form of government can render us secure. To suppose that any form of government will secure liberty or happiness without any virtue in the people is a chimerical idea."[58] And Tocqueville acknowledged that "the best possible laws cannot maintain a constitution in spite of the customs of a country."[59]

Economists often speak of concern for others as a rare commodity that must be husbanded carefully so that some supply remains when it is really needed. This reasoning suggests that political institutions should not be designed to rely on altruism, but rather to channel self-interest, a motivation that is abundant.[60]

Of course, the supply of altruism cannot be expanded infinitely. But the economists' view—an application of their discipline's general principle that preferences be taken as fixed—is an oversimplified account of much human behavior, from playing the piano to showing concern for others. Observing and practicing public-spirited behavior are likely to increase the extent and quality of public spirit. Experimental studies confirm ancient wisdom. "We become just by the practice of just actions," stated Aristotle. "Accustom yourself to do good, before long it will become your chief delight," it is written in the Talmud. We should not foreswear public spirit in the design of our political institutions for fear that it will run out. Even if altruism is in limited supply, what better place to use it than government, where joint decisions affecting others are made? Better, if need be, to rely on self-interest in the marketplace.

Public Spirit as a Political Norm

How can we explain the role of public spirit in the results of the political process and the behavior of participants in the process, given the thundering force of self-interest? The answer must be that people see government as an appropriate forum for the display of the concern for others.

Because political decisions involve the community as a whole, people tend to think about others when taking a stand. (In making personal decisions, on the other hand, people think mainly of themselves.) Furthermore, in a democratic society political choices cannot be made without the consent and participation of others. Political demands are typically made by groups of like-minded people. This practical need for cooperation reminds people of the importance of others in achieving one's goals. Moreover, to win the consent of others, political arguments must be expressed in terms broader than the self-interest of the individual or the group making the claim. When poor people demand increased welfare payments or journalists demand freedom from censorship, they must formulate their claims in terms of general ethical arguments about rights, justice, or the public interest, or at least in terms of the interest of some other groups.

It is unlikely that public spirit could be sustained simply by an agglomeration of individual decisions to regard public spirit as the appropriate motivation for political action. Rather we need a social norm that it is appropriate for people to try to do the right thing in public behavior and inappropriate simply to advance their personal interests.

Since behavior is often contagious, norms have a cascading effect. The norms influence the behavior of some people directly, and others are influenced as people imitate behavior they have seen. As many experiments have shown, the more that people observe altruistic behavior around them, the more likely they are to behave altruistically themselves, and vice versa. In one experiment, the presence of other people enthusiastically giving donations at a Volunteers of America table considerably increased donations from the public, while the presence of a mocking skeptic deterred giving.[61] In another experiment, students were more likely to volunteer for an activity if they saw other students volunteer, and motorists were more likely to stop to help somebody fix a flat tire if they had just driven past an experimenter's confederate who was fixing a flat tire.[62]

Norms promoting public spirit can also change the behavior of self-interested participants. Their use of "public interest" arguments is more than the compliment vice pays to virtue. Norms about public spirit in politics restrain the content of the demands that the self-interested can make. And, by implicitly accepting that their claims will be judged against a standard of what policy would be right, the self-interested open their case to scrutiny and make it easier to reject. Indeed, norms influence all of us. Our behavior consists of a complex set of motivations we do not completely understand. The norm of public spirit tips the scale further in that direction.

Some experiments that seem to show the dominance of self-interest have been marred by a failure to incorporate the role of norms. In one influential experiment on behavior in committees, subjects had to make a group decision about where to locate a point on a continuum. Each subject was assigned a preferred location, and results were interpreted to show that subjects' behavior was self-interested and not altruistic.[63] But the experimenters had refused to satisfy subjects' evident desire for norms. As the authors explained in reporting their findings, "Subjects regularly asked, 'What are we supposed to do?' ('Get what's best for ourselves?' 'Do what's fair?' etc.) We shrugged off such questions with a poker-faced, 'whatever you want.'"[64] Such normlessness is by no means characteristic of politics.

Norms are crucial. They can also be fragile. Negative descriptive conclusions about behavior in government threaten to undermine the norm prescribing public spirit. The cynicism of journalists—and even the writings of professors—can diminish public spirit simply by asserting its absence. Such critics thus make prophecies that threaten to become self-fulfilling. In fact, I believe, the political process is marked by a surprising level of public spirit. That knowledge can counteract the dissolution of norms that are necessary if the policy-making process is to work well.

CHAPTER 3

What Sort of Ideas Become Public Ideas?

Mark H. Moore

Gary Orren and Steven Kelman have argued that ideas about what is good for society, rather than selfish interests alone, explain much of political activity and policy making in America. In this chapter I explore four subsequent questions: where do we see the effects of these ideas? how do we know that any observed effects are the effects of public ideas and not private interests? what sorts of ideas become important? and how can such ideas be created? If one thinks of public policy as ideas that have power in guiding public actions rather than as an abstract set of techniques for developing and testing ideas, then these questions are the most fundamental in the field.

Some Ideas That Matter

To begin my analysis, I offer some examples, drawn from my professional experience, of ideas that seem to matter. I want to insist on these examples as evidence for the propositions I will put forward. But it is probably more accurate to see them as illustrations. My account of how these ideas have operated is impressionistic rather than well documented. The examples are drawn from a relatively narrow range of substantive fields (principally criminal justice) and are hence not necessarily representative of all fields of public policy. Still, as one participates in policy debates and observes organizations in action, one cannot help being impressed by the apparent power of public ideas. Here are seven examples that impressed me.

Alcoholism and Alcohol Policy

For the last several decades, alcohol policy has been shaped by the concept of alcoholism.[1] In this concept, the world is divided into two kinds of people: normal people and alcoholics who cannot reliably control their drinking and therefore experience unemployment, marital difficulties, and more than their share of ill health and accidents. Alcoholism is seen as a disease rather than as a moral failing. And virtually all of the society's alcohol problems can be attributed to the behavior and condition of the alcoholics.

With this diagnostic conception, the solution to the alcohol problem seems obvious: the goal of public policy must be to identify and treat alcoholics. A conservative strategy to achieve this goal is to wait for the alcoholics to identify themselves by experiencing problems and then refer them to treatment. A more aggressive strategy is to develop early detection programs to identify problem drinkers before they get into difficulty or become alcoholic. At the extreme, the society could develop genetic markers to identify individuals especially vulnerable to alcoholism and provide them with drugs or teach them techniques that will insulate them from problem drinking before any problems appear.[2] The common thread in these approaches is identifying individuals who are now alcoholics or at risk of becoming alcoholic.

These ideas undoubtedly capture an important part of the alcohol problem and the policies that might be effective in controlling it. They are consistent with some important facts about the epidemiology of alcohol use and with some important new developments in biochemistry.[3] They are also consistent with a spirit that prefers to see the problem of alcohol as a result of disease rather than moral failing. This point is particularly important in light of the current historical interpretations of Prohibition, which view the enterprise as not only a practical failure, but an inappropriate effort to impose middle-class values on an immigrant population.[4].

But what if some significant portion of the alcohol problem is produced not by alcoholics, and not even by "problem drinkers" or "proto-alcoholics," but instead by perfectly normal drinkers who drink unwisely and unluckily?[5] After all, ill-timed moments of drunkenness can produce very bad consequences, such as traffic accidents, drunken assaults, even disputes that become the basis for unemployment and divorce. Even if any individual bout of drunkenness is very unlikely to produce these results, so many people occasionally become drunk that these events may turn out to be significant in the overall problem.[6]

If unlucky or ill-timed drunkenness is an important factor, policy instruments designed to deal with alcoholics may well miss it.[7] Of course, if *everyone* is treated as being at risk of alcoholism, then the mechanisms of early detection and treatment should be successful. But there may be more efficient ways of going after the problems of drinking in the general population. For example, one could reduce the overall quantity of drinking through taxation or by limiting the availability of alcohol.[8] Or one could encourage the general citizenry to drink more wisely by passing laws prohibiting certain kinds of drinking behavior or offering health education programs. Or one could try to make the social and physical environment less hostile and dangerous to those who are occasionally or often drunk.[9] These are logically possible policies, but they are hard to recognize or take seriously if one is thinking primarily in terms of identifying and treating alcoholics.

To a degree, one can view this problem as nothing more than an analytical oversight. Two observations make the situation somewhat more sinister, however. First, few studies identify the importance of "normal" drinkers in society's overall alcohol problem. Indeed, this kind of understanding is made impossible by the practice of viewing anyone who has a problem with drinking as an alcoholic or proto-alcoholic. Second, as long as one thinks of the alcohol problem as lying among the alcoholics, it is hard to see it as being in the alcohol or in the general population. This deflects attention from some possibly significant pieces of the puzzle.

In fact, defining the alcohol problem as a problem of alcoholism produces a powerful political coalition uniting three constituencies: (1) the alcoholic beverage producers (who are not held responsible for the alcohol problem and can argue successfully against any new efforts at taxation or restriction of supplies); (2) the groups that "treat" alcoholics (to whom flow any public resources devoted to the solution of the problem); and (3) the general population of drinkers (who can rest assured that their drinking is not a problem). It is almost as if a conspiracy had arisen to keep the society ignorant of the role of nonalcoholic drinkers in causing the alcohol problem and of the potential value of policy instruments such as taxation, drunk driving laws, and public health education in dealing with it.

Dangerous Offenders and Selective Incapacitation

In recent years, crime policy has been heavily influenced by two closely related concepts: "dangerous offenders" and "selective incapacitation."[10] The basic idea is that a relatively small fraction of the criminal offenders accounts for a large proportion of the overall crime problem.[11] Consequently, an effective way to deal with the crime problem is to identify such offenders, increase the likelihood that they are arrested and successfully prosecuted, and lengthen their periods in confinement.[12] This basic idea is a very old one. Why has it now become powerful?

The most important answer is that the idea seems to solve an important contemporary problem: how best to use the nation's scarce prison capacity to control crime. The nation's prisons and jails are currently overcrowded, largely because more people have been arrested and successfully prosecuted for crimes.[13] A second factor crowding the nation's jails and prisons has been a policy shift from "indeterminate sentencing" (which allowed parole boards to adjust prison sentences and therefore to increase or decrease prison populations in response to immediate circumstances) to "determinate sentencing" (which took away this discretion and slightly increased the terms served for individual offenses). This shift in sentencing policy was in turn motivated by a widespread disillusionment with the practical potential of "rehabilitation" (a crucial supporting element of the policy of indeterminate sentencing) and with the justice of a sentencing scheme that left offenders convicted of the same offense serving different amounts of time in prison.[14]

The ideas of dangerous offenders and selective incapacitation seemed to point the way toward more effective use of prisons: if we could distinguish the most active, persistent, and dangerous offenders from the others, then we could use our existing prison capacity more effectively. The result would be either less crime or lower prison costs than if we failed to identify the most active offenders.

This proposal was put forward with some important scientific trappings. New evidence suggested that some offenders were much more active, persistent, and violent than others.[15] A simple system, apparently more accurate than its predecessors, was developed to identify the violent offenders on the basis of characteristics such as current offense, prior record, juvenile criminal record, drug abuse history, and patterns of legitimate employment.[16] A new analytic model made it possible to calculate how much better the society could do in terms of reduced crime or reduced prison populations if it was willing to pursue selective incapacitation as a principle of sentencing.[17] These features gave the old ideas some freshness and technical legitimacy that they would otherwise have lacked.

Of course, these concepts were attacked on all the usual powerful grounds—for example, that the evidence of concentration of offending in a minority of the criminal population was not credible, that the model predicting significant benefits from selective policies was based on inappropriate assumptions or was calculated incorrectly, that the predictions were too inaccurate to be tolerably just to individuals, that the predictive tests included inappropriate characteristics of individuals, that it was wrong to base sentencing decisions on predictions of future conduct, and that bail could not legitimately be used to control crimes by people who had not yet been convicted of an offense.[18] In the past, these criticisms had been sufficient to keep proposals for selective incapacitation off the agenda of criminal justice policy. Now, however, the criticisms seemed insufficient, and the concepts gained great prominence and standing.

Two other characteristics of the policy debate seemed unusual. First, no one seemed to notice that the criminal justice system was already behaving in a highly selective manner.[19] In reality, the concept of selective incapacitation was simply the mirror image of so-called rehabilitative sentencing, which proposed an early release for offenders who seemed to have rehabilitated themselves, while those not yet rehabilitated would remain incarcerated.[20] The goal of selective incapacitation—to keep dangerous offenders in prison a little longer than those who seemed less dangerous—was clearly the same. Parole boards had long used the same criteria in deciding who should be released as were now being proposed for selective incapacitation.[21] Thus some portion of the potential benefits of selective policies was already being exploited by the criminal justice system, and there was correspondingly less benefit to realize in the future.

Second, the policy debate about selective incapacitation generally focused on whether it was proper to use predictions in the criminal justice system. But one could equally well view the issue as one of discriminating between people who had been unusually persistent offenders in the past and others who seemed less persistent, more accidental offenders.[22] Such an approach would significantly alter the discussion of whether the policies were just, since it would eliminate the issue of prediction. It would also have important implications for how one constructed the discriminating tests, since the only relevant variables would be those related to prior criminal conduct. This, in turn, would reduce the practical value of the policies. But the point is that there was little possibility of even getting on the table the idea that the policy should be based on backward-looking discriminations rather than forward-looking predictions. The debate continued to focus on the issue of "prediction."

The Deinstitutionalization of Juvenile Offenders

In the late 1960s and early 1970s, the idea of deinstitutionalization began to influence the juvenile justice system.[23] This concept urged the abandonment of large institutions previously used to house delinquent children. Much of the opposition focused on the buildings themselves, which were large, often locked, and remote from the children's home communities. A powerful sociological theory predicted that this radical separation from the community and the official labeling of the children as delinquent would harden them in their criminal tendencies.[24]

These predictions gained credibility because they seemed consistent with two important facts. First, recidivism rates seemed intolerably high. Second, those who recidivated most quickly and disastrously were generally the offenders who had spent the most time in juvenile facilities.

In addition, it seemed impossible to run decent programs within such facilities. This view was supported by observations of conditions inside the institutions and by social psychological experiments. Inevitably, the professional staffs became "guards" and the children became "inmates."[25]

Opposed to the disappointing reality and dire sociological predictions of the institutions for delinquent children was a hope also rooted in a theory. This hope was that, for the most part, children had the determination and the capacity to grow into responsible citizenship.[26] The central problem was simply to avoid corrupting them. No elaborate process of exhortation, aid, and control was necessary to accomplish this task. To the extent that socializing efforts were required, they could be provided by indigenous community institutions rather than public bureaucracies. Such notions appealed not only to liberals optimistic about human capacities for spontaneous virtue, but also to fiscal conservatives, who saw an opportunity to save money for the state. After all, the institutions were quite expensive. If the liberals were prepared to retreat from the public provision of the services supplied in the institutions and to rely instead on private community capabilities, the fiscal conservatives would not protest.

These forces were sufficient to close the juvenile institutions in Massachusetts and reduce their use in other states. But there had been no real evidence that the institutions were exacerbating the problem of juvenile crime and recidivism, and no particular program or idea was proposed to replace the institutions. Over the years, states relied more on "community programs" and the "private sector" to supervise delinquent children. That may have increased the degree of connection between the children and their communities.[27] Moreover, there was much broader and wider experimentation with particular kinds of programs for supervising and rehabilitating delinquent children.[28] But there was no significant breakthrough in levels of juvenile crime or recidivism. Instead, suspicion increased that the juvenile justice system gave youthful offenders a free ride, and pressure arose to shrink the jurisdiction of the juvenile courts so that more crimes committed by children could be handled within the adult criminal courts.[29]

The Drug Enforcement Administration: Jailing Bad Guys

In 1974 President Richard Nixon created the Drug Enforcement Administration (DEA), which united several existing federal agencies focused on reducing the supply of drugs to illicit markets. The new agency included the Justice Department's Bureau of Narcotics and Dangerous Drugs (itself the product of an earlier reorganization that had combined the Treasury Department's Federal Bureau of Narcotics and the Food and Drug Administration's Bureau of Drug Abuse Control); two special organizations recently created to give special emphasis and new capabilities to drug enforcement—the Office of Drug Abuse Law Enforcement and the Office of National Narcotics Intelligence; and a portion of the U.S. Customs Agency that had been particularly active in investigating narcotics smuggling. The hope was that combining these diverse agencies might improve coordination and overall effectiveness in dealing with illegal drugs.[30]

In designing a successful supply reduction strategy, a variety of issues had to be resolved. First, which drugs should be the highest priority for enforcement action?[31] This issue had important implications for the overall style of the organization, because DEA confronted quite different kinds of supply systems and had to develop different strategies for controlling the supply to illicit markets.[32] Some drugs (such as barbiturates, amphetamines, and tranquilizers) had legitimate uses, and large domestic industries. To deal with these, DEA had to act like an effective regulatory agency establishing reasonable production quotas, imposing reporting burdens on legitimate suppliers, and so on. Other drugs (such as heroin, cocaine, and marijuana) had no legitimate uses: the supply systems were wholly illicit—most of them with international connections. To deal with these drugs, DEA relied heavily on criminal enforcement procedures such as informants, wiretaps, and undercover operations.

A second crucial issue was where to attack the illicit distribution systems.[33] Each strategy had its own advantages and disadvantages. Enforcement efforts in foreign countries would be "near the source," but "host countries" were of uncertain reliability. Some could not control areas dominated by drug dealers. Others were corrupted by drug money. Interdiction strategies might "stop the drugs at the border" and could exploit the special search and seizure powers that exist only at the international boundary. But how could the enforcement agencies cover 25,000 miles of unprotected borders and sift through millions of tons of imported goods in search of a ton or two of heroin? Domestic enforcement efforts "on the street" could attack drug distribution systems when they came into the open, but did not seem to make any lasting difference in the overall supply of drugs to illicit markets.

A third important strategic issue was what tactics and what sort of cases were most effective in immobilizing illicit trafficking networks. Traditional methods relied primarily on the use of informants and undercover buy operations. Newer approaches tried to make greater use of intelligence analyses and electronic surveillance, and to prosecute on the basis of conspiracy charges rather than the substantive offenses of sale and possession of narcotics.

In principle, the new organization, seeking a coherent and effective supply reduction strategy, could have usefully analyzed and debated these issues. It might even have conducted some planned experiments to find out what strategies worked. In practice, however, none of this was done because the organization had already decided on its mission. As one senior agent said during a major planning meeting, "As I see it, our job is simple: we put bad guys in jail." That characterization met with widespread agreement and obvious relief from the ambiguities of thinking about the issue in more complicated ways.[34]

Unfortunately, this formulation pre-empted all the other conversations and had a decisive effect on how they would be implicitly resolved. As it turned out, the drugs that received the highest priority were not necessarily those that created the worst social consequences for users, but those that were supplied by the biggest and baddest dealers. In practice, this meant heroin and cocaine. Dangerous drugs such as amphetamines and barbiturates were ignored as beneath the dignity of a "crime-fighting" organization. The focus of operations were principally domestic, since it was there that one could put most bad guys in jail. Moreover, both foreign operations and interdiction efforts were conceived principally as devices for immobilizing major traffickers. Crop eradication efforts overseas were neglected, as was the possibility of involving the military in interdiction efforts, since that would work against the basic notion of locking up bad guys. As for investigative tactics, the use of informants, undercover purchases, and substantive cases with seized drugs to display as evidence continued to dominate intelligence analysis, electronic surveillance, and conspiracy cases. This too was consistent with a straightforward approach to putting bad guys in jail.

This version of a supply reduction strategy is not necessarily wrong. But important issues had been pre-empted by a powerful idea of the organization's mission and style that drove out any other considerations. A new organization, instructed to rethink the nation's basic strategy to reduce the supply of drugs to illicit markets, had been guided by an old and unexamined idea.

*The Bureau of Alcohol, Tobacco, and Firearms: Revenue
Protection and Crime Fighting*

The Bureau of Alcohol, Tobacco, and Firearms (ATF) is a small unit within the U.S. Department of the Treasury, originally established to enforce Prohibition.[35] ATF's jurisdiction includes federal taxes and regulations covering alcohol, tobacco, firearms, and explosives.

Like DEA, ATF could have defined its mission in many different ways. Is its principal job to assure the collection of federal taxes on alcohol, tobacco, and firearms by monitoring the activity of federal licensees and suppressing those who do not pay appropriate taxes? Or should the central focus be on aiding the nation's fight against crime by using the bureau's regulatory powers and enforcement expertise to keep guns and explosives from dangerous people, and arresting those who possess these dangerous commodities illegally?[36]

A second major issue is the relative emphasis to be given to the various commodities under the bureau's jurisdiction. If revenue protection is the principal aim, then alcohol and tobacco are much more important than firearms and explosives. But if reducing crime is the aim, then guns and explosives seem more important than alcohol and tobacco, although the latter commodities are linked to crime as well.[37]

The overall style of the organization depends on its emphasis. If its primary goal is revenue protection, it will be largely a regulatory agency. Its staff will deal principally with federal licensees, monitoring activities and records. Most legal action will be through civil rather than criminal procedures. There will be little gun play. And, as it turns out, much of the organization's activities will be concentrated in the rural areas of the Southeast.

If the goal is crime control, on the other hand, the style of the organization will shift to criminal enforcement. Its staff will be largely agents who carry guns and have the power to arrest, rather than accountants and auditors. It will deal largely with those who are intentionally breaking federal law. It will rely on covert and aggressive methods to discover who these people are and to develop evidence against them. Finally, the work will shift geographically from rural areas of the Southeast (where federal salaries allow even midlevel federal officials to live like kings) to urban areas primarily in the Northeast, Midwest, and Far West (where federal salaries are far less appealing).

Between 1952 and 1978 these issues were fought out within ATF. Occasionally interest was shown by members of Congress and political appointees in Treasury or Justice. The balance of contending forces appears clearly in the statements made by ATF in the annual Congressional Appropriations Committee hearings. The table on the next page presents a chronology of the phrases ATF used to describe its basic mission. As one can see, the organization's mission moved toward crime control.

That shift seemed to reflect both external and internal factors. Crime was becoming a major national issue, and there was an increasing tolerance—even demand—for federal involvement in the fight against ordinary street crime. ATF leaders understood that this was a stronger current than any interest in improved tax collections, particularly since the taxes for which ATF was responsible accounted for a very small proportion of total federal revenues.

But the ATF leaders were also pushed by forces within the bureau. Over several decades, the enforcement side of the organization seemed to supply a larger and larger proportion of those who managed it.[38]

Overall ATF Mission Statements: 1969–1976

FY 1970
(1/8/69)

"The objective of the Alcohol and Tobacco Tax program is to *encourage the highest possible level of voluntary compliance with the Internal Revenue laws.* . . . The Permissive Program is concerned with the accurate determination and full collection of the revenue from legal activities. The principal function of the Enforcement program is to prevent the fradulent non-payment of taxes which results from the traffic in illicit liquor by the criminal community. An Enforcement function of growing significance is the investigation of violations of federal firearms control statutes." (emphasis added)

FY 1971
(1/23/70)

Same as above, but adds participation in organized crime Strike Forces as important features of enforcement.

FY 1972
(2/1/71)

Same as above, but adds, "The Enforcement function is directed [sic] toward suppression of the illicit manufacture, distribution and sale of distilled spirits without payment of tax, and curtailment of the illegal possession and use of firearms and explosives. . . . *in the nationwide attempt to reduce crime and violence.*" (emphasis added)

FY 1973
(1/21/72)

Same preamble, but criminal enforcement comes first. "The *Criminal Enforcement Function* has three significant objectives: (1) to prevent manufacture, distribution and sale of distilled spirits produced illegally; (2) to monitor the activities of the legal firearms industry by a system of licenses and occupational tax stamps and to apprehend violators (or prevent violations) of federal firearms control statutes. . . . and (3) the regulation of explosives through a license and permit system and the prevention or investigation of illegal uses of explosives. . . . The *Revenue Control Function* is charged with accurate determination and full collection of federal revenue due from the liquor or tobacco industries. It is also responsible for the effective administration of the consumer-related controls of the Federal Alcohol Administration Act and those ecological features concerning liquor plants and permittee premises which are controlled by the Environmental Protection Agency but have been delegated to the Service. This function also assisted in the administration of Phase I of the Economic Stabilization Program as a routine part of inspections."

FY 1974
(1/19/73)

"The objectives of the Bureau are to: (1) achieve maximum voluntary compliance with laws under ATF jurisdiction: (2) assure full collection of the revenue due from legal industries;

(3) suppress the traffic in illicit non-tax-paid distilled spirits; (4) eliminate illegal possession and use of firearms, destructive devices and explosives; (5) cooperate with federal, state and local law enforcement agencies to reduce crime and violence; and (6) cooperate with federal, state and local governmental agencies in the areas of industrial development, ecology, and consumer protection."

FY 1975
(1/24/74)
Same as above.

FY 1976
Same as above except (3) changes to "detect and neutralize traffic in illicit non-tax-paid distilled spirits."

FY 1977
(1/9/76)
Same as FY 1976.

FY 1978
(1/14/77)
"The mission of the Bureau is to: (1) reduce the misuse of firearms, to reduce the misuse and the unsafe or insecure storage of explosives, and to assist other law enforcement organizations, federal, state and local, in reducing crime and violence in which firearms and explosives are used, through effective enforcement of the firearms and explosive laws of the United States; (2) ensure that all revenue due under the alcohol and tobacco tax statutes is collected, and to obtain, to the maximum extent possible, voluntary compliance with those laws; (3) suppress illicit manufacture and sale of non-tax-paid alcoholic beverages; (4) suppress commercial bribery, consumer deception and other improper trade practices in the alcoholic beverage industry through effective administration and enforcement of the Federal Alcohol Administration Act; and (5) assure compliance with the wagering tax laws through effective enforcement of the criminal and forfeiture provisions of the Internal Revenue Code."

Source: Bureau of Alcohol, Tobacco and Firearms, Administration Services Division.

This trend preceded rather than followed the public interest in crime and was largely a reflection of the more aggressive, more flamboyant personalities of the criminal investigators. Since these characteristics were seen as attributes of leadership, managerial positions were more likely to go to enforcement agents than to those involved in regulatory activities. These managers quite naturally used these positions to incline ATF toward its crime control mission rather than its regulatory mission.

The Environmental Protection Agency: Pollution Abatement

The Environmental Protection Agency was, like DEA, an organizational effort to enable the nation to deal with a stubborn problem that seemed to require a sharper focus and more effective coordination.[39] The organization was assembled from many different operating units within the federal government, and its leader, William Ruckelshaus, was invited to plan an integrated attack on the nation's environmental problems.

The basic approach could have taken many different forms. Ruckelshaus could have opted for a relatively long period of study and development, arguing that the basic science tracing the relationship between pollution, environmental degradation, and health effects of a degraded environment was then too weak to justify particular actions. Or he could have concentrated on a particular medium. For example, at the time he took office, there was more capacity to deal with water problems than with air, noise, or solid waste. Or Ruckelshaus could have been guided by the links between concern about environmental degradation and quite different concerns and values. Some people cared about environmental issues because of a broad concern for "preservation," in some cases tied to a long-range practical concern about the quality of the gene pool, in others to a sense that nature had rights against man that could not be ignored. For other people, the environmental issue was largely an issue of aesthetics. Rivers that burned and dirty smogs that blocked out sunsets deprived people of simple aesthetic pleasures. To a third group, the environmental issue was largely one of health. Rather than wanting to preserve the environment for its own sake or make it beautiful, these people hoped to minimize the risk that they would get cancer or some other disease as a result of poisons released into the air and water. Thus Ruckelshaus could have defined the mission of EPA in terms of preservation, aesthetic, or health goals.

In determining the mission of EPA, Ruckelshaus was not without advice and pressures. President Nixon had indicated privately that he thought the environmental issue was a phony one. Moreover, his natural constituency was with business, and he was therefore reluctant to impose demands on business for environmental cleanup. From him, then, Ruckelshaus sensed a preference for doing as little as possible. The Congress was, as usual, divided. In the House, Jamie Whitten's appropriations subcommittee would review EPA's budget. His principal interest was in making sure that farmers would be allowed to continue using pesticides. Apart from that, he seemed inclined to respond to broad pressures to do something about the environment. In the Senate, the principal player was Senator Edmund Muskie, whose Public Works Committee was responsible for much of EPA's authorizing legislation. Muskie was then a candidate for the presidency and had made a great deal of political hay, both in his own state and nationally, by championing the environmental movement. He was determined to see action on environmental cleanup and also to criticize the Nixon administration's efforts in the area.[40]

In the internal administrative world, Ruckelshaus seemed to face a vacuum rather than a powerful force. Two major operations constituted the core of his agency. One was the water program transferred to EPA from the Department of the Interior. It had a great deal of money to provide subsidies for new sewage treatment plants and a reasonable data base describing the current state of the nation's waterways. On the other hand, it was dependent on the states to create plans involving specific obligations on polluters to cut back. Initially the EPA water program had no independent enforcement powers.[41] The air program had been transferred to EPA from the Department of Health, Education, and Welfare. Like the water program, it was dependent on the creation of state plans to establish specific liabilities on polluters. And very few of those state plans had been approved.[42] Over the medium term, these two programs would determine EPA's success, but in the short run they were remarkably weak. Scattered around these large programs were much smaller, more fragmented units that had not yet been effectively integrated into EPA. Indeed, the dominant impression of EPA at the outset was one of chaos and disintegration.[43] Finally, EPA seemed weak in some crucial functional areas. Its science base and capabilities appeared quite weak, as did its legal and enforcement capabilities.

Ruckelshaus's solution to the issue of EPA's mission was captured in a simple phrase. EPA's basic business, he said, was "pollution abatement."[44] This idea has several interesting properties. First, it seemed to balance the competing political priorities rather nicely. It reassured those concerned about economic growth, that there would be an incremental approach to cleanup, focusing first on the most flagrant violators. To those concerned about doing something to clean up the environment, it promised action after a decade of neglect. And it seemed to express the general sentiments of the broader public—that those who were making the environment dirty and dangerous should begin doing something, with the aid and encouragement of the government, to clean it up

The idea of pollution abatement also seemed to provide some guidance as to how the organization should be set up, which areas had to be built quickly and which could go slow. The most obvious implication was that EPA had to develop and use its enforcement capabilities. To deliver on the promise to abate pollution, someone had to be effectively sued. Thus Ruckelshaus created a separate Office of Enforcement, and the first person he hired was the head of that office.[45] The idea also implied that the most urgent operational step was to translate the general obligation to reduce pollution into specific liabilities for individual polluters. This depended on the setting of federal standards and the approval of state plans. To achieve this, Ruckelshaus left intact the water and air programs he inherited. As a result his organizational structure was partly functional (enforcement, science, and administration) and partly programmatic (water and air). But he tolerated this loss in administrative tidiness because he was convinced that the best way to get the standards out was to keep the existing organizations working on the problem.

Third, the concept of pollution abatement guided Ruckelshaus on specific policy decisions. Within the first few months in office, he had to decide which polluters to sue, whether to ban DDT, what standards should be set for air quality, and whether to fine the auto companies for violations of pollution standards for motor vehicles.[46] While each decision had to be confronted on its individual merits, the pattern of decisions also had to be consistent with EPA's overall mission. And that gave Ruckelshaus an entering bias, if not an answer, to each of these decisions: that the targets should be notorious polluters who could absorb the costs imposed by cleanup demands; that DDT as the symbol of environmental dangers for a decade should be banned (particularly because better pesticides were now available); that air quality standards should be set even though the science was weak, in order to build momentum for environmental cleanup; and that the most flagrant of the auto companies' violations should probably be fined, and they should be warned with respect to the others.

In retrospect, then, the resolution of EPA's mission had several important effects. It allowed EPA to survive, even flourish, in a potentially dangerous political situation. It resolved some basic organizational questions that set the agency on a long-run course of development. And it gave a bias to some specific decisions. Perhaps most interesting, EPA's impact on the actual course of environmental cleanup was probably more indirect than direct. By successfully championing the cause of pollution abatement, EPA fostered a general social movement in the direction of environmental protection. This had *political* implications in that the environmental voices remained powerful in Congress and state legislatures. But it also had *operational* significance, for it encouraged voluntary efforts to clean up whose effects were probably well beyond what EPA could have enforced directly with its weak legal authority and fledgling legal staff.

Drunk Driving: The Rise of Moralism

One of the most powerful political movements of recent years has been the emergence of grassroots concerns about drunk driving.[47] It has been expressed politically in the commitments of political candidates to crack down on drunk driving and in the passage of new legislation mandating prison terms for repeat drunk driving offenders. Administratively this concern has been reflected in increased levels of enforcement through more intrusive techniques such as checkpoints, closer surveillance of judicial decisions in drunk driving cases, and investments in new programs of education, treatment, and community service within which to manage convicted drunk drivers.

These initiatives seem to be guided by a simple conviction that it is wrong for drivers to expose themselves and others to the risks of death and physical injury associated with drunk driving.[48] The assumption is that drivers are capable of deciding whether or not to drive after drinking, and that it is their moral responsibility to decide not to impose that risk on the society. The moral character of this view also seems to allow others to comment on the drinker's decisions. Indeed, an explicit part of the campaigns against drunk driving is to mobilize third parties such as parents, friends, and neighbors to help prevent people from driving while intoxicated. That is the force behind the adjuration that "good friends don't let their friends drive while drunk." Finally, the movement seems predicated on the notion that the community as a whole can effectively and justly make this demand on individuals without worrying too much about the loss of liberty associated with the restriction.

It is difficult to assess how this idea gained such force. It was spread primarily by voluntary women's groups concerned about the safety of their children on the road. But why these groups should arise at this particular moment of our history remains unclear. The magnitude of the problem had not suddenly become worse. There was no new insight into the nature of the problem, no new technical invention that made it easier to detect drunk driving, no institution that suddenly needed drunk driving as a mission for itself. But whatever the mysterious origins of this idea, it seems that drunk driving has dropped, and with it many of the tragic accidents that drunk driving used to cause. While one can offer many different interpretations of how this effect occurred (including the incapacitation of drunk drivers, the general deterrent effects of the laws, and so on), it seems most likely that the grassroots movement changed many attitudes and practices of the general population. People attending parties seem more aware of the issue, and special arrangements are made to ensure that the people who drive are sober. In short, the idea that drunk driving is bad and avoidable has sustained a broad social movement that has changed the behavior of citizens.

Assessing the Impact of Public Ideas

It is one thing to observe that public actions are consistent with particular public ideas articulated by specific participants in the policy process. It is quite another to prove that the ideas are producing an independent effect on the public actions one observes. Indeed, the alternative hypothesis—that the particular ideas are nothing more than a smokescreen for the institutional and personal interests that are really animating and guiding action—has become quite familiar.

In principal, to determine whether and how public ideas influence public action, one would like to do a series of experiments in which public ideas that were more to less orthogonal to the play of interests were introduced into the domain of public deliberation and action, and measurements were taken of how often and to what degree the ideas shifted the nature of the discussion and the subsequent actions. But just to describe these conditions reveals the absurdity of a rigorous analytic approach to this question. There are many ill-defined terms in this analytic framework. And it is quite implausible that one could experiment with our own policy-making processes by systematically varying the character of the ideas available for discussion.

As a practical matter, then, one must rely on much cruder methods. My approach is to see whether this assertion—that so-called public ideas influence public deliberation and action—can survive a first-order skepticism based on the examples offered above. While such a method cannot produce anything like a proof, it may sharpen our perception of what the effect of public ideas would look like if it existed. The examples may show us the way.

Where Ideas Work: Ideas in Different Institutional Settings

One important lesson to be drawn from the examples is that public ideas have different kinds of influence at different stages of the policy process, and in different institutional settings. It is most natural to think of public ideas as being important in the context of policy debates—for example, within legislative committees, special task forces, or commissions, or more generally in the discussions among the "issue networks" concerned with specific policy issues.[49] The examples of alcoholism, selective incapacitation, and deinstitutionalization illustrate this kind of institutional setting. There is no specific organization whose entire mission is defined by these ideas. Instead, the ideas function as a broad mandate authorizing and guiding actions by many different organizations. Moreover, the focus is on deliberation and analysis rather than action.

In such institutional settings, ideas seem to guide public action in the same way that Kuhn's "paradigms" guide "normal" scientific inquiry.[50] The ideas define the conventional wisdom in the area, set out the questions for which evidence is necessary, suggest the alternative policies that are plausibly effective, and (most important), keep alternative formulations of the problem off the public agenda. Thus, for example, the concept of alcoholism effectively kept the issue of policies affecting the supply of alcohol off the government's agenda. No one seriously debated substantial increases in alcohol taxes, since it was obvious to them that higher taxes would not affect the consumption of alcoholics. The concept of selective incapacitation diverted attention from the issue of what should be done with the many minor and accidental criminal offenders who constituted the bulk of the criminal justice system's caseload.[51] And the concept of deinstitutionalization survived despite the absence of alternative means for dealing with juvenile offenders.

Perhaps "keeping ideas off the agenda" is too strong a formulation. But dominant ideas have certainly relegated competing definitions of the problem to relative obscurity. Those who advanced these alternative conceptions—that is, those who urged that public policy should be directed at occasional drinkers, that a portion of the crime problem was caused by accidental offenders, and that the society had not yet figured out how crime-committing juveniles could be properly supervised—often felt they were not only risking their reputation for knowledge in the area, but also trying the patience and tolerance of their audience.

Public ideas may also be particularly likely to exercise influence in organizations seeking to define their basic strategy or mission. In the case of DEA, the concept of "putting bad guys in jail" guided the organization's strategic and tactical thinking. The same was true for the concept of pollution abatement within EPA. In the case of ATF, the organization's mission was gradually shifted from revenue protection to crime fighting, and its focus shifted from alcohol to guns and bombs.

In this institutional setting, the public ideas give coherence and meaning to the work of the organizations and guide their investments for the future. Thus the idea that EPA was in the business of pollution abatement unified the diverse parts of the organization and indicated the crucial importance of establishing specific liabilities for reducing pollution and building the capacity for enforcement. Similarly the idea that ATF should join a national effort to control violent crime gave that agency a new raison d'être and justified a major shift in attention from alcohol taxation to pursuit of those who possessed guns and explosives illegally. The idea that DEA "put bad guys in jail" stunted the development of regulatory activities, foreign crop control programs, and intelligence analysis.

Note the difference in institutional setting between the policy and organizational strategy contexts. Policies are debated outside the context of particular organizations. The issue of an organization's basic mission, in contrast, is debated largely internally, with the occasional participation of oversight agencies in the executive and legislative branches.

There is only occasionally an exact one-to-one relationship between policies and organizations. Sometimes an organization is part of a policy—the part that implements a specific program. Other times, a policy is part of an organization—the specific way an organization chooses to carry out its broad purposes. "Issue networks" seem to work on policies. Organizational leaders seem to work on statements of organizational mission. Policies may make claims on parts of many organizations. Organizational missions seek to guide all activities within an organization.

A third institutional setting in which policy ideas seem to be important is in the mobilization of private individuals and agencies to help pursue public purposes in situations where no public organization can really command their actions. Examples include the cases of EPA and drunk driving. The concept of deinstitutionalization might also fit since it clearly generated some substantial responses from individuals and organizations outside the government. The problem was that, for a time at least, the response was too small.

In these settings, the public idea not only authorizes and guides governmental organizations, but animates private individuals and agencies. The concept of pollution abatement was important not only as an organizational mission but also as an invitation to many others, including polluters and those immediately affected by pollution, to join the cause. Similarly the idea that drunk driving is socially unacceptable allowed hosts, bartenders, parents, and friends all to discourage drunk driving with more self-confidence and conviction than they could when the issue was viewed as a matter of individual choice without moral significance. In short, the ideas may have generated social movements and new public norms guiding private actions.

The generation and support of social movements is probably the most interesting and least obvious context in which ideas might be powerful. Yet government acts principally through the actions of private individuals, and many policy problems are concerned with the question of how the government can motivate or encourage millions of individuals to do something differently in their lives. This is the issue in promoting voluntary compliance with the tax laws, in discouraging alcohol and drug abuse among teenagers, in eliminating racial bias from housing and labor markets, perhaps even in securing safer work places for the nation's workers.[52] It is also the context in which the effects of ideas are most clearly independent, for such ideas produce widely decentralized effects. So this third context is a particularly interesting one in which to see the potential power of ideas and to investigate ways of harnessing the power for specific public purposes.

The context of policy debates and forums has been well examined by political scientists who have studied the policy-making process.[53] The context of organizational mission has been explored by those who write about corporate strategy or organizational leadership.[54] The context of normative social movements has been researched by historians, sociologists, and social psychologists.[55] So far, however, these separate literatures have not been integrated in an effort to discern the independent effect of ideas.

The point of examining these different institutional settings is to prevent too narrow a search for the impact of public ideas. Ideas influence actions as well as deliberations. And their effect on actions is not restricted to their role in guiding particular organizations: significant public movements are sometimes stimulated and sustained by public ideas.

How Ideas Work: Ideas as Contexts for Social Action

Although the contexts within which ideas might produce material effects are different and offer different kinds of leverage to efforts to use ideas to guide public action, our examples suggest that ideas generally become influential in the same way: by establishing the context within which public policy is debated and executed. That is, the ideas simultaneously establish the assumptions, justifications, purposes, and means of public action. In doing so, they simultaneously authorize and instruct different sectors of the society to take actions on behalf of public purposes. The ideas create a reason for someone to take action by setting out the public value or necessity of the act and by giving the action a social meaning that is accessible to both the person who takes the action and others who are its audience or object. In this way ideas both motivate and direct action.

One can discern the effects of an idea by seeing which sectors of the society are motivated to take action or make investments guided by the idea. Like a spotlight, an idea illuminates and animates the particular parts of the world on which it focuses. When attention is directed to some possibilities for action, other possible modes are inevitably left in the shadows. But it is precisely that fact which reveals the power of a particular idea. When ideas become dominant in policy debates, when an organization develops a strong sense of mission, or when a social norm mobilizes private actions on behalf of public purposes and suppresses other possible approaches, ideas demonstrate their power to provide a context for public debate and action.

Some standard objections are often raised to the proposition that ideas produce material consequences in the world. It is worth reviewing these objections to refine our understanding of how ideas might be influential, as well as what sorts of proof about the independent power of ideas can be offered.

Post Hoc Rationalizations or Ex Ante Guides?

It is often asserted that ideas come after the fact as rationalizations rather than before the fact as guides. There are three possible answers to this objection.

Perhaps the most satisfying rebuttal is to find historical evidence that an influential idea existed in the minds of key actors before it became well known. Often such evidence is available. For example, the idea of selective incapacitation was explicitly set out and advocated by an important criminal justice researcher. The leaders who guided ATF toward "crime fighting" discussed that move with me as an explicit strategy. So did Ruckelshaus with respect to "pollution abatement." So there are often people who can plausibly claim authorship of an idea before it assumed a powerful institutional existence. (Of course, similar evidence might be available for many ideas that never became influential.)

Even if there is no evidence that key actors self-consciously adopted an idea before it became powerful, an influential idea may have been implicit in the minds of those who eventually gave it a powerful social existence, even if they never articulated it. In effect, they were able to express the idea only after it had appeared in the world, though in retrospect it is clear they were implicitly influenced by the idea all along. This seems to have been the case in DEA's strategy of "putting bad guys in jail." The problems with this explanation as an intellectual matter are its ad hoc quality and the difficulty of basing predictions on such a hypothesis. The proposition that people are influenced by implicit ideas is not necessarily wrong, but it is hard to prove it right.

A third rebuttal to the argument that ideas are mere rationalization is to concede that the ideas come after policies are adopted, but to insist that it is at this stage that the idea becomes powerful.[56] In essence the argument is that once an institution self-consciously adopts an idea, that idea then begins to exercise influence by preventing, delaying, or changing the form in which new ideas can emerge. The idea does not usher in or organize a set of activities, but sustains the current ways of doing things. Its influence supports the current pattern of activities and delays new developments and adaptations, rather than changing activities. None of our examples illustrate this point. But that is not necessarily surprising since it is easier to see the moment when things change than the moment when they should have changed and didn't.

A Mere Mask for Institutional Interests?

Even if one can produce evidence that a self-consciously developed idea gradually became influential, a second objection can be raised. This is the argument that ideas become powerful not because of their intellectual properties, such as accuracy, utility, or novelty, but because they balance competing political pressures. In this conception, a large, if not infinite, number of ideas is circulating at any given moment; the one that prevails is the one that can balance competing political and bureaucratic interests.

It would be foolish to deny that the success of an idea is related to the play of interests. Given the way the world operates, the power of an idea is inevitably linked with the power of the institutions whose interests it favors. The example of alcoholism suggests the potent role of institutional interests in sustaining a policy idea. So do the examples of DEA and ATF.

But what does "balance" mean? In one conception, political forces are competing but relatively static. In this world, the idea that becomes powerful is the one that ratifies and maintains the stalemate, exactly reflecting the relative power of the claimants. A more dynamic and fluid conception of political forces and the balance among them is also possible. As some forces wax and others wane, an idea may appear that disturbs the balance or rebalances the political forces. Such an idea would be connected to political forces but would not necessarily replicate their current balance exactly; it could exert influence by strengthening one emergent force at the expense of another. This seems to have been the case at both ATF and EPA. It also is an important part of the story of deinstitutionalization, which substantially changed the balance of political forces in the domain of juvenile justice.

The logic that guides the world of ideas is slightly different from that governing the world of political forces. Thus there is not always an idea available that accurately reflects the current balance of forces—or at least not one that has no important tensions and anomalies as an intellectual idea. Consequently, ideas cannot always be found to buttress the current arrangement of political forces. In this sense, our politics are often incoherent. As part of the armament of political contests, ideas can unbalance and rebalance political forces as well as keep them in alignment. Even though ideas must connect to political forces to become powerful, they are not necessarily slaves of an existing political balance. They can become active agents in reshaping the politics of particular issues.

Summary

Ideas matter because they establish the contexts within which policy debates are conducted, organizational activities are rendered coherent and meaningful, and people's actions are animated and directed. Ideas nominate particular people to do particular kinds of work and give them support for doing the indicated work. As the ideas change, the locus and nature of the society's work changes. The ideas are not always self-consciously known in advance, but once expressed and articulated they can have substantial power to continue one line of activity and investment and discourage others. Although related to existing political forces and institutions, they seem to follow a logic of their own, which sometimes unbalances or rebalances existing political forces.

The ideas that become powerful as contexts for public action are sometimes too simplistic and moralistic to provide useful guidance in addressing society's problems. These deficiencies pose an important normative challenge for those who would like to influence public policy by creating good and useful ideas.[57]

The Sorts of Ideas That Matter

In examining what sorts of ideas become influential public policies, it is useful to distinguish between their intellectual and contextual properties. The intellectual properties of an idea have to do with the differentiation between ends and means, the quality of the anlysis and evidence that lies behind the idea as a normative conception of how the society should deal with a particular problem, and perhaps even the methods used to produce the idea. The contextual properties of an idea have to do with how it fits within an ongoing historical discussion of a particular problem and how it accommodates or challenges the current politics of a given issue and the new interests that are advanced or retarded by the idea. Policy scientists and analysts generally focus on the intellectual properties of policy ideas. Sociologists and historians look more closely at their contextual properties.

Many ideas that become powerful lack the intellectual properties that policy analysts hold dear. Most such ideas are not very complex or differentiated. There is no clear separation of ends from means, of diagnosis from interventions, of assumptions from demonstrated facts, or of blame from causal effect. All are run together in a simple gestalt that indicates the nature of the problem, whose fault it is, and how it will be solved. These features are most obvious in the examples of alcoholism, selective incapacitation, and drunk driving.

Moreover, it is not clear reasoning or carefully developed and interpreted facts that make ideas convincing. Rather, ideas seem to become anchored in people's minds through illustrative anecdotes, simple diagrams and pictures, or connections with broad common-sense ideologies that define human nature and social responsibilities.[58] These connections cannot be dissolved simply through facts and logic. On the other hand, fact and logic can reinforce other sorts of connections to strengthen the hold of an idea. The example of deinstitutionalization illustrates this characteristic.

Turning to contextual properties, one intuitively feels much closer to the source of ideas' power as guides to public action. The ideas that become influential resonate with significant historical experiences. Alcohol policy, for example, was profoundly influenced by the society's understanding of the "lessons of Prohibition."[59]

Almost as important, the idea should have some obvious link to a current pressing problem. "Pollution abatement" was a particularly important idea in a world where rivers burned, beaches were blotted by oil slicks, and smog made people cough. "Dangerous offenders" would be a less potent idea in a world with plenty of prison space.

The particular way an idea balances political forces and identifies where blame is to be placed, and responsibilities for additional work created, is also quite important. The concept of "joining the nation's fight against crime" was quite welcome to ATF's criminal investigators, who felt stifled by the Treasury's concern about tax compliance and indifference to the opportunity to arrest bad guys. The concept of alcoholism was embraced by both the industry that claimed to know how to treat alcoholics and the alcoholic beverage industry, which used it to ward off increased regulatory efforts. The concepts of dangerous offenders and drunk driving were welcomed because they allowed the society to focus its attention (and wrath) on targets that were easy to attack.

Thus, to the extent that ideas distinguish heroes from villains, and those who must act from those who need not, and to the extent that these distinctions fit with the aspirations of the parties so identified, the ideas will become powerful. If powerful people are made heroes and weaker ones villains, and if work is allocated to people who want it and away from people who do not, an idea has a greater chance of becoming powerful.

This review suggests that the contextual properties of ideas are much more influential than their intellectual properties. Indeed, the intellectual properties that matter are those that qualify the idea in political and institutional terms, not scientific and intellectual terms. Those who would like policy ideas to meet intellectual tests may deplore the "irrationality" of a world that does not respond to the particular logic with which analysts are familiar. An alternative, more constructive, response would be to think about how one might enhance the contextual properties of ideas initially distinguished only in terms of their intellectual properties. How might ideas be self-consciously developed and used to improve the quality of public policy?

Creating Useful Policy Ideas

It is quite possible that ideas cannot be self-consciously produced and used to guide public action. It is almost certain that they cannot be produced single-handedly by an individual without reference to the existing institutional context. Yet it appears that some self-consciously developed and promoted ideas eventually produce significant effects on public policy. This is perhaps most evident in the context of defining an organizational strategy, where specific individuals—the organizational leaders— are expected to produce an idea that can motivate, direct, and explain their organization's purposes. In the context of policy deliberations too, ideas are explicitly invited and debated. This potential is perhaps least evident in the context of emerging social norms, though examples can be found even here. (I am thinking of Martin Luther King's dogged pursuit of voting rights, Ralph Nader's crusade for auto safety, and the "moral majority's" drive to "put God back in the classroom.")

If influential ideas can be produced, those who would shape public policy would benefit from knowing how to interact effectively with this world of ideas to enhance their quality and value. Our discussion suggests several rules.

Rules for Constructing Policy Ideas

The first rule is to diagnose what is already there. Those who would influence the world of ideas must understand both the intellectual and contextual properties of the ideas that are already in the field when they begin their work. Generally this involves an analysis of the intellectual history of the issue; an exploration of the intellectual properties of the new idea to see which values, facts, and policy approaches are emphasized and which neglected; and an analysis of the political and bureaucratic terrain to determine which concrete interests of politicians and bureaucrats are favored by the idea and which are neglected.[60] A particularly important part of this diagnosis is assessing the levels of conflict and fluidity in the institutional setting, since that will be a clue as to intellectual weaknesses in the prevailing ideas, as well as an indication that a new idea might be both feasible and necessary.

The second rule is to respect existing ideas and policies. A policy entrepreneur should give due regard to the value of the established ideas operating in a particular area. They are there for a reason, and sometimes the reason is a good one and still valid. Those who value ideas often emphasize the novelty or accuracy of an idea rather than its effectiveness in organizing the society's activities. But the old ideas may be accomplishing a great deal of social work by keeping policy debates, organizations, and the society in general focused on an important task. Thus it is important to think in terms of the utility of an idea. An idea that is old, somewhat confused, and not well worked out or supported is not necessarily a bad policy idea. Such ideas should be evaluated in terms of the useful social work they stimulate.

The third rule comes into effect only after diagnosis and evaluation reveal that the old ideas are significantly limited—for example, that some important value is not reflected in the old conception, that some new opportunity cannot be exploited, or that some emerging social problem is not effectively addressed by the old idea. Now the issue of how to construct a better (i.e., more useful) idea comes to the fore. A sound diagnostic analysis will already have suggested the many dimensions along which policy ideas in a particular area might be formulated. Imagining this "logical space" is a necessary part of seeing the limitations of the current idea.[61] So much of the hard intellectual work of imagining alternative formulations of the problem will have been done in the diagnosis stage.

The crucial remaining intellectual task is to shrink the complexity down to a relatively small number of dimensions. There is no intellectual rule that provides useful guidance on how to do this. Indeed, all the important intellectual standards, which require completeness and internal rigor, deplore the necessary simplification. Thus in deciding how to simplify the policy idea, one must turn to the standard of usefulness in a particular institutional context.

In judging the utility of alternative simplifications, one must consider their likely impact on patterns of thought, the location of responsibility, and the new activities and inventions that will be produced as the idea highlights areas not previously (or at least not recently) examined. The more potential value there seems to be, the more important the idea. Recognizing that the alcohol problem was not identical with the problem of alcoholism, for example, seemed to give the society new potential to explore alternative approaches. The concepts of dangerous offenders and selective incapacitation had less potential because they offered less room for social invention in dealing with the crime problem. Indeed, one had to work hard to keep this idea from *narrowing* the society's approach to crime.

In addition to gauging the potential value of the new opportunities created, one must judge the capacity of the policy idea to challenge the existing orthodoxy effectively. Can the new idea resonate with some forces and currents in the existing institutional context? If the idea is too exotic to be taken seriously, its value is essentially nil. On the other hand, an idea that does not challenge current patterns of thought and activity in useful directions is also without value. So there is an optimal distance from current conceptions that depends not only on the logical possibilities introduced by the new idea, but also on its ability to exploit or mobilize political and institutional forces.

Implications for the Practice of Policy Analysis and Design

Traditional ideas of how to analyze and design policies have emphasized clarity in the definition of problems and rigor in determining the optimal policy intervention.[62] They have also emphasized objectivity and distance from the existing political and institutional contexts. The ideas offered here would change the emphasis in crucial ways.

First, intellectual effort and power would be focused on imagining and systematically arraying alternative possible definitions of the problem, rather than reaching a conclusion given a definition of the problem. Abstract and rigorous thought would be valuable in enlarging the analyst's ideas of what the society has at stake and the various ways it might approach a particular policy issue.

Second, instead of encouraging a lofty indifference to the institutional context within which ideas are formulated, debated, and implemented, the concepts developed in this chapter would counsel a deep immersion in the institutional context. This immersion is a practical necessity, to make sure that the idea is formulated in a way that gets a hearing; in addition, the history and current tensions will provide important clues about the *intellectual* structure of the problem as well as its *institutional* structure. A political conflict is often the telltale sign of an important neglected value. A narrow bureaucratic capability can be interpreted as a sign of what the organization likes to do, knows how to do, or has learned to do through a long process of experimentation; this information may shed light on feasible program technologies and costs. Thus the institutional arrangements give analysts substantive information they need to do their analysis.

Third, the concept of policy analysis suggested here would de-emphasize the traditional criteria and focus instead on a new idea's value in challenging the society to perceive and deal with a problem differently, shifting the focus of responsibility for solving the problem or suggesting the potential of a different set of policy instruments and programs than are now employed.

I am not sure that all of these implications are correct. But if the essence of public policy is ideas that guide public action, and if my professional experience has not misled me as to what kinds of ideas can do this job, then we must change how we think about producing and evaluating policy ideas. Instead of thinking of ideas as scientific conclusions, we must recognize them as society's effort, groping in the dark, to help itself deal with intractable problems. To assist in this enterprise, we must not only sharpen our own vision of problems and possible approaches, but stay close to the society and its current understandings. Otherwise our ability to pose useful challenges will crumble into academic irrelevance.

CHAPTER 4

How Government Expresses Public Ideas

Philip B. Heymann

Earlier chapters have argued that ideas about what is good for society are critically important for mobilizing public action and that much public policy making thus depends on the persuasive power of the ideas underlying it. The implication is that policy makers are expressing and testing such public ideas all the time. In this chapter I examine the legitimacy of this expressive role.

Widely shared beliefs about the way social reality works are a powerful determinant of what is accepted, expected, and done in the relations among individuals, groups, institutions, and nations. So are the mandates and the suggestions of government. The two interact. Widely shared, well-defined beliefs shape the actions of government. But in areas where beliefs are not so clear, we derive a sense of what the common social understanding should be from government action. That sense in turn may be translated into actual more public understandings that influence future individual, group, and public actions and attitudes.

Inescapably, then, one of the great battlefields of government action itself (and not just of the politics that precedes and directs it) is the minds of the citizens. At stake are the beliefs and attitudes accepted by large or influential portions of the public. Government action has expressive purposes as important as its instrumental ones, as the presidency of Ronald Reagan forcefully reminds us.

But why was a reminder needed of something so seemingly obvious? Deeply embedded in our current American explanations of the roles of government for a free people is the notion that government is justified only in doing what citizens *need* done, perhaps because they cannot help themselves through private initiatives or cooperation. We have assumed that government legitimately acts only to meet existent needs, *not* to form views of the world we live in and thus create a sense of what is needed. The two goals may seem almost to merge as officials explain, instrumentally, why a particular action, institution, or rule is needed to meet some more fundamental, pre-existing need of citizens. But the instruments, in our familiar justifications of government, are temporary expedients generally thought to reflect nothing deeper about our condition, hardly deserving loyalty in themselves and often not even needing to be understood by nonspecialists. In our common ideology, the creation of shared views of our shared social reality and the demands it makes on us as individuals and as groups has never been thought a central role of government.

But it is, and it is a role fraught with dangers. The exercise of that role in areas where deeply held moral views are in conflict can lead to terrible and often unnecessary divisions within the society. Even where there are no passionate divisions, expressive government action can become a substitute for action or, more dangerously, a substitute for public demands for careful consideration of the complicated consequences of government choice in highly complex situations such as nuclear strategy. We must accept the legitimacy as well as the reality of expressive government action. But that acceptance frees officials to take cheap and foolish actions unless our politics also demands greater tolerance and honesty from our leaders.

Free-Wheeling Politics and Artificially Constrained Conceptions of the Role of Government

Citizens have views about what government should be doing in various domestic and foreign areas, as well as more general notions of the role of government in society. The latter, ideological notions influence the former, political ones. But sometimes the relationship is less straightforward. Even the clearest views about what government should not do may be set aside when they conflict with self-interest in a particular policy. Under the influence of interest even ideology may change. In addition, we try to exclude from our discussions about the proper roles of government something we know to be a major ingredient of our politics: the expressive function of government action.

In talking about how government should behave, we sometimes incorporate the ideology of welfare economics. Its basic units are individuals with presocial needs and desires who are motivated to action and cooperation by their effort to obtain personal satisfactions in the form of goods and services. In that paradigm individuals create private organizations to satisfy their pre-existing needs through a process of cooperative coming together that is facilitated by another artifact, law, including the law of contracts, corporations, and family. It is assumed that government should not act except where private organizations cannot be effective—that is, generally in situations of market failure that have been fairly well defined by microeconomists.

The paradigm of welfare economics is a special case of a much broader and more important category of models of what a government should do and how it should go about doing it. It is this broader "instrumental" category that dominates our talk about government and its proper role, although it provides only a very partial explanation of our politics. All models in this more general category share several characteristics regarding the choices government agencies must make.

Each model assumes, first, that government action is explained and justified as a response to problems and that the alternatives considered are chosen in light of the problem that stimulates action. Second, a defensible government process is supposed to incorporate a rational attempt to predict the consequences of the various alternatives. Often the prediction is based on particular assumptions about the self-interestedness of individuals and their focus on goods and services, but that is not essential to the broader model. An intelligent government choice requires, third, a rational process of assessing uncertainties and reacting to the risks they reveal. A false certainty based on an oversimplified model of reality would be grounds for serious criticism of the government choice.

The consequences predicted must be evaluated, and—a fourth characteristic of the model—the values be assumed to reflect the personal well-being of the individuals affected by the governmental action. Their interest is not conceived as the attainment of some preferred social state but rather as a solution to the far more limited problem that stimulated government action. Ultimately they are assumed to want whatever comes to them individually in the way of goods and services. This is what is to be maximized (although, without a basis for comparing the amount of happiness an event gives various people, this evaluation scheme leaves unresolved the difficult question of how the benefits and burdens will be distributed). Fifth, within this structure even lasting government processes, institutions, and laws are considered devices for cooperative action, to be designed and redesigned intelligently to that end. Politics and current government activity involve, we are led to assume, the use of resources or the direction of private activity to overcome the obstacles to private efforts to accomplish some cooperative end.

Although that description of the role of government may sound reasonable, each of the five characteristics of the general model is inconsistent with very important aspects of our experience of living together and accomplishing results jointly. Ignoring this "expressive" aspect of politics has serious consequences. If our discussions of objectives for government are constricted by the influence of a too limited, ideological model of what government should do, then the process of democratic debate is seriously distorted. And this is so even if our normal politics frequently manages to break loose from the constraints of the general model I have just described.

The Expressive Functions of Government

An alternative notion of the role of government activity in our society—one that emphasizes the expressive functions of government—is at least as realistic and important as the dominant paradigm. The reality and power of such a conception of government action become apparent as soon as one sees that each of the five requirements of the instrumental model is frequently ignored in real-world politics and governing—and for common, expressive reasons.

The Source or Motivation for Government Action

Very frequently, proposed solutions to societal "problems" precede the recognition or even existence of the problem to which they are later attached.[1] This does not happen because the solution is devised in response to some other real-world problem, not yet recognized by others. Rather, such solutions are expressive of a desired characteristic of the group or of group activity, not instrumental responses to any limited problem. For example, when I headed a bureau of the Department of State, I proposed to remove the four-year limitation on visitors' visas, so that they would be valid indefinitely. The proposal became realistic only when a balance of payments "problem" required some solution—such as encouraging travel to the United States by visitors from abroad. But my proposal originated in my desire to further a conception of the United States as an open society in which citizens would be freely exposed to the beliefs and experiences of people from every corner of the world.

In that sense much government activity is expressive of a generous society or a tough-minded society, of openness to change or respect for order, of a belief in excellence or a hatred of inequality. Consider what happens when proponents of a government program are confronted with evidence of its ineffectiveness. If shown that welfare does not help the recipients, a liberal would want the same money to be spent on the poorest welfare recipients in some other way or on some other disadvantaged group. If shown that the army's newest tank is a deathtrap for its occupants, the supporter of defense expenditures will want the same money transferred to another weapons system, perhaps a new ship. Liberals want to *express* generosity; hawks want to *express* determination. The death penalty says one thing; the exclusionary rule in criminal procedure says the contrary. Neither has much to do with danger on the streets, but both become the focus of our efforts to deal with that problem.

Attributing Consequences to Alternatives: Deeply Held Assumptions versus Open-Minded Predictions

The second step of our familiar model of government choice requires the careful prediction of the consequences of alternatives. But in many extremely important areas, this is not possible, even if it would make a difference to those recommending particular government actions. Frequently, perhaps generally, unproven and perhaps unprovable assumptions about human behavior are crucial to government choices. These assumptions are grounded more in our personal psychologies and histories, in our group memberships and accepted mythologies, than in any scientific evidence.

Consider, for example, the most important domestic problems: poverty, crime, lack of needed education. One's analysis of what should be done in these areas hinges on assumptions about moral responsibility for these evils. Are they primarily due to individual and family failures of character or to unjustified inequalities or denials of "true" opportunity in society? Liberals believe that all people are fundamentally very much the same and that social conditions create the observed differences. Conservatives believe that people are different in fundamentally important ways, such as their laziness, their tendency to take advantage of others, their willingness to break rules.

These presumptions, rooted in our personal lives and social experience, shape our approaches to many social issues. We cannot wait for a scientific resolution of the competing claims of nature and nurture before choosing our position on the death penalty. Conservative solutions differ radically from liberal ones; what one prescribes, the other regards as aggravating the harm. Yet the difference turns above all on whether one believes that failure is largely a matter of individual character or a responsibility of the larger society.

Pursuing these threads takes one very deep into the mind and social experience of the actor. Everything turns on judgments about two questions. First, can crime, ignorance, and poverty be traced largely to bad character and undisciplined choices, or are they caused by the harmful "lessons" imprinted on children by their painful experience of home and neighborhood and the absence of valuable lessons not available in their family and neighborhood life (i.e., to surrounding conditions for which the child is not responsible)? If the former, these are individual moral responsibilities; if the latter, they are social responsibilities with solutions in educational and economic policies. Second, where along this divide between the responsibilities of the individual and the state should the family be placed? Does the state bear any responsibilities for the crime and deprivation caused by failure of the family to play its role?

This conflict involves something even deeper than a profound disagreement about ultimate causes and something more firmly rooted than rational predictions about needed incentives. People differ in their attitudes toward the virtues and institutions required for self-sufficiency and getting ahead and those of sharing or responsibility for others. The roots of these differences may lie as deep as our various strategies for coming to terms with life's dangers and contingencies— whether by emphasizing that there is enough of the good things for the "producers" and "winners" in society or by remembering the dangers of failure, the risks of envy, and the value of sharing and generosity.

One's view of the extent to which responsibility for the nuclear arms race is shared—an unprovable proposition—profoundly shapes one's attitude toward new weapons systems from the Stealth bomber to Star Wars. If our actions are fueling the arms race needlessly, we must show restraint; if our enemies are trying to sneak an advantage that we may not detect until it is too late, we must push our own nuclear efforts ahead as fast as possible. Our judgments on these crucial assumptions (at least suspicious judgments) are likely to prove self-validating as our enemies respond. In any event, our judgments turn at least as much on the general attitudes toward enemies, opponents, and rivals that we absorbed in childhood as on a careful analysis of history or politics. Certainly the politics of the issue depends significantly on public judgments of how hostile parties behave and what creates the hostility.

Assessing Risks and Presumptions

Sometimes powerful presumptions seem to remove the need for rational prediction, as with our sense that a burden of proof "beyond a reasonable doubt" in a criminal case is wise *because* it is better to free nine guilty men than to imprison one innocent one. In many important government decisions, widely varying evaluations of the consequences create powerful presumptions about allocation of risk, making careful risk assessment irrelevant.

A good example is the debate about government response to environmental problems such as acid rain and threats to the ozone layer. Disagreements depend centrally on underlying judgments as to how much one should be willing to pay now to foreclose a very small chance of a very great catastrophe in the future. The partisans frequently differ so substantially on this underlying evaluation that careful calculation of probabilities and risks may not even enter into the argument. Similarly, careful calculation of risk has little to do with people's beliefs about requiring auto manufacturers to offer passive restraints to protect people who fail to use their seatbelts. Our views depend ultimately on our sense of the relative importance of individual responsibility and collective caring. In all these areas, ideas and values emerging from our childhood, our family life, our private associations, and our experience of living together have burrowed into the very core of efforts at analytic choice, largely replacing prediction or risk assessment.

Evaluation of Results: Summed Individual Satisfactions versus Desired Social States

The instrumental model that dominates discussions of the proper role of government evaluates activities in terms of their consequences for the private interests of affected individuals. But this scheme is too limited to capture the expressive quality of government action. Citizens want more from society than a collection of goods and services. And they see government as important to what society provides beyond goods and services.

People care about the nature of the society, including its political institutions, and not just about what it does for them as individuals. They want to live in a society that generally expresses their own values, in the structures and conceptions of family, state, friendship, the accepted grounds of respect, the sense of citizenship, the feeling for excellence, the attitudes toward loyalty, and so on. Most people have attitudes toward certain virtues and vices (e.g., generosity, self-reliance, cowardice) so strong that they would consider a society impoverished that lacked respect for these qualities. Most people have so deeply absorbed notions of morality that they would find themselves at confused cross-purposes with a society that embodied very different rules and expectations about work, extramarital sex, or squealing on friends, for example.

A too limited picture of what citizens want from society reflects a too limited model of what motivates individuals in everyday life. It is not valid to think about many individual needs and desires as if they preceded social life. They involve a desired (or feared) *relationship* with smaller or larger groups right up to the national level; and relationships are defined by what their participants think of them and believe they are. We live and die for love, respect, status, self-respect, a sense of belonging to valued groups—needs and desires that are socially defined and expressed. We live in fear of contempt, failure, ridicule, loss of love, and so on. Those who enjoy adequate food, clothing, and housing find that social rewards and punishments provide their motivations, direct their energies, and determine what goods and services are wanted for.

Social rewards and punishments are dispensed along pathways determined by custom and the relatively stable belief structure of enduring groups and institutions important to us. The pathways tell us what ways of behaving are acceptable, what is admired and rewarded, and when we can think well of ourselves. Children are first taught by their families about the conditions of receiving love, respect, success, and security. Further messages are conveyed by school and friends. Together they create both persistent social needs and beliefs about how desired social responses can be obtained.

What adults want most in life is a set of relationships with family and other loved ones, a position of respect and influence among friends and work associates, a sense of relative well-being in terms of wealth and independence, a sense of belonging to valued groups, and a pride in the groups to which they feel they inescapably belong. The things that matter are relationships defined by groups of people, institutions, and customs; and these relationships are closely tied to our sense of self and belonging.

By adulthood we have learned that the things that matter are largely socially dispensed and that we get them only through our relationships to social structures. We obtain what we need by orienting ourselves to available institutions, from accepted structures for male-female relations to citizenship in a nation; to the virtues recognized by groups and institutions we admire or belong to; to the ways of behavior that are accepted and admired; and to the attributes that bestow status with relevant institutions, groups, or social classes.

Private action takes such forms as accepting and playing roles; conforming to or challenging rules, mores, and expectations; teaching the young and persuading peers; and establishing status or challenging it. These actions create or preserve value for individuals and for the social structures with which they identify. The set of relevant alternatives includes all the ways of persuading, challenging, accommodating, and bringing like-minded people together that can shape attitudes, beliefs, and notions of acceptable behavior and institutional roles. The payoffs of action, the valued outcomes, are beliefs about social relationships and social structures that together define the good society.

A person concerned about the expressive function of group action cares about others' beliefs about proper behavior, virtues, certain institutions, social status, group membership, the status of groups, and so on. Those beliefs determine whether the others will behave in a predictable way and continue to accept the way the individual has organized his attitudes and behavior. That determines the safety of the institutions and groups whose welfare has become intertwined with his own.

The Functions of Law and Other Governmental Institutions

Against this background the institutions and rules of government action look very different from the devices for cooperation to which they are reduced by an instrumental perspective. Instrumental justifications for government action assume that the goal is to help individuals bring about some change in the world that benefits them. When the change requires cooperation, private institutions develop to do what private individuals cannot accomplish on their own. Government bodies and law become involved only when private institutions cannot bring about the necessary cooperation.

But the rules enforced by law are typically not the calculated result of citizens' conscious effort at cooperation. Rather they embody some part of the morality, custom, and ideology that shape our social life and define the pathways to social rewards or sanctions. Individuals recognize that others' behavior and the social rewards each enjoys depend crucially on *both* widely shared views about what is helpful to the group, what individual characteristics are admired, what is permissible conduct, *and* a common view of how the major groups within the society relate to each other and to those outside it. Debates about the rules of law are arguments about which views will be widely accepted—that is, what sort of society we purport to be. They involve differences about how we shall think of our relationship to each other (a matter that powerfully shapes informal social pressures on our conduct) as well as what actions we want the government to take in response to each other's actions (responses that are often impossible to guarantee because of the costs of official fact-finding). Law is just one aspect of the directions we take from our contemporaries and our predecessors—directions enforced by the social threats of losing economic opportunities and being excluded from groups that we need emotionally and practically, beginning with the family itself.

Our longer-lasting institutions and government processes are not empty boxes into which we can pour our present purposes. They come surrounded with meanings and expectations and imbued with particular understandings of their mission and how it relates to the nature of human beings and group behavior. For centuries, the major processes of democracy and the rule of law have been complex secular religions in the United States. As Mark Moore points out in Chapter Three, specialized government agencies (e.g., those dealing with spies, drugs, or offshore oil) preserve a panoply of coherently integrated assumptions, understandings, and values about particular policy areas, which in turn shape and preserve the coherence of those agencies.

In short, the expressive functions of government processes and institutions are something quite different from the planned use of resources to solve problems or the regulation of citizens' actions as they strive to accomplish their private ends. What matters is agreement or disagreement on customary or moral judgments, on membership and loyalty, on crucial social virtues, on matters of status and class. The agreement is expressed and made more permanent by various forms of government action, from authoritative legal pronouncements after due deliberation to embodiment of the agreement in structures that shape the thoughts and expectations of group members.

Each individual has a more or less organized world view composed of crucial attitudes and beliefs that shape his actions and social responses and set the measure of his sense of self-worth. His treatment by others with whom he interacts depends on where he fits in their world view. So does the respect and approval he enjoys from others important to him. For those reasons the individual must be greatly concerned with how well his world view corresponds to that of others (successful social living depends on this) and, where there are differences, whether others can be brought to see things more his way. In the language of economic analysis, expressive behavior is a world of omnipresent externalities. Everyone cares about other people's views of the institution, rule, status, or role with which he identifies. And government has great power to define, legitimate, and reconcile disparate world views.

The Nature of Expressive Governmental Action

Society is affected by new government actions or commitments of resources and by the threat of enforcement of particular laws. But it is still more influenced by government's impact on the pervasive structure of beliefs, attitudes, social rewards, and inhibitions that determine how individuals and groups will behave and what they will give to and expect from each other. Government influences this world of understandings and attitudes primarily through what it expresses.

Only through government expressive action can an entire society define its public attitudes, beliefs, and philosophies. The mechanisms of government influence on beliefs and attitudes are both psychological and sociological. Psychologically, political leaders play an important role in giving individuals a sense of worth in their work, an explanation for their frustrations, and a feeling of pride in belonging, along with a framework for relating these aspects of their personal lives to social institutions.

The other critical mechanism of government influence involves the sociology of knowledge. People are uncertain about the nature of social reality. Are citizens generally expected to cheat on their tax returns? What sexual behavior is currently expected of teenagers? The answers to these questions—the "truth" about social mores— and our own personal views both depend on what others generally believe and on the "laws of motion" that win people over to generally held beliefs or, occasionally, produce schisms. Government actions and the words of officials can seem a source of authority about these questions. In our secular society there is no higher shared authority.

Thus the authoritativeness of government actions (and even, to some extent, of government leaders) is likely to influence those who are uncertain about rules of behavior, status, or valued social institutions. And people's tendency to be affected by the prevalence of a particular view will multiply that effect. The passage of the Civil Rights Acts of 1964 and 1965 and the earlier leadership of Presidents Kennedy and Johnson illustrate government's influence on people's understandings about society—in this case with respect to the acceptability of racial discrimination. The same can be said of Ronald Reagan's efforts to change public views on the proper role of government and the embodiment of the new view in various budget and tax acts during his administration.

Political leaders, legislation, and government action convey two kinds of messages. At the level of general views about foreign enemies and domestic vices, proud traditions or lessons from failure, there is a lively competition for the minds of the undecided. Did the Great Society programs fail, and if so what can we learn from that? Did our effort in Vietnam fail, and if so what can we learn from that? Are the deficiencies in our society attributable to the undisciplined indulgence of noncontributors or to our cold indifference to those who are left behind? Is it more important to emphasize individualism or generosity? Officials, legislation, and governmental action say something about these questions. Although the questions, and their answers, are too general to determine specific actions by individuals or government agencies, they create the presumptions that justify otherwise arbitrary choices.

At a more specific level, government plays an expressive role in characterizing new events and situations. Thus government officials teach that a certain situation exemplifies a familiar virtue or vice, makes an accepted rule applicable, or should be understood in a particular framework or model of causal connections. Affirmative action is "remedying past wrongs" or "purposeful discrimination based on race." The Contras are "freedom fighters" like George Washington or "terrorists" like Abu Nidal. The MX missile is a "Peacekeeper" or a "white elephant." Abortion is "murder" or "free choice." Marijuana is a dangerous drug; alcohol consumption is an accepted social activity; the use of tobacco is "up to the individual" except where nonsmokers object. Different governments have conveyed different messages on such matters. In each case the message is really about how citizens should understand concrete situations and place them under the major premises we use for choice.

Such messages can be conveyed in several ways. At its most forceful, government sometimes compels action that can only be justified on the basis of a certain understanding of an otherwise ambiguous situation. Because marijuana is placed in the category of addictive drugs, smoking that substance is a crime, whereas drinking alcohol is considered a sociable activity. At its least forceful, government gives a meaning to ambiguous situations simply by not interfering with them. Charities are not to be taxed. Medicaid funds will not be used to fund abortions.

Between these extremes come two intermediate alternatives. The first is preaching. Urging individuals to act in a way that presupposes a particular major premise as to the value of their actions sends a clearer message than simply steering government programs around a particular, strongly felt issue. A still more powerful teaching device is to establish and fund a program whose justification plainly involves particular understandings about the likely behavior of individuals or organizations or assumes the desirability of certain forms of conduct.

The range of options can be illustrated by considering what government might do to encourage voter registration. At one extreme it might simply permit its own employees to leave work in order to register. Calling on people to register makes a more explicit statement about what is expected of citizens; establishing government programs for voter registration carries an even clearer message. Punishing a failure to vote would be the strongest form of government action.

In sum, governments influence the world views of citizens by placing situations, organizations (including other countries), and actions in one of the several frameworks of meaning—major premses—that are already part of most individuals' conceptual organization of their social reality. These sets of concepts suggest how things work and thus what is expected of them. They also provide categories of virtues and vices or highly motivating analogies readily transferrable to whatever is placed within that framework. Assigning new events to these categories makes it possible to shape individuals' reaction to them and develop political support for government action.

To a lesser extent, government action may broadly favor certain models of reality and values, thus encouraging acceptance of certain major premises and the variety of actions suggested by those premises. Thus, if people are uncertain about why we failed on a past occasion or what explains a record of success, government actions can encourage the acceptance of a particular view, as to what virtues are crucial or what misunderstanding of human nature was costly, thereby shaping their future behavior.

The Legitimacy of Expressive Governmental Action

If we assert that government activity can only be justified in instrumental terms, much of what we care about will be beyond the reach of government, and much of what government actually does will be unjustified. There is a world of rules, relationships, beliefs, mores, customs, groups, and institutions that are of immense importance in our daily lives. This world is not captured in the instrumental models of human interaction and governmental choice. It changes over time, in part because of the actions of government officials.

It seems clear that expressive action deserves a place among the legitimate roles of government. Our broader ideologies for society should have room for governmental actions motivated by the visions as well as the interests of groups. In particular, government should not be excluded from those whose concerns include the conditions of family life, community organization or disorganization, and private virtues. These matters of social relationship, which expressive government action influences, are of intense importance to individuals, in terms of both social rewards and knowing what to expect of others. In addition, there must be room in our democratic ideology for popular argument, based on analogies to the everyday experience of citizens, for and against alternative forms of government action in every area, from national security to welfare policy. Let me explain why we must legitimate expressive government action.

First, there is necessity. If government action significantly influences our beliefs about ourselves, the groups we value, the institutions we follow, and our predictions about the behavior of others, its expressive consequences cannot be ignored in democratic political choice and government decision. In a democracy those consequences seem so obvious to voters and to elected officials that they inevitably shape the field of promising possibilities for government action. Politicians know they will be made to pay at the polls for actions that, in what they say, disregard cherished values and institutions. So we might as well discuss this expressive aspect of government action directly.

Second, there is allegiance. Citizens' loyalty and acceptance of government actions depend in large measure on the expressive actions of government. To consider their society good, most people require more than an efficient capitalist economy and a decently responsive democratic system. Their loyalty and allegiance are to a far richer set of characteristics: beliefs about the ways we should behave or relate to others, virtues thought to be peculiarly American, a structure of nongovernment groups and institutions, national pride, and more— patriotism, generosity, initiative, rewards for merit, tolerance, courage.

Such virtues and the institutions that express them are as much the basis of national allegiance as political or economic theory. Part of what people want from their society is supplied by such government actions as the creation of a Peace Corps, symbolic of national generosity and idealism, and a manned space program, symbolic of courage, belief in progress, and pride in technological accomplishment.

Next and no less important, there is honesty and accountability. Officials cannot explain their own decisions without considering openly the expressive premises that underlie their choices. As we have seen, unexplored models of social reality are at the core of even our most determined efforts to be coolly analytic about the prediction and evaluation of consequences. *Every* model of social reality—and few government choices rely only on models of physical reality— carries a moral lesson; *every* scheme of evaluation of results must be defended in terms of a model of social reality. These matters deserve as much thought and discussion as any others.

Finally, there is the value of citizen involvement in collective choice. In every policy area, political actors must seek public support for their policies. A major form of expressive political action consists of attempts to influence citizens' beliefs so that they will support the government's action. To this end, the aims or likely consequences of a policy must often be described in terms that draw on the common-sense categories people use in everyday life.

There is an alternative, of course. Through experience people learn that experts have superior knowledge in particular areas and, if they have similar values, can be entrusted to act on our behalf in those areas. Thus government officials can ask the public to trust in their expertise and in their good will. Apparent success—even the absence of evident failure—may often be enough to maintain support for government expertise, so long as the officials are passably popular as individuals. But with failure comes the opportunity for an opposition appeal to common sense and familiar categories of understanding, which are likely to carry the day when claims of expert judgment are undercut by evidence of failure.

There is something healthy and democratic about the competition that familiar social understandings cn give to claims of expertise. If individuals fully participate in government choice in a democracy, it is because their leaders describe policies and themselves in terms that relate to citizens' everyday experience in shared social living and to the models and values citizens impose on that experience. Democracy lives in this marketplace of familiar understandings in a way that is consistent with public interestedness and the wisdom flowing from our experience of social life.

Expressive government action involves the effort to create or reinforce particular shared values about acceptable terms for living together and particular shared beliefs about the crucial relationships within the society and between the society and its neighbors. Whether the effort succeeds depends on how these values and beliefs relate to our more basic needs and to our prior understandings of the terms under which we live together. By expressing collective visions, political leaders often create the public desires for what they promise. The interests and values that motivate citizens do not always come from some source outside our social life and do not remain unaffected by the process of democratic discussion. The ultimate values reflected in expressive government action are generally experienced as "revealed" or "demonstrated" by political discussion and then reinforced by government action.

The citizen has a fuller, more central role in political processes that work in these expressive ways. When government urges private action or seeks support for its activities, citizens ask themselves why they should accept the associated costs. Of the four familiar answers, two are largely instrumental: (1) the benefits of this particular measure exceed its cost to you; (2) you will benefit indirectly (from the political process or from consistent application of the rule for choosing governmental activities—for example, economic efficiency). Two are largely expressive: (3) the measure addresses what you should see is a common danger or enemy; (4) the action will promote a particular vision of a better, stronger, or healthier society. In each case the answer depends on recourse to familiar, commonsensical models of the world and of social life. In the latter two cases, it requires an expressive exchange with citizens about what is to be valued or rejected. As interactive participants in these expressive efforts of government, citizens participate far more fully in democratic governance than when they are merely the passive beneficiaries or victims of actions taken by the state.

The Cost of Accepting the Legitimacy of Expressive Governmental Action

However unrealistic, a conception of the legitimate role of government that is almost entirely instrumental and ultimately based on the untraceable, irreducible desires of individuals has served us well in two respects. First, it has tended to suppress as unjustified various forms of government initiative that are extremely divisive. (Nevertheless divisive moral and social issues have often broken through in our politics.) Second, it has led us to demand more of government action than a showing that our collective heart is in the right place. The instrumental vision takes prediction of consequences and evaluation of results seriously, even though citizens in a democracy may be satisfied with good intentions and plausible, common-sense connections between actions and results. The inevitability that these expressive items will break through, the unanswerability of a demand that powerful human motivations be recognized in our government choices, and the democratic claim to participation in a discussion of all major choices—these may mean that we can no longer exclude expressive actions from our conception of the proper role of government. But there is a price to be paid for expanding our vision in this way.

The Consensus-Building Advantages of Assuming an Instrumental Role for Government Action

A debate about basic values is likely to be more divisive than discussions of government action couched in terms of instrumental efforts to satisfy individual preferences subject only to some consideration of equity and distribution. If deep divisions at a government level pose serious risks, then it may be wise to avoid having the government decide things that are deeply divisive. And there are such risks. Democracy may not work if many people identify very intensely with opposite sides of many issues. In the expressive world of meanings, people tend to form rival alliances and go to battle over such matters as abortion or the projection of American power abroad. Divisive issues are everywhere—the dangers of nuclear war, the role of women, even the visit of a president to a cemetery where Nazis are buried.

In the instrumental world of summed individual preferences there is a tendency to consensus built on efficiency, effectiveness, a sense of joint accomplishment in a growing pie, and shared resistance to waste. More particularly, there is a consensus-building quality in a decision-making approach that measures results in terms of the goods and services available to individuals. It assumes that all things of social life can be divided among individuals basically as buying power, without loss of meaning. It assumes that maximizing the store of good things is unequivocally good and that waste is unequivocally bad, that the political scheme can be relied on to revise the market's division as necessary. (And, although such redistribution is itself highly divisive, it can be handled separately from many other decisions that are based simply on enlarging or protecting the societal stockpile of goods.) These are plainly consensus-building assumptions.

Instrumental analysis eliminates some very divisive questions. Consider the currently prominent questions about social understandings, which involve how we define ourselves as a society, and what groups deserve respect. Whose view of the social welfare and family should prevail—that of the pro-choice or the pro-life people? What groups have been unfairly treated and deserve affirmative action protection? What outside forces are threatening? Is Nicaragua threatening? Angola? Is discipline or generosity a more important social value?

By their very nature views about social structures are intolerant; arguments demand converts. We care about what others believe is the role of the family or the obligation to pay taxes. We find the naiveté (or the insatiable suspicion) of others with regard to foreign enemies a positive danger. Indeed the danger of imperialism by religion—the dominant source of personal world views when our Constitution was written—led to a prohibition against the establishment of religion in our First Amendment. With the imperialism of visions of the social good and of social reality come both dangerous divisiveness and a willingness to stifle social innovation (which has, for example, brought about desperately needed changes in conceptions of race and gender roles). If these tendencies to divide and to repress dissent are linked to government powers of expression, there is real reason to fear the consequences of expressive governance.

A closely related point also favors the instrumental model: individualism offers some protection against the perverse enthusiasms of group membership or shared belief that have given rise in our century to the diseases of statism and racism, causing immense unhappiness throughout the world.

Simplistic and Ineffective Answers to Important Social Problems

A serious danger also lurks in the democratic practice of appealing to common understandings and widely held attitudes as a means of shaping government action. Often the world with which government deals is more complicated than our familiar understandings from everyday life. The expert judgment of policy elites is less likely to oversimplify complicated issues. The need to deal with complexity provides employment, prestige, and power for those who can claim to be experts. On the other hand, political action in the form of public mobilization uses very simple and powerful symbols.

Robert Reich has described the recent triumph of the great conservative philosophy of discipline, personal responsibility, and tough-mindedness over a faltering liberal philosophy of caring and an expanded, worldwide family.[2] But he shows that both philosophies are likely to mislead us in dealing with international relations and the world economy because neither has the precision of terms or the ability to handle complex relationships needed to describe accurately, and therefore prescribe usefully for, a world that is rapidly changing economically and militarily.

The world of expressive meanings, with its intimate, human, experiential categories, tempts us to deal with complicated human problems in models far too simple, with instruments far too blunt, and with attitudes far too crude. Unless one believes the world's evils are due primarily to a lack of the simple virtues or beloved institutions and will be cured by preaching the need for these, we must be constantly alert to the full complexity of the causes of our unhappiness. Social, economic, political, and strategic life is extremely complicated, though our popular pictures of it are simple. If government becomes the teacher of simple ways of understanding—really, misunderstanding—in a complicated and dangerous world, the price can be very high.

Another danger is that wallowing in expressive concerns can make us less effective in dealing with more concrete problems. Pursuing agreement when it is not necessary may represent a waste of energy. When agreement has been reached—for example, on the importance of motherhood and patriotism—repetition of the conceded point becomes an unattractive secular liturgy. Where there is need for action, the world of meanings is likely to be satisfied with symbols. Creating a federal Civil Rights Division may seem to be enough, even if it is woefully understaffed. There may be less anxiety about reducing the scope and costs of crime so long as a few very bad people are being sent to jail for a very long time or, better yet, executed. These are forms of dishonesty that thrive in the world of symbols.

When all is said and done, we do not need to agree about many of the characteristics of the good society; we can live with our disagreements even if the validity of our personal views seems extremely important to each of us. If we allow ourselves to be distracted by efforts to resolve issues we need not agree on, we may neglect issues that do have important consequences. The safety of the nation, the hunger and education of children, the availability of health care, the security of our streets—these matters truly depend on what governments do or fail to do.

In attending to the world of expressive meanings it is quite possible to lose track of the agenda of effective choices, becoming absorbed in arguments about prayer in the schools, abortion, or busing. There is something admirable about American pragmatism and its attention to a real world in which people live well or suffer, eat well or starve, have medical attention or lack it, and die old or young. Other countries spend more time arguing about the world of social understandings. We gain by our willingness to adopt simple definitions quickly (for example, of poverty) and then start counting people who fall in the category.

Making a Broader Conception of Legitimate Government Action Work

Government cannot abandon the world of expressive meanings to private enterprise. It cannot consider legitimate only what is instrumentally justified as satisfying the unexamined desires of individuals. That approach teaches the wrong lessons and is profoundly undemocratic.

Even the great risks that come with government characterizations of situations, actions, and institutions cannot justify a complete abandonment of expressive action by government officials. By word and action officials must teach social virtues and the value of institutions and rules in general terms; they must also be willing to apply the general lessons to concrete situations.

The real question is whether we can develop a politics that disciplines expressive government action without turning backward to an ideology of instrumentalism. What could be done to control the dangers of divisiveness inherent in expressive government action? This, after all, is an area of government activity almost unconstrained by the equal protection or due process clauses of the Constitution or the Bill of Rights. No court is likely to deny the president, a governor, or a legislature the right to support a particular disputed vision of social reality.

Expressive government action that places a particular situation in some familiar category of people's belief structure can generate public support for particular government choices. Often there is little problem in pursuing such benefits of expressive action. But the choice becomes a very serious one when the public is sharply divided as to the proper characterization of a particular situation, the causes and effects surrounding it, and the various possible government responses.

Slavery and segregation are the outstanding historical examples; abortion is the most important current one. In such situations the government can take either of two positions: it can add its moral weight to one of the competing characterizations, or it can press for mutual tolerance, encouraging each side to recognize that others can honestly believe in an alternative characterization of the situation.

There is surely no universally right answer to this government choice. Toleration of slavery and segregation was a national disgrace; intolerance of the views and practices of religious minorities was almost equally wrong. Government officials must recognize that repression is the likely result if the government throws its support behind one side of a debate where both sides feel their claims to set social direction are deeply moral. Except in situations of clear and dramatic moral importance, putting the credibility of the government behind one side is itself an immorality, although not an unfamiliar one in a country where so much political advantage can come from a dedicated constituency. But even the deepest divisions—civil war—have ultimately seemed preferable to tolerance of inhuman and clearly immoral conduct.

Can we expect that major government choices be explained and justified in the expressive terms of everyday social understandings, where values and predictions are intertwined and where unverifiable descriptions of one segment of the world are explained by (and explain) attitudes toward alternative choices? Here too we cannot expect too much nor should we accept too little.

The language of expressive government action depends on terms that many people will be able to understand and recognize as related to their past experience, and it requires quickly digestible connections. Citizens cannot spend a very long time on most public questions. Argument often proceeds by analogy rather than either induction from experience or deduction from an economic or other model of how society works. Citizens are asked to recognize the dominant importance of certain values or character traits in a particular situation. Or they are asked to accept the similarity of some new event to the models they have used to understand more familiar events. Or they may be asked to assimilate a new event or situation to some well-established attitude or belief.

What can we ask of officials who explain government activity through such arguments by analogy? We must be aware that politicians are tempted to exercise leadership by entering into a comforting psychological or social relationship with citizens, without any necessary regard to the truth of the models on which their proposals are based. When a comforting analogy is substituted for a true one, the currency of democratic discussion is debased. When a simple explanation is substituted for the more difficult one needed to account for the complexity of a situation, the listener is belittled and the truth is disguised. We must point out such deceptions angrily, yet accept discussion in terms of analogies to familiar situations where they represent a careful and honest effort to make the facts comprehensible to a wider public.

We must, in short, develop a tradition of politics that includes vigorous criticism of the looser forms of expressive utterance. Even in expressive debate we should demand that the facts be accurately and fully conveyed, the problem defined with sufficient clarity that alternative frameworks are obvious, and principles or values applied consistently. We must watch for and reject the unexplained leap from platitudes to action-inciting characterizations of events, parties, or situations. Even when the argument is not instrumental but expressive there is a need for intermediate-level premises and an exploration of the connections along the line.

There is ultimately no better guarantee against the dangers of divisiveness, oversimplification, and ineffectiveness than public insistence on three crucial virtues in government. From government officials we must accept a wide range of expressive actions but at the same time demand (1) tolerance of the social visions and characterizations of others; (2) respect for the complexity of social life and the causal patterns that explain it; and (3) impatience with ineffectiveness or hypocrisy in the name of symbolic victories. The country's welfare depends on our insistence that officials show and teach these virtues. For these qualities alone can offset the dangers of accepting the legitimacy of more than instrumental governmental action and the value of more than privately held, undebatable desires.

CHAPTER 5

The Political Theory of the Procedural Republic

Michael J. Sandel

Public policy is not a sovereign subject but a subfield of political theory. No government official or policy analyst, however expert, has yet devised a way of resolving public questions without relying on a theory of the public interest.

But what theory of the public interest is appropriate to an administrative state that is also a democratic state? How can unelected officials govern by a vision of the public interest without imposing their values on democratic institutions? As the scope of government has grown, so have worries about the legitimacy of administrative discretion.

In recent decades, the solution has been sought in the idea of the administrative *process*.[1] The administrative state would "strive to remain neutral among competing conceptions of the good," while securing the capacity of individuals and associations to realize their chosen ends.[2] This ideal of the neutral state finds expression in two familiar theories of the public interest. The first, the utilitarian view, conceives the public interest as the sum of individual preferences, a calculus performed by interest-group bargaining or cost-benefit analysis.[3] The second, the rights-oriented view, would constrain utilitarian considerations by insisting on certain individual rights and entitlements.[4] Both ways of conceiving the public interest seek to reconcile democracy and the administrative state by making it unnecessary for public officials to affirm a substantive conception of public purposes or ends.

Yet doubts persist about the legitimacy of the bureaucratic state, calling into question those theories of the public interest that aspire to neutrality. Several chapters in this volume explore the practical difficulties of understanding the public interest in this way. Here, I examine some of the difficulties as they arise within political theory.

My aim is to connect a certain debate in political theory with a certain development in our political practice. The debate is the one between rights-based liberalism and its communitarian, or civic republican, critics. The development is the advent in the United States of what might be called the "procedural republic," a public life animated by the rights-based liberal ethic. In the modern American welfare state, it seems, the liberal dimensions of our tradition have crowded out the republican dimensions, with adverse consequences for the democratic prospect and the legitimacy of the regime. In this chapter, I will first identify the liberal and civic republican theories at issue in contemporary political philosophy and then employ these contrasting theories in an interpretation of the American political condition. I hope ultimately to show that we can illuminate our political practice by identifying the contending political theories and self-images it embodies.

Liberal Political Theory

Liberals often take pride in defending what they oppose—pornography, for example, or unpopular views.[5] They say the state should not impose on its citizens a preferred way of life, but should leave them as free as possible to choose their own values and ends, consistent with a similar liberty for others. This commitment to freedom of choice requires liberals constantly to distinguish between permission and praise, between allowing a practice and endorsing it. It is one thing to allow pornography, they argue, something else to affirm it.

Conservatives sometimes exploit this distinction by ignoring it. They charge that those who would allow abortions favor abortion, that opponents of school prayer oppose prayer, that those who defend the rights of communists sympathize with their cause. And in a pattern of argument familiar in our politics, liberals reply by invoking higher principles; it is not that they dislike pornography less, but rather that they value toleration or freedom of choice or fair procedures more.

But in contemporary debate, the liberal rejoinder seems increasingly fragile, its moral basis increasingly unclear. Why should toleration and freedom of choice prevail when other important values are also at stake? Too often the answer implies some version of moral relativism, the idea that it is wrong to "legislate morality" because all morality is merely subjective. "Who is to say what is literature and what is filth? That is a value judgment, and whose values should decide?"

Relativism usually appears less as a claim than as a question. ("Who is to judge?") But it is a question that can also be asked of the values that liberals defend. Toleration and freedom and fairness are values too, and they can hardly be defended by the claim that no values can be defended. So it is a mistake to affirm liberal values by arguing that all values are merely subjective. The relativist defense of liberalism is no defense at all.

What then can be the moral basis of the higher principles the liberal invokes? Recent political philosophy has offered two main alternatives—one utilitarian, the other Kantian. The utilitarian view, following John Stuart Mill, defends liberal principles in the name of maximizing the general welfare. The state should not impose on its citizens a preferred way of life, even for their own good, because doing so will reduce the sum of human happiness, at least in the long run; better that people choose for themselves, even if, on occasion, they get it wrong. "The only freedom which deserves the name," writes Mill, "is that of pursuing our own good in our own way, so long as we do not attempt to deprive others of theirs, or impede their efforts to obtain it." He adds that his argument does not depend on any notion of abstract right, only on the principle of the greatest good for the greatest number. "I regard utility as the ultimate appeal on all ethical questions; but it must be utility in the largest sense, grounded on the permanent interests of man as a progressive being."[6]

Many objections have been raised against utilitarianism as a general doctrine of moral philosophy. Some have questioned the concept of utility and the assumption that all human goods are in principle commensurable. Others have objected that by reducing all values to preferences and desires, utilitarians are unable to admit qualitative distinctions of worth, unable to distinguish noble desires from base ones. But most recent debate has focused on whether utilitarianism offers a convincing basis for liberal principles, including respect for individual rights.

In one respect, utilitarianism would seem well suited to liberal purposes. Maximizing utility does not require judging people's values, only aggregating them. And the willingness to aggregate preferences without judging them suggests a tolerant spirit, even a democratic one. When people go to the polls, we count their votes whatever they are.

But the utilitarian calculus is not always as liberal as it first appears. If enough cheering Romans pack the Coliseum to watch a lion devour a Christian, the collective pleasure of the Romans will surely outweigh the pain of the Christian, intense though it be. Or if a big majority abhors a small religion and wants it banned, the balance of preferences will favor suppression, not toleration. Utilitarians sometimes defend individual rights on the grounds that respecting them now will serve utility in the long run. But this calculation is precarious and contingent. It hardly secures the liberal promise not to impose on some the values of others. Just as the majority will is an inadequate instrument of liberal politics—by itself it fails to secure individual rights—so the utilitarian philosophy is an inadequate foundation for liberal principles.

The case against utilitarianism was made most powerfully by Kant. He argued that empirical principles, such as utility, were unfit to serve as basis for the moral law. A wholly instrumental defense of freedom and rights not only leaves rights vulnerable, but fails to respect the inherent dignity of persons. The utilitarian calculus treats people as means to the happiness of others, not as ends in themselves, worthy of respect.[7]

Contemporary liberals extend Kant's argument with the claim that utilitarianism fails to take seriously the distinction between persons. In seeking above all to maximize the general welfare, the utilitarian treats society as a whole as if it were a single person; it conflates our many, diverse desires into a single system of desires and tries to maximize. It is indifferent to the distribution of satisfactions among persons, except insofar as this may affect the overall sum. But this fails to respect our plurality and distinctness. It uses some as means to the happiness of all, and so fails to respect each as an end in himself.

Modern-day Kantians reject the utilitarian approach in favor of an ethic that takes rights more seriously. In their view, certain rights are so fundamental that even the general welfare cannot override them. As John Rawls writes, "Each person possesses an inviolability founded on justice that even the welfare of society as a whole cannot override... The rights secured by justice are not subject to political bargaining or to the calculus of social interests."[8]

So Kantian liberals need an account of rights that does not depend on utilitarian considerations. Moreover, they need an account that does not depend on any particular conception of the good, that does not presuppose the superiority of one way of life over others. Only a justification neutral about ends could preserve the liberal resolve not to favor any particular ends or to impose on some the values of others.

But what sort of justification could this be? How is it possible to affirm certain liberties and rights as fundamental without embracing some vision of the good life, without endorsing some ends over others? It would seem we are back to the relativist predicament—to affirm liberal principles without embracing any particular ends.

The solution proposed by Kantian liberals is to draw a distinction between the "right" and the "good"—between a framework of basic rights and liberties, and the conceptions of the good that people may choose to pursue within the framework. It is one thing for the state to support a fair framework, they argue, something else to affirm some particular ends. For example, it is one thing to defend the right to free speech so that people may be free to form their own opinions and choose their own ends, but something else to support it on the grounds that a life of political discussion is inherently worthier than a life unconcerned with public affairs, or that free speech will increase the general welfare. Only the first defense is available in the Kantian view, resting as it does on the ideal of a neutral framework.

Now the commitment to a framework of rights neutral among ends can be seen as a kind of value—in this sense the Kantian liberal is no relativist—but its value consists precisely in its refusal to affirm a preferred way of life or conception of the good. For Kantian liberals, then, the right is prior to the good, and in two senses. First, individual rights cannot be sacrificed for the sake of the general good; second, the principles of justice that specify these rights cannot be premised on any particular vision of the good life. What justifies the rights is not that they maximize the general welfare or otherwise promote the good, but rather that they comprise a fair framework within which individuals and groups can choose their own values and ends, consistent with a similar liberty for others.

Of course, proponents of the rights-based ethic notoriously disagree about what rights are fundamental and about what political arrangements the ideal of the neutral framework requires. Egalitarian liberals support the welfare state and favor a scheme of civil liberties together with certain social and economic rights—rights to welfare, education, health care, and so on. Libertarian liberals defend the market economy and claim that redistributive policies violate people's rights; they favor a scheme of civil liberties combined with a strict regime of private property rights. But whether egalitarian or libertarian, rights-based liberalism begins with the claim that we are separate, individual persons, each with our own aims, interests, and conceptions of the good, and seeks a framework of rights that will enable us to realize our capacity as free moral agents, consistent with a similar liberty for others.

The Claims of Community

Within academic philosophy, the last decade or so has seen the ascendance of the rights-based ethic over the utilitarian one, due in large part to the influence of John Rawls's important work, *A Theory of Justice.* In the debate between utilitarian and rights-based theories, the rights-based ethic has come to prevail. The legal philosopher H.L.A. Hart recently described the shift from "the old faith that some form of utilitarianism must capture the essence of political morality" to the new faith that "the truth must lie with a doctrine of basic human rights, protecting specific basic liberties and interests of individuals. . . . Whereas not so long ago great energy and much ingenuity of many philosophers were devoted to making some form of utilitarianism work, latterly such energies and ingenuity have been devoted to the articulation of theories of basic rights."[9]

But in philosophy as in life, the new faith becomes the old orthodoxy before long. Even as it has come to prevail over its utilitarian rival, the rights-based ethic has recently faced a growing challenge from a different direction, from a view that gives fuller expresssion to the claims of citizenship and community than the liberal vision allows. Recalling the arguments of Hegel against Kant, the communitarian critics of modern liberalism question the claim for the priority of the right over the good, and the picture of the freely choosing individual it embodies. Following Aristotle, they argue that we cannot justify political arrangements without reference to common purposes and ends, and that we cannot conceive our personhood without reference to our role as citizens and as participants in a common life.

This debate reflects two contrasting pictures of the self. The rights-based ethic and the conception of the person it embodies were shaped in large part in the encounter with utilitarianism. Where utilitarians conflate our many desires into a single system of desire, Kantians insist on the separateness of persons. Where the utilitarian self is simply defined as the sum of its desires, the Kantian self is a choosing self, independent of the desires and ends it may have at any moment. As Rawls writes, "The self is prior to the ends which are affirmed by it; even a dominant end must be chosen from among numerous possibilities."[10]

The priority of the self over its ends means I am never defined by my aims and attachments, but always capable of standing back to survey and assess and possibly to revise them. This is what it means to be a free and independent self, capable of choice. And this is the vision of the self that finds expression in the ideal of the state as a neutral framework. On the rights-based ethic, it is precisely because we are essentially separate, independent selves that we need a neutral framework, a framework of rights that refuses to choose among competing purposes and ends. If the self is prior to its ends, then the right must be prior to the good.

Communitarian critics of rights-based liberalism say we cannot conceive ourselves as independent in this way, as bearers of selves wholly detached from our aims and attachments. They say that certain of our roles are partly constitutive of the persons we are—as citizens of a country or members of a movement or partisans of a cause. But if we are partly defined by the communities we inhabit, then we must also be implicated in the purposes and ends characteristic of those communities. As Alasdair MacIntyre writes, "what is good for me has to be the good for one who inhabits these roles."[11] Open-ended though it be, the story of my life is always embedded in the story of those communities from which I derive my identity—whether family or city, people or nation, party or cause. On the communitarian view, these stories make a moral difference, not only a psychological one. They situate us in the world and give our lives their moral particularity.

What is at stake for politics in the debate between unencumbered selves and situated ones? What are the practical differences between a politics of rights and a politics of the common good? On some issues, the two theories may produce different arguments for similar policies. For example, the civil rights movement of the 1960s might be justified by liberals in the name of human dignity and respect for persons, and by communitarians in the name of recognizing the full membership of fellow citizens wrongly excluded from the common life of the nation. And while liberals might support public education in hopes of equipping students to become autonomous individuals, capable of choosing their own ends and pursuing them effectively, communitarians might support public education in hopes of equipping students to become good citizens, capable of contributing meaningfully to public deliberations and pursuits.

On other issues, the two ethics might lead to different policies. Communitarians would be more likely than liberals to allow a town to ban pornographic bookstores, on the grounds that pornography offends its way of life and the values that sustain it. But a politics of the common good does not always part company with liberalism in favor of conservative policies. For example, communitarians would be more willing than some rights-oriented liberals to see states enact laws regulating plant closings, to protect their communities from the disruptive effects of capital mobility and sudden industrial change. More generally, where the liberal regards the expansion of individual rights and entitlements as unqualified moral and political progress, the communitarian is troubled by the tendency of liberal programs to displace politics from smaller forms of association to more comprehensive ones. Where libertarian liberals defend the private economy and egalitarian liberals defend the welfare state, communitarians worry about the concentration of power in both the corporate economy and the bureaucratic state, and the erosion of those intermediate forms of community that have at times sustained a more vital public life.

Liberals often argue that a politics of the common good, drawing as it must on particular loyalties, obligations, and traditions, opens the way to prejudice and intolerance. The modern nation-state is not the Athenian *polis*, they point out; the scale and diversity of modern life have rendered the Aristotelian political ethic nostalgic at best and dangerous at worst. Any attempt to govern by a vision of the common good is likely to lead to a slippery slope of totalitarian temptations.

Communitarians reply that intolerance flourishes most where forms of life are dislocated, roots unsettled, traditions undone. In our day, the totalitarian impulse has sprung less from the convictions of confidently situated selves than from the confusions of atomized, dislocated, frustrated selves, at sea in a world where common meanings have lost their force. As Hannah Arendt has written, "What makes mass society so difficult to bear is not the number of people involved, or at least not primarily, but the fact that the world between them has lost its power to gather them together, to relate and to separate them."[12] Insofar as our public life has withered, our sense of common involvement diminished, we lie vulnerable to the mass politics of totalitarian solutions. So responds the party of the common good to the party of rights. If the party of the common good is correct, our most pressing moral and political project is to revitalize those civic republican possibilities implicit in our tradition but fading in our time.

Theory in Practice

How might the contrast between the liberal and communitarian, or civic republican, theories we have been considering help illuminate our present political condition? We might begin by locating these theories in the political history of the American republic. Both the liberal and the republican conceptions have been present throughout, but in differing measure, with shifting importance. Broadly speaking, the republican strand was most evident from the time of the founding to the late nineteenth century; by the mid- to late twentieth century, the liberal conception came increasingly to predominate, gradually crowding out republican dimensions. I shall try in this section to identify three moments in the transition from the republican to the liberal public philosophy: (1) the civic republic, (2) the national republic, (3) the procedural republic.

Civic Republic

The ideological origins of American politics are the subject of lively and voluminous debate among intellectual historians. Some emphasize the Lockean liberal sources of American political thought, others the civic republican influences.[13] But beyond the question of who influenced the founders' thought is the further question of what kind of political life they actually lived. It is clear that the assumptions embodied in the practice of eighteenth-century American politics, the ideas and institutions that together constitute the "civic republic," differ from those of the modern liberal political order in several respects. First, liberty in the civic republic was defined not in opposition to democracy, as an individual's guarantee against what the majority might will, but as a function of democracy, of democratic institutions and dispersed power. In the eighteenth century, civil liberty referred not to a set of personal rights, in the sense of immunities, as in the modern "right to privacy," but, in Hamilton's words, "to a share in the government." Civil liberty was public or political liberty, "equivalent to democracy or government by the people themselves." It was not primarily individual but "the freedom of bodies politic, or States."[14]

Second, the terms of relation between the individual and the nation were not direct and unmediated, but indirect, mediated by decentralized forms of political association, participation, and allegiance. As

Laurence Tribe points out, "it was largely through the preservation of boundaries between and among institutions that the rights of persons were to be secured."[15] Perhaps the most vivid constitutional expression of this fact is that the Bill of Rights did not apply to the states and was not understood to create individual immunities from all government action. When James Madison proposed, in 1789, a constitutional amendment providing that "no State shall infringe the equal rights of conscience, nor the freedom of speech or of the press, nor of the right of trial by jury in criminal cases," the liberal, rights-based ethic found its clearest early expression. But Madison's proposal was rejected by the Senate and did not succeed until the Fourteenth Amendment was passed some seventy-nine years later.

Finally, the early republic was a place where the possibility of civic virtue was a live concern. Some saw civic virtue as essential to the preservation of liberty; others despaired of virtue and sought to design institutions that could function without it.[16] But as Tocqueville found in his visit to the New England townships, public life functioned in part as an education in citizenship: "Town meetings are to liberty what primary schools are to science; they bring it within the people's reach, they teach men how to use and how to enjoy it. A nation may establish a free government, but without municipal institutions it cannot have the spirit of liberty."[17]

National Republic

The transition to the national and ultimately the procedural republic begins to unfold from the end of the Civil War to the turn of the century.[18] As national markets and large-scale enterprise displaced a decentralized economy, the decentralized political forms of the early republic became outmoded as well. If democracy was to survive, the concentration of economic power would have to be met by a similar concentration of political power. But the Progressives understood, or some of them did, that the success of democracy required more than the centralization of government; it also required the nationalization of politics. The primary form of political community had to be recast on a national scale. For Herbert Croly, writing in 1909, the "nationalizing of American political, economic, and social life" was "an essentially formative and enlightening political transformation." We would become more of a democracy only as we became "more of a nation . . . in ideas, in institutions, and in spirit."[19]

This nationalizing project would be consummated in the New Deal, but for the democratic tradition in America, the embrace of the nation was a decisive departure. From Jefferson to the populists, the party of democracy in American political debate had been, roughly speaking, the party of the provinces, of decentralized power, of small-town and small-scale America. And against them had stood the party of the nation—first Federalists, then Whigs, then the Republicans of Lincoln—a party that spoke for the consolidation of the union. It was thus the historic achievement of the New Deal to unite, in a single party and political program, what Samuel Beer has called "liberalism and the national idea."[20]

What matters for our purpose is that in the twentieth century liberalism made its peace with concentrated power. But it was understood at the start that the terms of this peace required a strong sense of national community, morally and politically, to underwrite the extended involvements of a modern industrial order. If a virtuous republic of small-scale, democratic communities was no longer a possibility, a national republic seemed democracy's next best hope. This was still, in principle at least, a politics of the common good. It looked to the nation not as a neutral framework for the play of competing interests, but rather as a formative community, concerned to shape a common life suited to the scale of modern social and economic forms.

But by the mid- to late twentieth century, the national republic had run its course. Except for extraordinary moments, such as war, the nation proved too vast a scale across which to cultivate the shared self-understandings necessary to community in the formative, or constitutive sense. And yet, given the scale of economic and political life, there seemed no turning back. If so extended a republic could not sustain a politics of the common good, a different sort of legitimating ethic would have to be found. And so the gradual shift, in our practices and institutions, from a public philosophy of common purposes to one of fair procedures, from the national republic to the procedural republic.

Procedural Republic

The procedural republic represents the triumph of a liberal public philosophy over a republican one, with adverse consequences for democratic politics and the legitimacy of the regime. It reverses the terms of relation between liberty and democracy, transforms the relation of the individual and nation-state, and tends to undercut the kind of community on which it nonetheless depends. Liberty in the procedural republic is defined not as a function of democracy but in opposition to democracy, as an individual's guarantee against what the majority might will. I am free insofar as I am the bearer of rights, where rights are trumps.[21]

Unlike the liberty of the early republic, the modern version permits, even requires, concentrated power. This has at least partly to do with the universalizing logic of rights. Insofar as I have a right, whether to free speech or a minimum income, its provision cannot be left to the vagaries of local preferences but must be assured at the most comprehensive level of political association. It cannot be one thing in New York and another in Alabama. As rights and entitlements expand, politics is therefore displaced from smaller forms of association and relocated at the most universal form—in our case, the nation. And even as politics flows to the nation, power shifts away from democratic institutions (such as legislatures and political parties), toward institutions designed to be insulated from democratic pressures and hence better equipped to dispense and defend individual rights (notably the judiciary and bureaucracy).

These institutional developments may begin to account for the sense of powerlessness that the welfare state fails to address and in some ways doubtless deepens. But a further clue to our condition may lie in the vision of the unencumbered self that animates the liberal ethic. It is a striking feature of the welfare state that it offers a powerful promise of individual rights and also demands of its citizens a high measure of mutual engagement. But the self-image that attends the rights cannot sustain the engagement. As bearers of rights, where rights are trumps, we think of ourselves as freely choosing, individual selves, unbound by obligations antecedent to rights or to the agreements we make. And yet, as citizens of the procedural republic that secures these rights, we find ourselves implicated willy-nilly in a formidable array of dependencies and expectations that we did not choose and increasingly reject.

In our public life, we are more entangled but less attached than ever before. It is as though the unencumbered self presupposed by the liberal ethic had begun to come true—less liberated than disempowered, entangled in a network of obligations and involvements unassociated with any act of will and yet unmediated by those common identifications or expansive self-definitions that would make them tolerable. As the scale of social and political organization has become more comprehensive, the terms of our collective identity have become more fragmented, and the forms of political life have outrun the common purposes needed to sustain them.

CHAPTER 6

Policy Making in a Democracy

Robert B. Reich

So far in this volume it has been argued that citizens are motivated to act according to ideas about what is good for society; that such ideas determine how public problems are defined and understood; that government depends on such ideas for mobilizing public action; that, in consequence, policy makers find themselves espousing substantive conceptions of the public good (although the expression is often implicit); and that this role, in turn, raises questions about the place of policy making in a democratic society. If conceptions about what is good for society are different from mere aggregations of selfish wants, where should policy makers look for guidance about what they should do? What is the relationship between policy making and democracy? In this chapter I offer tentative responses to these questions, grounded in the idea of public deliberation.

For the typical public manager who heads a bureaucracy charged with implementing the law, public debate is not something to be invited. It is difficult enough to divine what the legislature had in mind when it enacted the law, how the governor or president wants it to be interpreted and administered, and what course is consistent with sound public policy. It is harder still to commandeer the resources necessary to implement the program, to overcome bureaucratic inertia and institutional rigidity, and to ensure that a system for producing the desired result is actually in place and working. In the midst of these challenges, public controversy is not particularly welcome. The tacit operating rule holds that the best public is a quiescent one; the manager should work quietly, get the job done without disturbing the peace, and reassure everyone "out there" that there is no reason to be concerned or involved.

But sometimes, I believe, higher-level public managers have an obligation to stimulate public debate about what they do. Public deliberation can help the manager clarify ambiguous mandates. More importantly, it can help the public discover latent contradictions and commonalities in what it wants to achieve. Thus the public manager's job is not only, or simply, to make policy choices and implement them. It is also to participate in a system of democratic governance in which public values are continuously rearticulated and recreated.

The first part of this chapter considers the problem of administrative discretion in its historical context. The next section examines the two techniques of constraining administrative discretion that have come to dominate our thinking about responsive government. In the third section I will show why these two dominant forms have failed to solve the problem of administrative discretion in a democracy. The fourth section suggests why public deliberation may, at least on occasion, offer a desirable alternative to the dominant forms. The final sections will examine some applications of this errant concept and the lessons they reveal about the possibilities and limits of public delibertion.

The Problem of Administrative Discretion

Nonelected public managers at the higher reaches of administration—commissioners, secretaries, agency heads, division chiefs, bureau directors—rarely can rely on unambiguous legislative mandates. The statutes that authorize them to take action are often written in vague language, unhelpful for difficult cases of a sort the legislative drafters never contemplated or did not wish to highlight for fear that explication might jeopardize a delicate compromise. The legislators may have had conflicting ideas about how the law should be implemented and decided to leave the task to those who would be closer to the facts and circumstances of particular applications. Or they may simply have wanted an administrator to take the political heat for doing something too unpopular to be codified explicitly in legislation. Or the legislators may have felt that the issue was not sufficiently important to merit their time and resources.

As a result, higher-level public managers are likely to have significant discretion over many of the problems they pursue, solutions they devise, and strategies they choose for implementing such solutions. To be sure, they will need to keep in touch with key legislators and elected officials within the executive branch who have an interest in the policy area—periodically informing them of plans, seeking their approval of broad purposes and strategies, and reporting on important problems and accomplishments. But despite these informal ties, public managers will have considerable running room. There are typically too many decisions to be made, over too wide a range of issues, for even informal ties to bind. Administrative discretion is endemic.

Given this range of discretion, it may seem curious that so little thought has been given to the relationship between administrative performance and democratic values. It is particularly curious in light of the extraordinary attention devoted to the parallel problem facing the judiciary—the other domain of nonelected discretion in government. A seemingly endless stream of critical commentary has sought to reconcile judge-made law with democratic values. Although the *Federalist* described the judiciary as the "least dangerous branch" of government, having no direct influence over "the sword or the purse,"[1] generations of scholars and commentators have fretted over where judges should find their substantive conception of the public interest— whether from some transcendant notion of natural law, principles deducible from the common law, historical inquiries into what the framers of the Constitution (or the drafters of various statutes) "really" had in mind, or some set of "neutral principles" that reconcile and give consistent meaning to various constitutional and common law provisions.[2]

At the very least, the public has come to expect that judges will justify their decisions by reference to general principles lying beyond the particular situation confronting them, reflecting some intelligible and coherent normative ideas—or that they will refrain from deciding at all. Judges are in the business of articulating public values, within a form of argumentation and logic fundamentally concerned with how such values can and should be found. Judicial opinions are attempts at stating public ideas—trying them out first on other judges, who are either persuaded by them or compelled to say why they are not. This ongoing conversation among judges, as they grapple with public ideas in differing contexts, is a form of public deliberation. Judicial opinions are arguments for public legitimacy. The ultimate test of such an articulation is how persuasive the public finds the argument.

History may explain the different treatments accorded judges and administrators. Judicial discretion has been long understood as a potential threat to democratic values. Not so administrative discretion. In the half-century before World War II, the standard American attitude toward administrative discretion vacillated between efforts to improve its exercise and to deny its existence. Initially, the two coexisted quite peacefully. Administrative action was seen less as an act of discretion than as an application of expertise—the discovery of the best means of executing preordained public goals. No less a Progressive reformer than Woodrow Wilson saw public administration as a "detailed and systematic execution of public law" in which discretion was confined to the expert choice of means for carrying out policies decided on by elected officials.[3] Fellow political scientists Frank Goodnow and Charles Beard called for a science of administration through which public administrators could use their knowledge of administration and the tools of social science to serve the public interest.[4] By 1914 several American universities were offering one-year master's degrees in public administration, and by 1924 the first semi-independent school for training public officials was founded at Syracuse University.

As these Progressive era ideals found expression in independent administrative agencies, some members of the legal community grew concerned about the extraordinary delegation of legislative-like responsibilities these schemes implied. Legal scholars like Ernst Freund warned that broad grants of administrative discretion to set rates and standards would reduce public accountability and cause democratic institutions to atrophy.[5] With increasing enthusiasm—culminating in the Supreme Court's determination that Title I of the National Recovery Act of 1933 represented an unconstitutional delegation of congressional authority—the federal courts struck down statutes that contained broad delegations of administrative responsibility.[6]

This conceptual tension between the benefits of administrative expertise and the evils of administrative discretion continued into the 1930s. New Dealers like Felix Frankfurter and James Landis, among others, saw in the development of administrative agencies a capacity to solve social and economic problems quickly and efficiently, applying systematic knowledge to public issues. These New Deal theorists of public administration perceived no conflict between their vision and democratic ideas: elected representatives would define the broad goals and problems to be addressed; the agencies would solve them. Others, however, particularly those sitting on the federal courts, took a dimmer view.

By the middle of the decade, under pressure from Franklin D. Roosevelt, the courts relented. Most broad delegations of authority would thereafter be declared constitutional. But it was not just

Roosevelt's threat to pack the Supreme Court that tipped the scales at the time. Public opinion was solidly behind the ideal of administrative expertise. From the depths of the Depression the public goals seemed self-evident—to get the economy moving again and ameliorate some of the worst suffering. The challenge was to discover and implement solutions. And this was manifestly a job for expert judgment. If not delegated to expert agencies, that job could only be handled by the courts, through case-by-case adjudication of specific applications of broad statutes. But the courts lacked the expertise, they could not be counted on to act quickly, and they had no capacity to solve the inevitable problems of implementation.[7] The logic of the reformers seemed irrefutable.

In reality, of course, no sharp line could be drawn between ends and means, between making policy and implementing it. During the Depression decade of the 1930s and the subsequent war years, there was a broad consensus about the problems that needed to be solved. This left considerable room for administrative discretion that *looked* like implementation. After peace and prosperity had been substantially attained, the next set of goals—having more to do with the quality of the life Americans would lead thereafter—was less clear-cut. Accordingly, administrative discretion began looking more like policy making. This shift in public perceptions, in turn, brought into sharper focus the problem of reconciling discretion with democratic values.

There was another reason why the American public became more sensitive to administrative discretion after 1945. The fresh experience of fascism, Soviet totalitarianism, and then McCarthyism at home caused many to view with alarm any scheme of governance that permitted moral absolutism or smacked of social engineering. To Americans who had emerged from the shadow of demagoguery, the virtue of American democracy appeared to lie in political pluralism and ethical relativism.[8] Political scientists of the era slipped gingerly from description to prescription: American politics was pluralist, composed of shifting and overlapping groups whose leaders bargained with one another; the vast majority of Americans were members of one or more of these groups, even if they remained mostly uninvolved. These features helped to explain why democracy had survived so well in the United States, by contrast to many other nations; these features were thus desirable prerequisites for democracy.[9] Economists began to entertain a similar vision of democracy as a contest among leaders to represent the interests of competing groups.[10]

Broad grants of administrative discretion to the "experts" seemed dangerously inconsistent with these newly discovered democratic virtues. Accordingly, the postwar intellectual and political agenda turned toward *reducing* administrative discretion rather than justifying and enlarging on it. But this proved no mean task. Given the complexities of modern government, legislatures could not simply reclaim responsibilities of the sort they had been delegating to administrators. At the same time, given the premises of pluralism and relativism, it was quite impossible to construct a set of substantive standards to guide administrators in discovering the public interest. For there was no longer assumed to be any unified "public interest" capable of discovery. What passed for the public interest at any moment was now thought to be the product of an ongoing competition among groups for power and influence.

One needed some means of reconciling the practical necessity of administrative discretion with this emerging pluralist norm—a way to retain the broadly delegated authority of administrators to make choices in the public interest, while radically limiting their substantive discretion over where the "public interest" might lie. The solution was found in the idea of administrative process. Henceforth, public administrators were to be managers of neutral processes designed to discover the best ("optimal") public policies. Their substantive expertise about a particular set of public problems was to be transformed into procedural expertise about a set of techniques applicable to all sorts of public problems. At the same time, new emphasis was to given to the details of making administrative decisions. Public managers would have to follow certain preordained steps for gathering evidence and arriving at conclusions. The Administrative Procedure Act of 1946 and its subsequent amendments codified the prevailing expectations. The burgeoning field of administrative law thereafter concerned itself primarily with the procedural steps judges should demand of public administrators, rather than with the substance of what administrators ought to do. The effect was to treat administrative law as the consequence of judicial review rather than as a set of substantive standards of public administration.

Even the words used to describe the responsibilities of administrators subtly changed. Instead of finding the "common good" or the "public interest," the new language of public management saw the task in pluralist terms—making "tradeoffs," "balancing" interests, engaging in "policy choices," and weighing the costs and benefits. Graduate schools of public administration henceforth would pay less attention to the purposes and methods of governance than to the techniques of making and implementing public policy. Courses in "analysis" and "implementation" would frame the core curricula.[11]

The Two Paradigms

The postwar transformation of public administration centered on two related but conceptually distinct procedural visions of how public managers should decide what to do. The first entailed *intermediating among interest groups;* the second, *maximizing net benefits.* Intermediation was the direct intellectual descendant of pluralist theory. Maximization was a stepchild, claiming equal descent from decision theory and microeconomics. Together the two procedural visions embodied the postwar shift from a description of how democratic institutions work to a powerful set of norms for how public decision making should be organized.

Interest Group Intermediation

Interest group intermediation took as its starting point the prevailing pluralist understanding of American politics, along with its prescriptive tilt. The job of the public manager, according to this vision, was to accommodate—to the extent possible—the varying demands placed on government by competing groups. The public manager was a referee, an intermediary, a skillful practitioner of negotiation and compromise. He was to be accessible to all organized interests while making no independent judgment of the merits of their claims. Since, in this view, the "public interest" was simply an amalgamation and reconciliation of these claims, the manager succeeded to the extent that the competing groups were placated.

In time, as the rather self-congratulatory pluralist theories of the 1950s and early 1960s gave way to a deepening critique of the American "administrative state" for its insensitivity to less organized interests and its corresponding tendency to be captured by dominant interests, the job of the manager-as-intermediator was refined. The central challenge came to be understood as ensuring that *all* those who might be affected by agency action were represented in decision-making deliberations—including interests dispersed so widely and thinly over the population that they might otherwise go unexpressed.

The federal courts took an early, active role in this refinement. As early as 1966 the Court of Appeals for the District of Columbia Circuit ruled that, within a license renewal proceeding, the Federal Communica-

tions Commission was obliged to permit the intervention of spokesmen for significant segments of the listening public. The basis for the
ruling was that, since consideration of such viewpoints was necessary
to ensure a decision responsive to public needs, failure to allow intervention rendered decisions arbitrary and capricious. The court noted that
in "recent years, the concept that public participation in decisions which
involve the public interest is not only valuable but indispensable has
gained increasing support."[12] Subsequent court decisions required that
an agency seek out representatives of opposing views, that it affirma-
tively consider all such views, and that it also consider alternate policy
choices in light of their impact on all affected interests.[13] State courts
imposed similar requirements on state agencies. Public participation
was further aided by several statutes that provided funding for interest
groups to be represented in agency proceedings. The Federal Trade
Commission Improvement Act of 1975, for example, authorized the
FTC to pay attorneys' fees and costs of rule-making participation to
any group representing an interest that "would not otherwise be
represented in such a proceeding" and whose representation "is
necessary for a fair determination of the rule-making proceeding."[14]

As opportunities for participation grew, the task of interest group
intermediation became more open to public scrutiny—or rather to the
scrutiny of organized groups with the resources to ferret out
information from the government. Courts required, for example, that
all relevant information from agency files or consultants' reports be
disclosed to all participants for comment, that agency announcements
of proposed rule making give the agency's view of the issues, and that
agency decision makers generally refrain from communicating in
secret with participants.[15] Moreover, in the 1976 Government in the
Sunshine Act, Congress declared it "the policy of the United States that
the public is entitled to the fullest practicable information regarding the
decisionmaking processes of the Federal Government." The act
required that, with limited exceptions, agencies make their decisions in
public.[16]

These developments tended to formalize the administrative process, making it resemble a trial court proceeding. But their more
consequential effect was to impose ever more severe penalties on a
public manager who failed to reach a workable compromise with
groups that had the resources to challenge his decision in the courts, on
some procedural ground. The penalty they could threaten was delay;
litigation could drag on for years. Procedural formality thereby upped
the ante, making accommodation all the more important.

Accommodation was possible largely because participation was conditioned on specific, concrete, and self-serving claims, rather than on general views about what policies were in the "public interest." To be sure, these self-interested claims typically were encased within arguments appealing to general principles of law or public interest that tended to favor the claimants' position. But it was well understood that the purpose of the inquiry was not to discover the public interest directly, only to find it indirectly by identifying programs or solutions that accommodated most groups. The courts would not guarantee groups espousing so-called ideological interests—who had no selfish stake in the outcome—a right to participate in the proceedings. Participation was conditioned on a showing that the proposed agency action might cause some material "injury in fact" to members of the group, or that the group's interest was specifically protected by the statute in question.

This condition aided accommodation in two ways. First and most obviously, it limited participation. If the proceedings were open to anyone who claimed to know what was best for the public, there might be no efficient way of reaching agreement among so large a crowd. Even more importantly, the requirement that participants have experienced a concrete injury ensured that grievances could be remedied and compromises devised. There would be no efficient way to bargain with parties espousing purely "ideological" views about what was good for the community or the nation, because there would be no obvious means of compensating them for their potential loss. Their injuries would involve values rather than palpable harms. Such values are often impossible to measure or rank, and they have an all-or-nothing quality that makes them stubbornly resistant to tradeoffs. They cannot be compromised easily without losing their inherent moral character.[17]

Net Benefit Maximization

Net benefit maximization proceeded along a different route. This paradigm took as its starting point the decision-making tools that had been successfully applied in World War II for allocating resources and planning strategy, and added to them microeconomic theory, which supplied the idea of allocative efficiency. But the shift from description to prescription was as complete as in the preceding vision. How people acted in the market to satisfy their desires was taken as a model for how public managers should decide what to do. In this view government intervention was justified primarily when it would result in an allocation of goods and services better matched to what people want than the outcome generated by market forces alone (as under conditions of natural monopoly or other forms of "market failure"). Even when allocative efficiency was not the goal of a given intervention, consideration of economic effects presumably would lead to a more efficient intervention—that is, one that achieved its goal at minimal cost.

Here the public manager was less a referee than an analyst. His responsibilities were, first, to determine that the market had somehow failed and that intervention might improve overall efficiency; second, to structure the decision-making process so as to make explicit the public problem at issue, alternative means of remedying it, and the consequences and tradeoffs associated with each solution; and third, to choose the policy option yielding the highest net benefits—where there was the greatest social utility. Along the way he (or his staff) might employ a range of analytic tools: probability theory, to deal with uncertainty; econometric, queuing, diffusion, and demographic models, to help predict the remote consequences of particular actions; linear programming, to perform complex resource allocation computations; discounting, to measure future outcomes in terms of present values; and other variations on game theory, statistics, and mathematics. Social science data derived from empirical experiments and field studies might be applicable to these analytic processes, of course, particularly to anticipate the consequences of various alternatives. But unlike his prewar predecessors who wielded substantive expertise, the public manager who sought to maximize net benefits relied primarily on procedural expertise. His focus was on how to organize the process of discovering the optimal policy.

Net benefit maximization became a cornerstone of regulatory reform efforts. Between 1965 and 1980, Congress passed approximately forty new laws—on health, education, transportation, housing, the environment, and agriculture—that required evaluations of the economic impact of regulations proposed under them. Six of these laws specifically authorized funding of, or required that a fixed percentage of the agency program budget be set aside for, such evaluations.[18] In addition, the Ford, Carter, and Reagan administrations actively pursued economic impact analysis. Executive orders required that agencies subject major regulations to a "regulatory analysis" that contained a succinct statement of the problem requiring federal action, the major ways of dealing with it, analysis of the economic effects of the proposed regulation and of alternative approaches considered, and a justification of the approach selected. These analyses were to be reviewed by groups within the Office of Management and Budget, or affiliated with the Council of Economic Advisors, to ensure that major regulations were justifiable in terms of costs and benefits.[19] Similar efforts cropped up among the states. At the same time, and with increasing boldness, the courts also embraced net benefit maximization. They deemed evidence "insufficient" or the process of decision making "arbitrary and capricious" when an agency disregarded important economic effects of its actions, artificially narrowed options, failed to set forth its theories, or employed faulty analysis and a weak chain of analytic reasoning.[20]

Net benefit maximization shared with interest group intermediation the central premise that the "public interest" could—and should—be defined only by reference to the disparate, selfish preferences of individuals. But rather than uncritically accept the preferences articulated by and through group leaders, net benefit maximizers sought to measure preferences directly by observing how people behaved. If people were simply asked what they wanted, their responses would not necessarily reflect tradeoffs implied in the choice. A preferable course was to observe how people expressed their priorities within the numerous market transactions of their daily lives. If the policy at issue concerned something that was not traded on the market, like clean air, the net benefit maximizer would seek a surrogate measure of citizens' willingness to pay for such a good, like the price of homes in a nonpolluted area of town relative to housing prices in a polluted section nearby.

Policies that would make one group of people worse off and another group better off posed a special problem. Interest group intermediators attempted to solve it by pitting the groups against one another, presumably until an accommodation occurred through which the gainers shared some of their benefits with the losers. This approach still left open the possibility that certain groups might have more organizational strength than others and thus could impose substantial (although perhaps widely dispersed) costs on the others for the sake of relatively small gains for themselves. Net benefit maximizers sought to solve the problem through cost-benefit analysis; policies would be chosen that conferred larger benefits on some than losses for others. Because there is no theoretically defensible means of determining that the wants of one group of people are either stronger or more worthy than those of another, net benefit maximizers felt more confident about these decisions if the two groups—the gainers and the losers— started in roughly equivalent circumstances or, if not, the resulting redistribution at least moved them closer together.[21] But such judgments ultimately rested on a pluralist vision as well—one that perceived individuals as members of groups, the members as possessing certain common characteristics, and the groups existing in some specific and identifiable relationship to one another. These perceptions, in turn, could be drawn reliably only from the ways in which the groups actually organized themselves—what criteria defined their memberships, how they described their central purposes, and how they characterized themselves.

The Two Paradigms in Practice

These two approaches to policy making—interest group intermediation and net benefit maximization—have coexisted uneasily. Both have rested on the same pluralist vision and understood the "public interest" as nothing more (or other) than the disparate sentiments of diverse groups of people about what they want for themselves, combined with procedural norms for weighing and balancing such interests. And from a strictly theoretical perspective (ignoring agency and transaction problems) there is no difference in outcome between the two methods. After all, any "solution" whose benefits exceed its costs would enable those who gain from it to compensate those who lose (or who receive none of the direct benefits) and still come out ahead. Since actual compensation would cause losers and nongainers to acquiesce to the change, the mere fact of unanimous agreement to a compromise would signal that it is efficient.

As a practical matter, however, the two approaches have diverged in several ways. The first involves the objectives to be sought by government intervention. Interest group intermediators have assumed that the objective will emerge only from the interactions of divergent participants and cannot be fully defined in advance. This lack of definition enables each of the participating groups to believe (or at least its leader to claim to his clients and constituents) that the intervention served the group's purposes. As a result, the public goal of the government action is established after the fact, if at all. But net benefit maximizers have required that the objective be articulated as specifically and narrowly as possible in advance, so that alternative (and less costly) means of attaining it can be considered.

A second divergence has to do with evidence. Interest group intermediators have assumed that the facts at issue are the articulated preferences of parties likely to be affected by the rule. Relevant evidence therefore properly includes a substantial amount of testimony by group representatives about what the group wants and needs. On the other hand, net benefit maximizers have not concerned themselves with articulated preferences. The facts at issue are the potential overall costs and benefits of the proposed action and its alternatives. Articulated preferences offer a poor means of measuring these values.

A final divergence concerns the criteria for a good decision. Interest group intermediators have believed the best decision is the one most acceptable (or least objectionable) to the groups affected—that outcome to which the greatest number of participants ultimately subscribe most enthusiastically. But net benefit maximizers have believed the best decision is the most efficient one—that which maximizes benefits for a given cost or minimizes costs for a given benefit. Negotiation and compromise have nothing to do with it; an efficient solution might be unpopular with many participants.

To get a concrete sense of these differences, imagine a town in a river valley periodically subject to flooding. The public manager has a broad statutory mandate to "manage the environment" or "manage water resources"; or perhaps he is a city manager charged with overseeing the local government. If he views his role as interest group intermediator, he would listen to the complaints of various group representatives who came to his office—business and civic associations representing downstream merchants and householders who want a dam constructed. He also would listen to residents of the less populous area upstream, who would lose their businesses and homes if a dam turned the upstream area into a reservoir. The intermediator's objective is neither to stop the downstream flooding nor to save upstream homes, but only to reach an accommodation that basically satisfies the various groups. Our manager-as-intermediator also might solicit the participation of other, less organized groups, such as lower-income people who now rent houses on the flood plain (whose rents would substantially increase if the land values were to rise). The resulting decision would reflect a great deal of negotiation. The dam may be built; but if so, upstream owners will be paid for their land and their moving expenses, and perhaps given an additional "sweetener," and some of the poorer renters downstream will be allocated parcels of the new land made habitable as a result of the project.

A manager who viewed his role as net benefit maximizer would proceed quite differently. He would be open to the possibility of a dam project, since the market cannot be expected on its own to generate a "public good" like a dam. But he would carefully examine the costs and benefits of building it or taking any other measure to reduce downstream flooding. He might gather evidence of the market values of property on the flood plain, above it, and upstream—thereby discovering how much money people in principle would be willing to spend to avoid flooding, on the one hand, or to live in the rural area upstream that would be permanently flooded by construction of a dam. In the end, let us suppose, the administrator decides that the benefits of the dam far outweigh the costs. The dam will be built. But upstream landowners will not necessarily be paid anything (beyond the "just compensation" required by the Fifth Amendment to the Constitution) since actual compensation need not be paid to make the outcome efficient, and there is no particular income difference between upstream and downstream owners that might justify such a payment. Poorer renters downstream will receive a cash transfer instead of an allocation of the newly habitable public lands; such a transfer will represent a more efficient redistribution than a donation of the land, since the poor can then choose how they wish to spend it.

It is hardly surprising that these two different approaches have, in practice, resulted in something of a hybrid. While the formal language of policy making increasingly has borrowed forms of argument and analysis from net benefit maximization, the actual process of coming to a decision has rested ever more firmly on interest group intermediation. Each participating group typically submits its own data and analysis tending to support a definition of the problem and a proposed solution that best serves its wants. To return to our example, upstream homeowners could be expected to submit data and analyses suggesting that the periodic costs of downstream flooding are really quite minor, while the costs of damming the river and flooding upstream would be high, and that, in any event, the problem could be alleviated simply by building a drainage canal. Downstream owners, on the other hand, would submit data and analyses tending to show that the costs of failing to remedy the problem are higher than those of building the dam, and that there are no less costly alternatives. Typically the public manager would compromise among these competing estimates, choosing a set of valuations approximately halfway between those offered by the competing camps (thereby practicing interest group intermediation while applying the form of net benefit maximization.)[22]

Ironically, the hybrid of the two procedural visions occasionally has thwarted both. The strategic use of the *form* of net benefit maximization in the *process* of intermediation has tended to exacerbate a central problem of intermediation: the underrepresentation of poor and diffused interests. The very insistence on analytic argument has altered the rules of the game; proffered "views" are no longer assertions of preference for certain outcomes, but estimates of costs and benefits, and predictions about future consequences. Wealthy and well-organized groups have been able to offer sophisticated analyses and rebut alternative (often less sophisticated) analyses supplied by less well-endowed groups. The very complexity of the analysis has tended to discourage the involvement of a wider range of participants, who feel that they have nothing legitimate to add to this form of public debate.

At the same time, the commingling of the two approaches has aggravated a central problem of net benefit maximization, which is the interpersonal comparisons of utilities implied when some people gain and others lose from a policy deemed to maximize net social benefits. The analytic form of argument has obscured the actual patterns of group organization and membership lying behind it. This in turn has made it more difficult to judge whether groups of gainers and losers are in roughly equivalent circumstances to begin with, or whether the resulting redistribution brings them closer together.

The net result of these conceptual impasses has been to undermine further the legitimacy of administrative decision making and subject it to repeated criticism both for failing to respond adequately to affected interests *and* for failing to yield efficient solutions. Proposals for reform have cycled back and forth between interest group intermediation and net benefit maximization as the inadequacies of first one, then the other vision are exposed. Not surprisingly, the resulting policy decisions have often lacked broad and sustained public support.

The Problem of Neutrality

The muddle into which both types of policy making have fallen is due, I believe, to difficulties lying deeper than the problems of reconciling them or the technical challenges of accommodating diffused interests and comparing the utilities of different groups. These are symptoms of a more profound failure to reflect an authentic governmental character—that is, to inspire confidence among citizens that the decisions of public managers are genuinely in the "public interest."

Both procedural devices are premised on the view that democracy is simply (or largely) a matter of putting public authority to the service of what individual people want. These individual preferences in turn are assumed to exist apart from any process designed to discover and respond to them—outside any social experience with democratic governance. Both interest group intermediation and net benefit maximization share a view of democracy in which relevant communications all flow in one direction: from individuals' preferences to public officials, whose job it is to accommodate or aggregate them. The formal democratic process of electing representatives is only the most traditional manifestation of this communications system. Since elected representatives cannot or will not fully instruct public managers in what to do, the formal process has needed to be enlarged and supplemented by a separate system that links individual preferences more directly to administrative decision making: hence interest group intermediation and net benefit maximization.[23]

This view of the place of public management in a democracy suffers from two related difficulties. First, it is inaccurate. Individual preferences do not arise outside and apart from their social context, but are influenced by both the process and the substance of policy making. Communications move in both directions, from citizen to policy maker and from policy maker to citizen, and then horizontally among citizens. The acts of seeking to discover what people want and then responding to such findings inevitably shape people's subsequent desires. Occasionally these effects are so profound that neither interest group intermediation nor net benefit maximization can do its job, even in the limited terms of linking public authority to selfish wants. In addition, this view of policy making is normatively suspect. It leaves out some of the most important aspects of democratic governance, which involve public deliberation over public issues and the ensuing discovery of public ideas. As we will see, these two shortcomings are connected. For it is only through public deliberation that the shared understandings that animate public policy can be examined and the tacit assumptions about what is wanted can be revised.

Consider, first, the possible effects of interest group intermediation on the way a citizenry understands what is important to its collective life, what problems it must address, what is at stake in such decisions, and its capacities to deal with such problems in the future. Returning to our earlier example, suppose the intermediator has sought out the views of citizen groups on construction of a dam. He has been willing to listen to spokesmen of any established organization, and he has actively encouraged the leaders of other, less prominent groups to proffer their views as well. He has listened to the president of the local Chamber of Commerce, the head of the Downtown Merchant's Association, the chairman of the Board of Realtors, the leader of the Upper Valley Homeowners Association, and a variety of other groups representing homeowners and merchants, living upstream and downstream from the proposed dam. Each group leader has presented formal testimony; some have filed reports, analyses, and extensive commentary. The local media have duly reported their views. Editorialists, commentators, and political leaders have begun to take sides in the emerging controversy. It is soon understood as a contest between upstreamers and downstreamers.

But note that the controversy itself has been shaped largely by how representatives of the various groups have expressed their views about what their constituents want for themselves. These spokespeople have identified the key issues and arguments, defined the relevant constituencies, and structured the emerging debate. The public might have developed a very different understanding about what was at stake had a different set of representatives and groups participated—for example, downstream tenants or those who loved to fish and hike in the upstream woodlands. Rather than a contest between upstreamers and downstreamers, the controversy might have been understood as one between economic growth and environmental conservation, or between land speculators and poor renters, or all of these and more—a decision rich with implications, potentially creating all sorts of gainers and losers. Each of these frames would have caused a different set of issues to be explored in the media and in various public forums, a different set of arguments and questions to be considered by the public, and a different set of connections to be made to other issues and values lying at the perimeter.

The implicit selection of certain groups and leaders to participate has subtly altered the configuration of influence and political authority in the community. These groups and those who have spoken on their behalf are now seen as having access to power, and this perception feeds on itself. Earlier there were probably many *incipient* groupings in the community, since at any point in time there is a variety of ways in which citizens might join together to express different constellations of concerns. Many of these fledgling organizations and leaders were presumably weak—disorganized, lacking a clear focus, as yet incapable of generating strong support and a dedicated following. Those that become recognized as participants in the decision making process, however, find their roles legitimized and strengthened. The groups and leaders that were encouraged to participate have now become semiofficial channels through which community views are expressed; accordingly, their focus and support are both enhanced. As issues arise in the future, these groups and their leaders will be among the first to be consulted. Incipient groups and leaders that were not selected or encouraged to participate, on the other hand, suffer a corresponding decline in influence and status. Citizens have less reason to involve themselves in such groups or support such leaders next time because they are perceived to lack standing to articulate public views.

Finally, the act of participation has rendered the articulated concerns appropriate subjects of public debate and, by implication, public action. Their very expression has legitimized them. The concerns of downstream merchants now have a clear place on the public agenda; the periodic flooding to which they are exposed has been transformed from an act of nature causing private loss into a public problem open to public remedy. To the extent possible, these concerns must now be accommodated in the eventual decision. For under interest group intermediation, the primary criterion of a good decision is that it addresses such articulated concerns. There are no principled limits to, or goals for, public involvement apart from this. Once they become legitimate subjects of public debate and action, such concerns will remain on the public agenda, to be accommodated in future decisions as well. The welfare of downstream merchants has now become a public goal.

In all these ways, the interest group intermediator is an active participant in the political development of the community. By recognizing "established" groups and leaders, and subtly encouraging others to participate, the intermediator effectively shapes public understandings of what is at stake, perceptions of who has power in the community, and assumptions about what subjects merit public concern. In this way he alters the political future. To view him merely as a neutral intermediator dramatically understates his true role.

Net benefit maximization is no less influential. But here it is the initial selection of objectives to be achieved and options to be weighed, rather than the groups and leaders to participate, that shapes public perceptions about what is at stake; and it is the choice of proxy for "willingness to pay" that affects how the public values these stakes.

Let us return to our example, but this time with our public manager as a net benefit maximizer. To analyze the problem and measure public preferences for different solutions, he first must simplify it. Asking himself how the costs of downstream flooding can most efficiently be reduced, he estimates the costs and benefits of three alternatives: a dam, a drainage canal, and a dike along the edge of the river. The cost of the dam will include the loss of upstream wilderness that will be flooded. The manager estimates this loss by adding to the market value of the land its recreational value, calculated by estimating how many people visit the wilderness area in a given time period, how much money they spend to get there, and how much more they would have to spend to travel to alternative wilderness areas. Assume that after estimating the costs and benefits of each alternative he concludes that the dam will generate the greatest net benefits, and the dam is constructed.

The issue is not the "correctness" of his conclusion about the social utility of a dam relative to the other alternatives, although that will be how opponents of the dam will approach the subject. Any formal analysis necessarily entails a somewhat simplified characterization of reality and a host of choices about how and what to simplify. Of more enduring consequence is the effect of such choices on the social utility function itself. Like the intermediator's implicit choices of whom to encourage to participate, these net benefit maximizing choices reverberate through the community because they have public authority behind them. They influence the way people in the community come to think about the problem, its possible solutions, and the values at stake in the decision.

To state the objective as reducing the costs of downstream flooding, for example, constitutes an important public act. That technical objective is transformed into a public goal to which the community attaches its collective aspirations and around which citizens mobilize. Just as mere participation serves a legitimizing function in interest group intermediation, such a statement of objective legitimates a whole class of similar problems as appropriate subjects for public action—for example, acts of nature (rock slides, dust storms, tornadoes) that periodically imperil the area or hardships that periodically befall those who live downstream. It simultaneously makes other ways of thinking about the issue less legitimate—for example, the thought that periodic flooding is not really a public problem at all, since downstream owners have always coped with it.

The identification of alternative solutions also sends powerful social messages that will influence the way people think about, and act on, similar problems in the future. One such message is that appropriate solutions are to be found in complex engineering projects, rather than in social endeavors like organizing a voluntary brigade to clean up after each flood. Another, related message is that the identification of alternative solutions is primarily a technical task for which the average person has no particular competence or relevant knowledge. Together these messages may tend to discourage social responses that draw inspiration and energy from citizens' sense of their shared responsibility for community problems and their competence in devising solutions.

Finally, the methods used by the net benefit maximizer to evaluate the alternatives affect the way citizens come to view certain attributes of their lives. The official act of placing a monetary value on the upstream wilderness, for example, constitutes a powerful public statement that feelings toward such wilderness *can* be expressed in monetary terms. It thereby transforms wilderness areas into consumer goods whose worth depends on how well they satisfy us, rather than entities with their own constitutive values, whose worth to us is bound up in the belief that a monetary value cannot be placed on them. The further assumption that "willingness to pay" to travel to such a wilderness area is the proper measure of how we value it, moreover, dismisses as irrelevant any positive feelings people have simply because the wilderness area exists there upstream. It suggests that the only grounds for complaint or despair, should the area disappear, derive from the direct and personal loss of access to it. Together, such ideas— that wilderness areas should be valued in terms of how well they satisfy people, and then only on the basis of people's direct and personal experience with them—are powerful social norms that may influence how citizens think about their environment in the future.[24]

The *substantive* decisions that emerge from both types of policy making, or some hybrid of the two, also influence future preferences.

These decisions alter the world that people experience. To return to our example, the experience of future generations in the community will be quite different if the dam is constructed. People will then grow to adulthood without enjoying relatively easy access to the upstream wilderness. Not knowing what experiences they have missed, they will never learn to place the same high value on accessible wilderness as earlier generations did. Because their relationship with the environment is likely to be more attenuated, they will probably be more willing to make subsequent decisions that sacrifice the environment to other values. If the dam is not built, the experience of future generations will not change in this way. Over time, the divergence between the two paths of decisions (and the preferences on which they are based) would grow larger. Several generations hence, the descendants of the dam builders are likely to live in a profoundly different setting and to have different norms, espouse different causes, dream different dreams. The decision to build the dam, then, does not just reflect the values of the present generation; it sets a trajectory of future values.

Even the choice of a policy instrument can generate powerful social signals that shape future norms. As we have seen, for example, the net benefit maximizer typically prefers to give the poor cash rather than a scarce commodity—like a portion of the downstream lands rendered habitable by construction of the dam—on the rationale that it is more efficient to let individuals decide how to spend the cash than to give them something that might not exactly meet their needs. But this view ignores the quite different public perceptions attached to the two transfers. The transfer of newly habitable land has a clear social meaning. The land is indelibly "public"; it was created through public action aimed at improving the habitability of the entire downstream area. This particular parcel could have been used for a park or a school, but the public has chosen instead to give it to those in need. It is thus a particular gift, reflecting a particular sort of public generosity, linked to particular public purposes. The homes that the poor can now build in this area will continually remind the community of these purposes and thus shape the way the public thinks about future projects of a similar sort. A simple transfer of cash would be devoid of these social meanings—so devoid, in fact, that it might not summon sufficient political support to be authorized in the first place.[25]

In sum, both the process and the substance of policy decisions generate social learning about public values and set the stage for future public choices. They give rise to new understandings and expectations;

they shape policy debates in other, related policy areas; they reconfigure social ideals. It is therefore misleading to view the job of public
managers simply as responding to pre-existing preferences, expressed
either through group leaders or market transactions. Their responsibility is much broader and more subtle.

Civic Discovery

Within the context of either interest group intermediation or net
benefit maximization, disagreements among people are assumed to
derive from incompatible preferences—conflicts among selfish desires.
The challenge to the public manager under these circumstances is
thought to be a technical one: either to intermediate among groups
until an accommodation is reached or to measure people's willingness
to pay for certain things (and avoid other things) and then maximize
their combined welfare. As we have seen, neither of these techniques is
entirely neutral; both can alter how the initial problems are perceived
and solutions understood. In addition, neither creates an opportunity
for the public to deliberate about what is good for society. Yet it is
through such deliberation that opinions can be revised, premises
altered, and common interests discovered.

To return once again to our example, imagine now that the public
manager eschews both types of conventional policy making. Instead of
assuming that he must decide whether the dam should be built, he sees
the occasion as an opportunity for the public to deliberate over what it
wants. Accordingly, he announces that various people living and
working downstream are complaining about periodic flooding of the
river. He then encourages and instigates the convening of various
forums—in community centers, schools, churches, and workplaces—
where citizens are to discuss whether there is a problem and, if so, what
it is and what should be done about it. The public manager does not
specifically define the problem or set an objective at the start. He
merely discloses the complaints. Nor does he take formal control of the
discussions or determine who should speak for whom. At this stage he
views his job as generating debate, even controversy. He wants to
bring into the open the fact that certain members of the community are
disgruntled and create possibilities for the public to understand in
various ways what is at stake. He wants to make the community
conscious of tensions within it, and responsible for dealing with them.

In short, he wants the community to use this as an occasion to debate its future. Several different kinds of civic discovery may ensue.

The problem and its solutions may be redefined. During the course of such deliberations, people may discover that their initial assumptions about the nature of the problem and its alternative solutions are wrong or inappropriate. Through sharing information about what concerns them and seeking common solutions to those concerns, they come to see that the issue should not be defined as whether to build the dam, but how best to relocate people off the flood plain. Viewed this way, a potentially sharp conflict within the community is transformed into a project that almost everyone can support (even though it may be no one's most preferred outcome). Had the public manager sought to make the decision on the basis of the interest groups through which people express their wants, or through measurements of their willingness to pay, this possibility for redefining the issue and garnering widespread support would have been overlooked.

Voluntary action may be generated. Their consideration of the plight of the downstream residents and businesses may lead others to volunteer time and money to the effort—erecting dikes, digging drainage canals, or relocating people and businesses. This willingness to volunteer stems from the discovery that others are also willing to lend a hand. Had there been no such deliberation, individuals might not have recognized how they could voluntarily help remedy the situation. Those who were inclined to help might have assumed that their charitable impulses were not widely shared, so that it would have been futile to act on them. The discovery empowers people, together, to take voluntary action.

Preferences may be legitimized. Some people may discover that there are many others like them who have not visited the upstream wilderness, but who nevertheless share a deep feeling for it and wish it to be preserved. Had there been no such deliberation, each might have continued to assume that his feelings were somehow illegitimate since they were not based on direct experience—and for this reason were not measurable on a willingness-to-pay scale and did not fit within an established interest group. Indeed, people might have denied having such feelings, regarding them as invalid or immature. But the discovery emboldens these people to admit and express such views, and seek to persuade others of their validity.

Individual preferences may be influenced by considerations of what is good for society. Some people may discover a conflict between their personal, pecuniary interests in the problem and their hopes for their community. A downstream property owner who realizes that the dam would increase property values downstream, enhancing his personal wealth, may nevertheless believe it would be bad for the community. The dam would continue to be a divisive issue for years to come; future generations would no longer have access to the unspoiled wilderness areas upstream; and too many people would move to the downstream area, eventually overloading the roads, schools, and sewage lines. The citizen may still choose to favor his own pecuniary interest. Public deliberation does not guarantee that people will become more altruistic. But the deliberation at least creates the opportunity for such weighing and balancing. Had there been no such deliberation, the downstream owner might never have considered the future of the community.

Deeper conflicts may be discovered. People may discover that their disagreements run much deeper than previously imagined. Those who want to preserve the upstream wilderness also want to minimize downstream development and preserve parks and open spaces within and around the city; downstream owners who want the dam also favor extensive development. The discovery of this more fundamental conflict might have been avoided (or delayed, or denied) had the public manager decided whether to build the dam on the basis of interest group demands or willingness to pay.

In these ways, public deliberation provides an opportunity for people to discover shared values about what is good for the community, and deeper conflicts among those understandings. Deliberation does not automatically generate these public ideas, of course; it simply allows them to arise. Policy making based on interest group intermediation or net benefit maximization, by contrast, offers no such opportunity. The self-interested preferences of individuals as expressed through their market transactions do not reflect potential public ideas. Interest groups, for their part, are instrumental devices for fulfilling the individual desires of their members, not bodies for deliberating what is good for society; their leaders are paid to be advocates and conduits, not statesmen.

The failure of conventional techniques of policy making to permit civic discovery may suggest that there are no shared values to be discovered in the first place. And this message—that the "public interest" is no more than an accommodation or aggregation of individual interests—may have a corrosive effect on civic life. It may invalidate whatever potential exists for the creation of shared commitments and in so doing may stunt the discovery of public ideas. Such a failure may in turn call into question the inherent legitimacy of the policy descisions that result. For such policies are then supported only by debatable facts, inferences, and tradeoffs. They lack any authentic governmental character beyond accommodation or aggregation. Those who disagree with the procedures or conclusions on which the policies are based have every reason to disregard them whenever the opportunity arises. Under these circumstances disobedience is not a social act reflecting on one's membership in a community, but merely another expression of preference.

Real-World Applications

Can public managers realistically hope to enhance public deliberation and social learning about what is good for society? Some real-world illustrations will suggest both the possibilities and limitations of such a role.

Ruckelshaus and Tacoma

Under the Clean Air Act Amendments of 1970, the Environmental Protection Agency (EPA) is required to issue national emissions standards for hazardous air pollutants, so as to provide an "ample margin of safety" to protect the public health.[26] Congress gave EPA no guidance for deciding how much safety is "ample," however. Evan a small exposure to certain hazardous pollutants can pose substantial health risks. But to ban any air pollutant that caused even a small risk to health would substantially impair the national economy.

The problem received national attention in 1983 when the agency was trying to decide what, if anything, should be done about inorganic arsenic, a cancer-causing pollutant produced when arsenic-content ore is smelted into copper. The issue was dramatized especially in the area around Tacoma, Washington, where the American Smelting and Refining Company (Asarco) operated a copper smelter. The EPA had concluded that if Asarco's emissions were not controlled, approximately four new cases of lung cancer would be contracted each year in the area; even the best available pollution control equipment would still emit enough inorganic arsenic into the air to cause one cancer death a year. But the cost of such equipment would render the plant uneconomical, forcing the company to close it. The closing would have a devastating effect on the local economy: Asarco employed 570 workers with an annual payroll of about $23 million, and the company purchased $12 million of goods from local suppliers.

William Ruckelshaus, then administrator of the EPA, decided that the citizens of the Tacoma area ought to wrestle with the problem in a series of public meetings held during the summer of 1983. EPA officials began each meeting by explaining how the agency had estimated the health risks; they then divided the audience into three groups for more informal discussion with agency officials and staff. Some of the ensuing discussion concerned technical questions of measurement and emissions control, but many of the citizens' questions concerned the possible effects of the emissions on their gardens, animals, and overall quality of life. As the dean of the University of Washington School of Public Health observed, "the personal nature of the complaints and questions made a striking counterpoint to the presentations of meteorological models and health effects extrapolations."

These meetings, together with the national attention that Ruckelshaus had deliberately drawn to them, generated considerable and often unfavorable press coverage. In one editorial entitled "Mr. Ruckelshaus a Caesar," the *New York Times* argued that it was "inexcusable . . . for him to impose such an impossible choice on Tacomans." The *Los Angeles Times* pointed out the difficulties in "taking a community's pulse. . . . [Should he] poll the community . . . [or] count the pros and cons at the massive hearing?" Ruckelshaus was not surprised by the controversy. "Listen, I know people don't like these kinds of decisions," he said. "Welcome to the world of regulation. People have demanded to be involved and now I have involved them, and they say, 'don't ask that question.' What's the alternative? Don't involve them? Then you are accused of doing something nefarious."

By 1985, the EPA still had not promulgated regulations for arsenic emissions, but declining world copper prices in the interim had forced the closure of the Asarco smelter. What then did Ruckelshaus accomplish? For one thing, the problem was redefined. Instead of focusing on how best to control hazardous air pollutants, citizens began to ask how they could diversify a local economy and attract industry that would not generate such substantial hazards. Attendance at the meetings, along with massive media exposure, had personalized the controversy in ways that induced people to look at it differently. As area residents heard a tearful woman, diagnosed as ultrasensitive to arsenic, describe how she and her husband had to sell their farm at a severe loss and leave the area, or saw copper workers in danger of losing their jobs, energies shifted from "winning" to changing the way the problem was understood and finding workable solutions. As Ruckelshaus described it, "Even the residents of Vashon Island, who were directly exposed to the pollution and yet had no employment or financial stake in the smelter, began to ask whether there was a means of keeping the smelter going while reducing pollution levels. They saw the workers from the smelter—encountered them in flesh and blood— and began incorporating the workers' perspective into their own solutions."

Several participants attacked the fundamental perception of "the environment versus jobs issue," arguing that discussion should focus instead on the development of new pollution control technologies that could control arsenic emissions and allow the plant to stay open. Others argued that Tacoma would do better to diversify its employment base and that the real problem was the local economy's dependence on a few industries like copper. Gradually, for many participants, the goal came to be understood as finding new jobs for the Asarco workers and new industry for the region, by attracting and developing nonpolluting businesses.[27] This view gained substantial support. By 1985, when the Asarco smelter closed down, Tacoma already had begun the task of diversifying its economy.

For Ruckelshaus, the value of the Tacoma experiment also included social learning about the health risks of pollution and the enormous costs of eliminating them altogether, not only in Tacoma but also in other communities that saw what occurred there. The deliberation in Tacoma thus helped launch a national debate over environmental policy, giving the public a deeper understanding about what would have to be sacrificed to reduce risks to health. Looking back more than a year later, after he had left the EPA, Ruckelshaus assessed the Tacoma experiment:

Perhaps I underestimated how difficult it would be to get people to take responsibility, to educate themselves and one another about such a difficult issue. Probably not more than a relatively few citizens of Tacoma learned that for issues like this there is no "right" answer. . . . They would have to decide what they wanted for their community. They would have to determine their own future. But even if a handful learned this lesson, then you have a basis for others learning it. You have the beginnings of a tradition of public deliberation about hard issues. And you also have all the other people in the country who watched what happened there in Tacoma, and indirectly learned the same lesson from it.[28]

Pertschuk and Children's Advertising

In 1914 Congress created the Federal Trade Commission (FTC) as an independent agency to ferret out "unfair and deceptive acts and practices in commerce," but it left to the agency the task of defining these vague terms.[29] In 1977, Senator Warren Magnuson, chairman of the Senate Commerce Committee, which oversaw the FTC, suggested that the agency, under the direction of its new chairman, Michael Pertschuk, should look into the issue of advertising directed at children as a possible "unfair act." Magnuson knew very little about the subject and had only vaguest of concerns." Now, we've all been interested here in children's advertising," he said when Pertschuk first came to the Commission. "It's a difficult, complex subject. . . . I would hope that you would take a good, long look. . . . I hate to narrow this down, but the abuses seem to be in children's advertising, advertising directed to children."

Pertschuk saw in the issue a perfect means of raising consciousness about public susceptibility to advertising in general and in particular the vulnerability of young children to commercial inducements to buy sugary cereals and candy. Accordingly the Commission launched a preliminary investigation, and by April 1978 was considering several possible remedies: a ban on the number of advertisements for sugared products that could be directed at children during a certain period of time, or on a particular medium; controls on the kinds of advertising techniques that could be used; a requirement that nutritional information be disclosed in such advertisements; a ban on advertisements for sugar-coated products; and a ban on all children's advertising. The proposals drew significant media attention. Pertschuk received even more when he gave strongly worded speeches and provocative interviews about the dangers of advertising directed at children.

The proposals and Pertschuk's speeches and interviews set off a firestorm of criticism from industry groups. Broadcasters, advertisers, cereal manufacturers, grocery manufacturers, and sugar producers all felt threatened and counterattacked through the press and their lobbyists in Congress. The *Washington Post* editorialized that the FTC was aiming to be the "national nanny" and that it had no business interfering in an area of parental responsibility. One lobbyist felt that the Commission's confrontational strategy had contributed to the tumult. "We could have gotten some of the more enlightened companies to say, let's go in and bargain a little bit, and get half a loaf," he observed. "But they got everyone 100 percent against them, willing to commit war chests and time, the personal time of chief executive officers, saying, we cannot allow this to happen. They basically accused well-known businessmen of deliberately trying to foreshorten the lives of kids."

In the end, Congress reined in the FTC. Indeed the Commission's powers to issue all rules were curtailed; the agency's appropriations were reduced and its credibility severely crippled. What then did the campaign accomplish? Looking back several years later, Michael Pertschuk regretted the tactics, but not the goals.

I suppose we made some mistakes. We came on too strong. If the goal was to preserve and develop the FTC's powers over the long haul, then Kidvid was a disaster. . . . But I'm not sure that was or should be the goal. After all, the FTC is merely a shell. It changes its color with every new administration. Why should I worry about its powers over the long term? The real goal was to get issues like children's advertising out there in front of the public. . . . I wanted to stir up a debate, get people thinking. You know, that's one of the most important things we can do, get the public to grapple with hard issues. And they did. The public had a chance to understand children's advertising, the press played it up. . . . We probably should have gone easier with it, given the issue more time to boil. But even so, you look around now in the stores, you see a lot less sugary cereal. You watch cartoons on Saturday morning, you see a lot fewer advertisements for sugary cereals and candy. Was consciousness raised about advertising directed toward children? Yes, and I think we contributed.[30]

Bennett and Educational Reform

Our final illustration concerns William Bennett, who became secretary of education in 1985.[31] The Department of Education administers a wide variety of programs, but they are tightly connected to individual congressional committees and to state and local programs. Most educational policy in the United States is determined at the state and local levels, where the bulk of the money is raised and spent. Accordingly a secretary of education has quite limited scope to affect change directly. Bennett, however, was determined to raise issues about American education that might affect change indirectly, through public debate. He began boldly, perhaps too boldly. At his first news conference, when announcing tighter standards for student loans, Bennett opined that students should help meet tuition by "stereo divestiture, automobile divestiture, three weeks at the beach divestiture." The speech infuriated many middle-class parents who relied on the student loan program and angered several members of Congress who had long supported it. By the end of Bennett's first month in office, the *Washington Post* ran an article entitled "Another Watt?" referring to the former secretary of interior's tendency to offend.

In subsequent months, however, Bennett's pronouncements were accompanied by detailed position papers and proposals for changes in various department regulations. Among other things, he advocated improved teacher training, higher standards for promoting students to the next grades, a return to "basics" in the classroom, educational vouchers as a means of generating competition among schools and giving students a choice of where to attend, a reconsideration of the place of religion in public education, and a rethinking of the tenets of bilingual education. Amid much press attention, Bennett traveled around the country, sitting and teaching in public classrooms and continuing to raise issues about educational policy. As his credibility increased, many of his ideas gained begrudging respect, even from groups that opposed him, like the National Educational Association and the American Federation of Teachers. Prominent politicians were picking up some of his themes. By March 1986, *Newsweek* remarked that Bennett's style was "guaranteed to win some enemies . . . but even critics recognize its usefulness. As Diane Ravitch, a professor at Teachers College of Columbia says: 'The main role of the Secretary of Education is to keep the attention of the country focused on education.' By that standard, Bennett has been a resounding success. He has turned his office into a bully pulpit . . . He has barnstormed the country." One of Bennett's assistants explained the overall strategy:

Bennett sees himself as in the business of raising the level of debate, focussing the public's attention where it hasn't been focussed before. We've had to be sufficiently controversial to get the attention, but solid enough to gain the public's respect. It's a delicate balance. . . . It's okay to get the front-page story the next day, but you really want the feature stories that follow a few days or weeks later, that set out the arguments on both sides, and the editorials. The subject gradually becomes a respectable topic of debate. Politicians pick up the ideas. University presidents talk about them. . . . You know, most people think of speeches and position papers and all that stuff as being in the service of specific regulations or legislation. Around here, it's the other way around. The specific policies are in the service of raising issues.[32]

Lessons

In each of the situations described above, a public manager sought to stimulate public deliberation over what was good for society rather than to decide specific policy. Each felt that public learning was at least as important a part of his job as policy making, because the public had to understand and decide for itself what value it was to place on certain issues lying within the manager's domain. Deliberation was worthwhile both in itself and because it could clarify ambiguous mandates and perhaps even move Congress to a different course of action. Rather than view debate and controversy as managerial failures that made policy making and implementation more difficult, these managers saw them as natural and desirable aspects of the formation of public values, contributing to society's self-understanding.

Were they successful? The answer depends on what is meant by success. Each succeeded in stimulating debate and focusing attention. There is some evidence—scattered, impressionistic—that each succeeded in altering the terms of public debate, engendering some sorts of civic discovery. Each insisted that such public deliberation was crucial to his mission. Ruckelshaus made the point explicitly: "My view is that these are the kinds of tough, balancing questions that we're involved in here in this country in trying to regulate all kinds of hazardous substances . . . [T]he societal issue is what risks are we willing to take and for what benefits? . . . For me to sit here in Washington and tell the people of Tacoma what is an acceptable risk would be at best arrogant and at worst inexcusable."[33]

But there were costs. Ruckelshaus's Tacoma experiment reduced his credibility with environmentalists, whose support he vitally needed on other EPA projects. Pertschuck almost destroyed the Federal Trade Commission. Bennett spent so much time and energy in instigating debate that he had none left for legislative battles. All three managers faced a hostile press.

The cases also suggest that public deliberation is not easy to manage well. Public managers and the public at large often tend to equate administrative effectiveness with active decision making and successful implementation. These are concrete achievements that can be measured and on which reputations can be built. The nurturing of social learning about public values, on the other hand, is an elusive undertaking. A manager who tentatively advances several proposals and stirs controversy about them may appear indecisive or indifferent at best, as did Ruckelshaus, or he may be cast as a villain, as was Pertschuk. Moreover the public will wish to avoid facing difficult issues and examining the values bound up in them. Many people will resent the tensions and ambiguities inherent in such deliberation. They would prefer that the public manager take responsibility for making such decisions, as did many Tacomans, or that unsettling problems and questions not be raised at all.

There will also be procedural obstacles. To instigate public discourse the manager will have to make speeches, stage events, and use the press artfully. But in doing so he may deflect public attention from the issue to himself. It is far easier to attract the public's curiosity to a personality than to a substantive problem. Ruckelshaus, Pertschuk, and Bennett all became the focus of the media. Ruckelshaus managed to refocus on the issues; Pertschuk never quite pulled it off; Bennett, at this writing, is still struggling with the problem. The manager must also contend with well-established interest groups, whose strong advocacy can drown out any semblance of public thought. Their easy dominance of the media and of legislatures can push issues back off the table or reconfigure them into older debates. Ruckelshaus avoided this by staging his event in Tacoma, far from the center of organized group activity on the Potomac. Much of Pertschuck's message was jammed by the trade associations and major corporations that waged war against the FTC. Bennett took his show on the road, where established groups could not override his message, but teachers' lobbies and textbook manufacturers continually sought to define the issues he raised in ways they could control.

Public deliberation will take up inordinate time and resources (all three of our managers were almost consumed by it), and it can easily cycle out of control. There is no guarantee that the resulting social learning will yield a clear consensus at the end. Instead the process may exacerbate divisions within the community and make it more difficult to achieve consensus in the future. The FTC debacle made it more difficult for the Carter administration as a whole to gain the cooperation of the business community later on issues for which its support was needed.

The experience of public deliberation is not likely to be enjoyable for either politicians or agency employees. Politicians will resent a process that is beyond their control, often involving issues they would rather not have to deal with (that is why those issues were handed over to the public manager in the first place). All three of our public managers met with hostility from important congressional committees. Agency employees, for their part, are unlikely to understand the importance of fostering public discourse rather than getting on with the job of making policy. Their jobs and reputations depend on getting something done (or undone), and they will have little role in instigating or managing the debate. Furthermore, they will have to live with the results, often long after the top manager has left. Pertschuk's employees did not appreciate his willingness to sacrifice the agency's powers to the more immediate goal of raising the public's consciousness.

Lastly, there are lingering doubts about the propriety of nonelected bureaucrats' taking on this sort of responsibility. The line between ideological chest-thumping and the instigation of public debate can be a narrow one, easily missed even by managers who sincerely believe they are letting the public decide. Ruckelshaus stayed well to one side, but Pertschuk and Bennett both approached the line. James Watt, Reagan's errant secretary of the interior, seemed to have crossed it. Although there is no clear guide for where the line should be drawn, the cases examined here suggest a rule of thumb. The public manager may be in a better position than a legislator or senior elected official to foster a national debate over certain value-laden issues when the manager deals with specific applications of general principles. It is through detailed and vivid applications that the public comes to understand the principles and the tradeoffs and stakes they imply. Tacoma dramatically illustrated the principle that the cost of achieving zero health risk is prohibitive. Advertising directed at children was a less specific application, and Congress could have instigated a similar public deliberation. Similarly with many of the issues that Bennett sought to dramatize.

For all these reasons, prudence is advised. The public manager should not completely abandon interest group intermediation and net benefit maximization in favor of public deliberations. Each of the more traditional techniques has its place, especially for the vast majority of comparatively routine decisions, which are not fundamentally bound up with public values and are unlikely to have important effects on future choices.

But public managers must be willing to venture occasionally into the third sphere, in which public deliberation takes prominence. As we have seen, they have little choice in the matter. Enabling statutes are often vague, as was Congress's requirement that the EPA ensure an "ample margin of safety" for hazardous emissions or that the FTC ban "unfair" advertising. In certain areas of policy making, any decision is likely to have profound effects on how people understand and value the objects of policy. Instigating deliberation on controversial issues may sometimes be the only way for a public manager to effect change. In these circumstances, it is wise to allow, or even invite, some public discourse rather than to aim single-mindedly at making a decision. Public managers must understand that public debate and controversy over a domain within their control are not necessarily to be avoided. Although heated discourse may make their jobs somewhat less comfortable, it comes with the territory.

CHAPTER 7

Policy Analysis and Public Deliberation

Giandomenico Majone

Robert Reich suggests in Chapter Six that public deliberation may be a crucial aspect of public administration in a democracy. Here I ask: What can policy analysis contribute to the process of public deliberation? To answer this question one must distinguish two types of policy analysis. The first focuses on the problem of allocating public resources among competing ends. To achieve an optimal allocation the policy maker must specify the objective that is sought; lay out the alternatives that can accomplish the objective; evaluate the costs and benefits of each alternative; and choose the course of action that maximizes net benefits. An instrumental conception of rationality underlies this maximizing approach to policy analysis: rationality consists of choosing the best means to a given end.

The second type of policy analysis derives from a different, much older conception of rationality as a process of finding acceptable reasons, discovering warrants for one's beliefs or actions. Analysts of this school recognize that public policy is made of language and that argument is central in all stages of the policy process. Hence they are less concerned with maximization than with determining which assumptions and arguments would provide a conceptual basis for a certain policy or assessing the persuasiveness of the evidence that supports a proposal.

The central problem for this type of policy analysis is how to improve the quality of public discourse. The two approaches rely on different concepts and patterns of reasoning. Analysis-as-maximization employs the basic categories of microeconomics and the logic of choice—decision making, objectives, alternatives, preferences, criteria, tradeoffs—whereas analysis-as-argument uses categories borrowed from jurisprudence, history, ethics, and rhetoric: evidence, conclusion, context, metaphor, analogy, values, audience, persuasion. One type of analysis favors formal methods of proof while the other uses a mode of reasoning (traditionally called argumentation) that does not start with axioms or "hard facts" but with contestable and shifting points of view. Given the ambiguous basis from which it starts, argumentation cannot produce formal proofs, only conclusions that are more or less convincing to the members of an audience. Its problem is how to base plausible inferences on values or opinions when hard facts are not available.

In some areas of the production and delivery of public services, reliable data are available and formal quantitative techniques can discover the most efficient use of the available resources. In such situations technical policy analysis makes valuable contributions to public management. In authoritarian regimes policy analysis is not allowed to go beyond managerial problems. But in a democracy, where almost every aspect of public policy is a legitimate topic of debate, analysts who stick to the task of working out unique solutions to well-defined technical problems deny themselves any significant role in the policy process.

By restricting the role of reason to discovering appropriate means to achieve given ends, instrumental rationality relegates values, criteria, judgments, and opinions to the domain of the irrational or the purely subjective. Analysis-as-argument holds that such a narrow view of rationality goes against the grain of a democratic system of government by discussion, and that any topic relevant to public discussion is an appropriate subject for informed debate. The main task of policy analysis, so conceived, is not to determine theoretically correct solutions, but to raise issues, probe assumptions, stimulate debate, and especially to educate citizens to distinguish between good and bad reasons. In fact, this is precisely what analysts and experts often do; their practice is generally much better than their theory. The purpose of this chapter is to bring the theory of policy analysis closer to its practice and to relate both theory and practice to the nature of policy making in a democracy.

Government By Discussion

According to classical liberal theory, democratic government is a system of government by discussion. "The key to democracy," Lord Lindsay writes, "is the potency of discussion. A good discussion can draw out wisdom which is attainable in no other way . . . If the freedom of discussion is safeguarded and fostered, there is no necessity for the most urbanized of constituencies to become a mob."[1] Such a system of government is calculated to elicit the thought, the will, and the general capacity of each citizen. It does not rest on mere number or quantity, but on the quality of the process it engages and on the value of the process for every participant.[2]

The process of discussion develops sequentially in separate but interconnected forums: in political parties, as they formulate their programs and identify the issues for electoral debate; in the electorate, as it discusses issues and candidates, and expresses a majority in favor of one of the programs; in the legislature, where the majority attempts to translate the programs into law, in constant debate with the opposition; in the executive branch, where the discussion of new policies is carried forward to the chief executive and the cabinet; and in the courts, where the adversary system provides powerful incentives for agencies and interested parties to present the strongest arguments for their respective positions. Although debate and persuasion are involved at every stage of the process, each organ of public deliberation—political parties, electorate, legislature, executive, courts—performs a specific function. They debate an issue in different forms and from different points of view. But since they all discuss the same issue they are all interconnected, and all contribute to the overall solution.[3]

Government by discussion is a plant of singular delicacy, as Walter Bagehot put it. A method of governance based on the interchange and mutual criticism of competing ideas and on the common acceptance of the idea that wins the competitive struggle is constantly exposed to a number of serious threats. For this reason, public deliberation has been carefully institutionalized in all modern democracies, with elaborate codes of electoral, parliamentary, administrative, and judicial procedure. For example, electoral laws have the effect of regularizing citizen input to the policy-making process, so as to limit other forms of participation, such as political protest or mass demonstration. Texts like *Jefferson's Manual of Parliamentary Practice* and *Robert's Rules of Order* are the fruit of centuries of experience in coping with the practical problems of public deliberation.[4]

The history of democratic government might well be described as the history of the various procedures devised to institutionalize and regulate public deliberation, with the goal of ensuring the hearing of every opinion without compromising the need to reach a conclusion. In addition to procedural safeguards, various substantive conditions must also be satisfied. Common deliberation presupposes some common ground; without shared values and understandings, discussion quickly degenerates in unending dispute. Some measure of social equality and of equal access to information are also highly desirable, since the ideal discussion takes place among equals. But the most basic prerequisite of public deliberation is that the members of the community agree to focus the debate on some issues of general interest. Before the dialectic of conflicting positions can unfold, there must be widespread agreement about the nature of the central problems then facing the community.

The power of public ideas is nowhere more visible than at the focusing stage of public debate. Consider, for example, how the idea of poverty—the cluster of concepts, assumptions, values, perceptions, and images—changed during the early phase of the industrial revolution in England. The optimism of Adam Smith gave way to the pessimism of Ricardo and Malthus, the bitterness of the 1830s to the social consciousness of the 1840s and the spirit of reconciliation of the 1850s. At each stage there were heated debates about the nature of poverty and what should or could be done about it. Yet, as historian Gertrude Himmelfarb writes, "even as the ideological battles were being most seriously waged ... there were significant respects in which most of the parties in the dispute were in agreement, sharing the same moral and intellectual assumptions about poverty, making the same distinctions among the poor, focusing on the same group of poor as 'the social problem' and using the same vocabulary to describe that group and that problem."[5]

The agreement to regard a social condition as an issue for public debate and collective action, rather than "the way things are," presupposes a preliminary agreement about norms or standards of what is morally and politically acceptable. A policy problem is a condition that does not meet some standards: poverty is not a problem for a society that believes that the poor are always with us, or that they get precisely what they deserve.[6] Hence a discussion of the role of policy analysis in democratic policy making must begin with norm setting.

Norm Setting

It is often held that public deliberation, like public policy, is primarily concerned with setting goals and finding the means to achieve the defined goals. But the most significant function of both public deliberation and policy making is setting the norms that determine when certain conditions are to be regarded as policy problems. In this sense, norm setting is more basic than goal setting. The emphasis on goal setting derives from the instrumental conception of rationality as goal-directed behavior. According to this conception, rational policy analysis cannot begin until the relevant values have been stipulated, either by an authoritative policy maker or through the aggregation of citizen preferences in the political process.

In fact, these values are neither given nor constant, but often are themselves a function of the policy-making process they are supposed to guide. Thus, many of the problems that a democratic government is expected to consider today, from sex discrimination to insurance against sickness and unemployment, were not regarded as policy problems a century ago. And for the long-established policy concerns, like the relief of extreme poverty, the norms have radically changed. Yet the process that has modified the norms is the same historical process that those norms have guided.[7]

Far from waiting passively for the stipulation of public values to be served, policy analysts and scholars are often deeply involved in the norm-setting process. For example, the policy innovation represented by pollution control laws with clear goals and timetables to achieve them (such as the 1970 Clean Air Act and the 1972 Federal Water Pollution Control Act) was significantly influenced by the theory of "agency capture" proposed by political scientists and economists more than a decade earlier. These scholars believed that vague statutory language had led to the capture of the regulatory agencies by business. The growth of broadly delegated authority and increased bureaucratic discretion had corrupted liberalism into a system of competition among interest groups and reduced the power of the electorate. The proposed remedy was statutes that have clear goals, set fixed deadlines for achieving them, and empower citizen groups to take slow-moving agencies to court. As political scientist Marver Bernstein argued, statutes of this character institutionalize the sentiments of the citizens originally mobilized for the purpose of passing the legislation. Armed with strict legal authority, a regulatory agency is less likely to decline and perform inadequately, even if its activities no longer command general interest or attention.[8]

The ideas of Bernstein, Lowi, and other scholars were incorporated in influential textbooks and were eventually adopted by Congress in the popularized versions provided by members of the Ralph Nader organization. The ultimate result was a radical resetting of norms relating to environmental and health protection. Judged by the new norms, the traditional regulatory structure—based on informal negotiation with industry, weak enforcement by state agencies, and a large measure of administrative discretion—suddenly appeared inadequate and prone tò corruption. A major shift from decentralized regulation and voluntary compliance toward regulation at the national level by means of legally enforceable environmental standards was the legislative response to the new values.

Norm setting must be distinguished from norm using—the search for solutions that satisfy current norms. This distinction is similar to, but not identical with, the traditional dichotomy of policy and administration. It is sometimes said that political leaders make policy while the task of administrators and experts is to find the appropriate means to implement the policy. This formulation suggests that policy settles everything down to a certain point while administration deals with everything below that point. In fact, however, policy and administration do not occupy two separate spheres of action. They interact throughout the entire policy-making process.

Legislative mandates are often so vague, ambiguous, or contradictory that there are no clear standards for the administrators to apply. Even when the statutes attempt to define objectives with great precision, as the environmental laws of the early 1970s did, available technical and scientific knowledge may be insufficient to indicate unambiguously a unique best way to achieve the goals. Then it becomes necessary to introduce additional criteria for choosing among alternative solutions. Because uncertainty is so pervasive in public policy, the values of administrators and experts inevitably count a great deal.

Hence, although we may identify norm setting with policy and norm using with administration, we must be careful not to imply that policy and administration occupy two completely separate spheres or are the responsibility of two completely separate groups of people. Norm setting is not the prerogative of high-level policy makers, and administrators and experts do not deal only with means to politically designated ends. In fact, as political scientist Charles W. Anderson writes, "the actual role of policy professionalism in contemporary government is probably more prescriptive than instrumental. The setting of standards of good practice is a large part of what professionalism means. Most policy professions are such precisely because they provide standards for public policy. In such diverse fields as forestry, public health, nutrition and welfare, the essential function of the expert is often that of setting criteria for the definition of public objectives and the appraisal of public programs."[9] As the following example shows, experts may play an important role in setting standards for public policy even when they appear to be dealing with purely factual questions.[10]

In 1974 an environmental group, the Environmental Defense Fund, petitioned the Environmental Protection Agency (EPA) for suspension and cancellation of two chemical pesticides, Aldrin and Dieldrin (A/D). The administrative law judge hearing the case of EPA recommended that A/D be suspended because of the carcinogenic risk the pesticides posed, and this recommendation was endorsed by the administrator of EPA. When the decision was upheld in the appeals court, Shell Chemical Company, the producer of A/D, withdrew from the cancellation hearings.

During the cancellation hearings it became clear that there was no agreement over the standards for inferring carcinogenicity. Shell's experts argued that certain strict criteria had to be satisfied before a substance could be considered carcinogenic. For example, tumors should develop in two or more animal species exposed to the substance in the laboratory; there should be proof that the tumors are substance-related; data should be available proving the existence of at least one human cancer. EPA's case against A/D rested on different criteria of carcinogenicity. According to EPA's experts, a carcinogen is any agent that increases the induction of tumors in people or animals; a carcinogenic agent may be identified through analysis of experiments on animals or on the basis of properly conducted epidemiological studies; any substance that produces tumors in one animal species in appropriately conducted tests must be considered a carcinogenic hazard to man.

Neither set of criteria could be dismissed as being unreasonable or contrary to the rules of scientific evidence. Consequently a choice between them had to be made on nonscientific grounds. For example, in objecting to Shell's criterion requiring demonstration of at least one A/D-induced human cancer, the EPA's experts maintained that since animal tests were sufficient to predict carcinogenic risk, it was ethically unjustifiable to wait for the demonstration of human harm. They also argued that it was prudent to regard positive evidence of tumors in one animal species as indicating negative results in other species. By introducing standards of evidence that departed significantly from the more traditional toxicologic criteria used by Shell's experts, the EPA's experts were effectively setting new norms for public policy concerning carcinogenic risk.

Assessing Feasibility

Focusing public attention on a problematic condition and setting the norms to evaluate that condition and the facts relevant to it are only the initial stages in the process of public deliberation. The purpose of the next stage of debate is to fashion mutual understandings about the boundaries of the possible in public policy. Here too policy analysis can play a crucial role, first by identifying the relevant constraints and then by devising methods for removing or taking advantage of them when possible.

The conventional wisdom about the role of knowledge and analysis in the policy process has been aptly summarized as follows: "A problem exists; information or understanding is needed to generate a solution to the problem or to select among alternative solutions; research provides the missing knowledge; the decisionmakers then reach a solution."[11] In fact, however, the relationship between knowledge and policy is much less direct. Knowledge, especially theoretical knowledge, plays mainly a negative or critical role in practical affairs: it tells the practitioner what cannot, rather than what can, be done. Scientific theories do not tell engineers how to achieve particular goals, for example; rather, they show why certain goals are impossible in principle. The second law of thermodynamics shows the impossibility of constructing an engine that will operate with 100 percent efficiency. Similarly, the possibility of a perpetual motion machine, which has fired the imagination of so many visionaries and cranks in the past, is ruled out by the law of conservation of energy.

Entire branches of physics are based on very general impossibility principles or "postulates of impotence," and it has been argued that all physical science and perhaps all natural science could some day be derived from a small number of such postulates. "A postulate of impotence," Sir Edmund Whittaker writes, "is not the direct result of an experiment, or any finite number of experiments; it does not mention any measurement, or any numerical relation or analytical equation; it is the assertion of a conviction that all attempts to do a certain thing, however made, are bound to fail."[12]

The logical character of such impossibility principles is not fundamentally different from that of many generalizations in the social sciences, such as the "law" of supply and demand or the three basic principles of organizational control formulated by Anthony Downs (no one can fully control the behavior of a large organization; the larger an organization becomes, the weaker is the control over its actions exercised by those at the top; the larger an organization becomes, the poorer is the coordination among its actions).[13] The obviousness of these generalizations does not reduce their importance. Although, like the physical postulates of impotence, they cannot be proved, to disregard them would be courting disaster.

In public policy debates, the tendency to equate the desirable with the feasible is both more common and more difficult to correct than in science and technology. Particularly in the area of social policy, public opinion is often divided over questions of feasibility, with conservatives overstating and liberals underestimating the constraints on collective action.

An important part of the job of policy analysts, therefore, is to improve the quality of public deliberation by helping policy makers and the general public avoid both reckless underestimation and harsh overstatement of the limitations on the possible in public policy. A competent feasibility assessment of a new proposal would identify the major actual or potential constraints (including political or administrative feasibility), evaluate their significance for different implementation strategies, separate real constraints from fictitious obstacles, and estimate the costs and benefits of relaxing those constraints that are not absolutely fixed.

The latter task is particularly important since the analyst's job is not only to calculate optimal solutions within given constraints, but to push out the boundaries of the possible. Doing this requires both objective analysis and persuasion. What is possible within given constraints often depends on what the political system considers fair or acceptable. Hence many policy constraints can be eased only by changing attitudes, values, and cognitive beliefs.

When assessing policy feasibility it is not always easy to distinguish between constraints that are actually binding and those that can be relaxed by changing attitudes and values, and may turn out to be blessings in disguise. With the exception of physical impossibilities, policy feasibility is not an objective property but depends on such factors as time, motivation, skill, and imagination. In the short run technology, institutions, organizational capabilities, financial resources, and (in the very short run) even administrative routines and standard operating procedures must be taken as given. With sufficient time and motivation, however, technological and institutional obstacles can be removed, laws revised, capacities increased, procedures changed, and new skills learned.

By skillful and imaginative analysis it is often possible to take advantage of constraints. In fact, learning depends to a large extent on the skillful exploitation of constraints. Organisms can learn and adapt only to the extent that their environment is constrained; once a constraint has been recognized they can usually take advantage of this knowledge. The familiar phenomenon of friction is a good example of how a constraint may turn out to be, at least in some respects, a blessing in disguise. To mechanical engineers friction represents a pervasive and costly limitation. A significant portion of the power used in running machinery (about 20 percent for a modern automobile) is spent in overcoming friction. At the same time, friction is highly desirable in certain circumstances. Without it the wheels of a car would skid instead of rotating; we could not walk with ordinary shoes, but would need suction pads to cling to the floor; knots would be ineffective since it is friction between the interlocking parts of the knot that hold it together; and a nail hammered into a piece of wood would be immediately squeezed out like a pip between our fingers.

It is not difficult to find social analogues of this engineering example. Without severe resource constraints, countries like Japan and Switzerland might not have discovered the new ways of achieving economic growth that brought them to such a high level of industrial development. Similarly, the absence of a tradition of high craftsmanship and the relative scarcity of skilled labor may have accelerated development in the United States in the nineteenth century by stimulating the introduction of capital-intensive, skilled labor-saving techniques.[14]

For more recent examples, consider the constraints imposed on industry by environmental and health regulation. Regulatory restrictions have undoubtedly increased production costs in the short run and may have caused the loss of jobs in some marginal firms. However, a few countries (Japan being again a notable example) have taken advantage of environmental constraints and developed a new industry exporting pollution-control technologies and equipment worldwide. Similarly in the United States the threat of a ban on the use of chlorofluorocarbons in nonessential aerosol applications, combined with strong consumer pressure, has stimulated product innovation. The inventor of the first workable aerosol valve was able to present his device just one day after the Environmental Protection Agency and the Food and Drug Administration proposed their ban in May 1977.[15]

As these examples show, regulatory constraints can stimulate the new technical advances needed to channel economic growth away from hazardous industries and materials toward safer forms of production and employment. Hence policy feasibility may be analyzed from two different but complementary perspectives. On the one hand, overly ambitious goals must be tested against constraints since trying to do something inherently impossible is always a corrupting enterprise, as political philosopher Michael Oakshott once observed. On the other hand, short-run constraints should not become convenient excuses for passively accepting the status quo. In many cases the boundaries of the possible in public policy can be pushed out by devising methods of relaxing constraints or learning how to use them creatively.

Policy Evaluation

Assessing policy feasibility is only one aspect of a continuous process of evaluation in which all members of a democratic community are engaged. Citizens, legislators, administrators, judges, experts, the media—all contribute their particular perspectives and evaluation criteria. This multiplicity of viewpoints is not only unavoidable in a pluralistic society, but also necessary to the vitality of a system of government by discussion. Nevertheless, as Northrop Frye remarked in the context of literary criticism, there seems to be no reason why the larger understanding to which these separate perspectives contribute should remain forever invisible to them, like the coral atoll to the polyp.

Comprehensive policy evaluation should also be possible. It would recognize the validity of the different perspectives but would also seek, by making those perspectives more aware of one another, to reach a level of understanding and appreciation that is more than the sum of the separate evaluations. The purpose is not to construct a grand model combining all the partial perspectives into one general criterion of good policy—a weighted combination, so to speak, of equity, efficiency, effectiveness, legality, legitimacy, and any other relevant standard—but to contribute to a shared understanding of the multiple perspectives involved.

In constructing a comprehensive policy evaluation, one must distinguish the various organs or forums of evaluation—the electorate, the courts, public administration, and so on—and the evaluative criteria they use. In addition, there are three aspects of policy making that may be evaluated: the political and resource inputs, the transforming process, and the outcomes. To understand the general logic of evaluation it is convenient to examine input, process, and output separately. Most evaluations involve all three modes, in proportions that depend on the nature of the activity evaluated.

The common-sense view of evaluation (whether of a car or of a school program) is summarized in the slogan "only results count." Evaluation by results (also called payoff evaluation) proceeds by comparing a set of benchmarks or goals and a set of outcomes. In the case of an educational program, for example, one would appraise the difference between pre- and post-tests, or between experimental and control groups, on a number of criteria. In the case of a predictive policy model, one would compare its output (predictions) with actual developments.

Perhaps the best example of pure evaluation by results is the pricing of goods like apples or automobiles in a competitive market. The price system evaluates products quite precisely, without requiring that the buyer have any detailed information about either inputs or production processes. As this example suggests, outcome evaluation can be very efficient; it typically requires less information than alternative modes and evaluates performance less obtrusively—that is, with less direct interference with people's activities and internal decisions. Moreover, because such evaluations are usually expressed in quantitative terms—by prices, quantities, success rates, or similar outcome indicators—they can be more easily compared across products, functions, or activities.

This explains the strong intuitive appeal of evaluation by results. Indeed, one may well wonder why any other form of evaluation is needed at all. But outcome evaluation can be successfully performed only under rather special conditions. The most basic requirement is that it be possible to measure, with reasonable precision, the quality or level of the output or performance. If the indicator of performance is expressed by the distance between goals and outcomes, goals have to be clearly defined, outcomes must be unambiguously measurable, and the measuring instrument should be reliable. When joint or interdependent activities, such as teamwork, are evaluated, it should also be possible to measure separately the individual contributions to the final result, so that both rewards and joint costs may be allocated according to the different marginal contributions. Finally, to evaluate activities involving special skills, like managerial or professional decisions, it may be necessary to distinguish between results due to chance and those that can be attributed to skill or foresight.

These are stringent conditions, not often satisfied in practice, even approximately. When they are not satisfied, other modes of evaluation must be used. Evaluation by inputs focuses on the quantity and quality of the resources available to perform a certain task: number and technical quality of the staff, available information, level of funding, political support, and so on. These are indirect indicators of performance, at best. Unless one can assume a definite relationship between inputs and outputs—a well-defined production function, in the language of the economist—input variables are a poor proxy for what we are really interested in knowing: how effective is a given program? how good is particular policy?

But in some situations, input variables are the only information an evaluator has to work with—for example, when the problem is to estimate the likely results of a new project or to assess the feasibility of a new program. Moreover, for the purpose of control, input variables are often strategically more important than knowledge of outputs. The detailed rules of public accounting, which severely restrict the freedom of public managers to substitute one input for another in response to changing circumstances and new opportunities, are a good example of evaluation and control by inputs.

When knowledge of input variables is not sufficient to assess performance and results are difficult to measure, evaluation must focus on process variables. Evaluations of school programs, for example, generally consider such process variables as course content, grading procedures, teaching methods, and teacher-student interactions, rather than relying exclusively on students' performance in standardized tests, as in pure outcome evaluation.

To view process evaluation simply as an inferior substitute for "true" evaluation is to misconceive its real function and to underestimate its importance. Process evaluation is concerned not only with what decisions are made, but also with how they are made. If the correctness of a decision can be determined unambiguously, the decision process is unimportant—only results count. But when the factual and value premises are controversial, when there is no agreement on criteria and no satisfactory measure of the outcomes, then process acquires a special significance.

Consider judicial decisions. Even when the evidence is insufficient to allow absolute certainty of correctness, some decision must be reached and accepted as legitimate by all interested parties. Clearly, a system that must guarantee the decidability of all problems presented to it cannot also guarantee the correctness of the solutions. Legal procedures are designed to force a decision under all circumstances while ensuring, as much as possible, its legitimacy. Legitimacy is a quality that predisposes people to accept decisions that are yet substantively indeterminate and hence depend on procedural consideration rather than actual results.

Procedural considerations also play a much more important role in science than nineteenth-century positivists were willing to admit. What distinguishes a scientific from a nonscientific theory is not its "truth," which is always tentative at best, but the scientist's adherence to certain rules. Since there can be no demonstrative certainty for the conclusions of empirical science, their acceptance by the scientific community can only be established procedurally, by satisfying certain methodological and professional criteria—the rules of the scientific game. Generally speaking, the importance of process grows with the complexity of the problems to be solved. As sociologist Talcott Parsons has argued, only procedural primacy allows a social system to cope with a wide variety of changing circumstances and types of cases without prior commitment to specific solutions.[16]

The literature of evaluation research has often called for the development of methods emphasizing outcome rather than process. But unless outcomes can be adequately measured, outcome evaluation may be even less satisfactory than other modes and may actually decrease rather than improve the quality of performance. Peter Blau offers several interesting examples of this problem in his classic study of an employment agency. For example, when the number of interviews completed by a subordinate was the only evidence the supervisor had for evaluating him, "the interviewer's interest in a good rating demanded that he maximize the number of interviews and therefore prohibited spending much time on locating jobs for clients. This rudimentary statistical record interfered with the agency's objective of finding jobs for clients in a period of job scarcity."[17]

Even the more comprehensive system of monitoring introduced later produced serious displacements of organizational goals:

As instruments intended to further the achievement of organizational objectives, statistical records constrained interviewers to think of maximizing the indices as their major goal, sometimes at the expense of these very objectives. They avoided operations that would take up time without helping them to improve their record, such as interviewing clients for whom application forms had to be made out, and wasted their own and the public's time on activities intended only to raise the figures on their record. Their concentration on this goal, since it was important for their ratings, made them unresponsive to requests from clients that would interfere with its attainment. Preoccupation with productivity also affected the interpersonal relations among interviewers, and this constituted the most serious dysfunction of statistical reports.[18]

Similarly, the practice of using preset output goals in evaluating medical services creates a risk that the goals will not be interpreted as guidelines, but as commandments to be violated at the physician's risk. The physician begins to practice "defensive medicine," being afraid to depart from the codified conventional wisdom.[19] Experience with merit pay for teachers also illustrates the limitations of evaluation by results. The intent was to encourage better teaching in the public schools by raising teacher salaries on the basis of performance rather than such traditional (input) criteria as years of experience and educational credentials. The system has been tried in many school systems but as recent research has shown, it has failed in most cases; an important reason has been the difficulty of measuring teacher performance objectively.[20]

Even when the necessary conditions for outcome evaluation are satisfied, prudent managers try to avoid too narrow a focus on results. They know that the best outcome measures never capture more than a small fraction of the total domain of performance that is important to the organization. For example, sales volume is an unambiguous and robust output measure, but it tends to focus the attention of salespeople too narrowly on maximizing sales in the short run, so that they ignore functions that may have a large effect on future sales. People on straight commission have no incentive to arrange stocks, take inventory, or train new salespeople who become their competitors, and their supervisor cannot affect their salary by taking into account the other, unmeasured goals. Hence commission payment tends to be found in sales areas (like cosmetics, major appliances, and furniture) where the requirement of a relatively high degree of expertise encourages salespeople to develop something like professional norms, or where knowledgeable and active clients can replace professional norms as a source of evaluation and control. Some companies even prohibit the maintenance of sales volume records for individual salespeople.[21] Thus even the relatively simple activities of a department store are evaluated by criteria more refined than the mere comparison of results with predetermined standards of success.

The issue of government accountability reveals the limitations of outcome evaluation in extreme form. In the past it may have been possible to agree on a few stable standards—maintaining law and order and a stable currency at home, peace abroad—for evaluating government activities. But as these activities have expanded and the time span on which judgments of performance should be based has lengthened, the record of any particular administration becomes much less conclusive and the evaluative criteria more controversial. In such conditions confidence in government depends less on the relation between some measurable outcomes and a predetermined standard of success and correspondingly more on methods of evaluation that can provide more information than the simple judgment of success or failure. For example, evaluation should also provide information about the constraints facing policymakers.

Evaluation by results implies a clear separation of process and outcomes, of means and ends, and a strictly utilitarian position with respect to the means: the choice of means is a matter of indifference as long as the goals are reached. But in the realm of public policy, means are seldom value neutral and must always be evaluated in terms of procedural criteria. The problem of unemployment cannot be solved by putting people in labor camps, and even criminals are entitled to due process in a democratic society. Thus comprehensive policy evaluation must be concerned with process as much as with outcomes. It should also be more concerned with the potential for learning, with policy evolution and institutional change, than with short-run results.

As collective action has become more complex, the time span on which judgments of performance should be based has been lengthening. To evaluate an ambitious effort to produce significant change in the behavior of a large number of people, for example, a limited time frame is inappropriate, since it neglects both the severity of the initial administrative problems and the possibility of learning by doing. Thus evaluation studies conducted a few years after passage of the Elementary and Secondary Education Act produced widespread evidence that compensatory education produced no improvement in disadvantaged students' basic learning skills. Yet studies conducted after a decade of implementation revealed significant improvements in the administration of the program and a number of instances of substantial improvements in educational performances. The new findings suggest that there was a pattern of learning by program administrators and their congressional supporters as they identified obstacles and then devised various strategies to deal with them.[22]

To sum up, comprehensive policy evaluation must consider not only the results but also the process and, where necessary, the inputs of public policy. Process criteria are important because they protect the institutions of public deliberation against the eroding influence of utilitarian principles and short-run considerations. In the long run the effectiveness of public policy depends more on improving the learning capacity of the various organs of deliberation than on optimizing achievement of immediate goals. The real challenge for evaluation research and policy analysis is to develop methods of assessment that emphasize learning and adaptation rather than expressing summary judgments of pass or fail.

Deliberation, Analysis, and Persuasion

We have distinguished several stages of public deliberation—focusing, norm setting, feasibility assessment, policy evaluation—and have given examples of the contribution that ideas and analysis can make at each stage of the process. At several points it has been suggested that because facts and values are so closely intertwined in policy making, factual arguments unaided by persuasion can seldom play a significant role in the public debate. We conclude this chapter by examining in greater detail the relationship between analysis and persuasion in the context of public debate.

Persuasion is widely regarded as a dishonest or merely "rationalizing" use of arguments; it is propaganda, brainwashing, a method of "winning friends and influencing people" through manipulation. Persuasion can indeed be used in these ways, but we focus here on a variety of persuasion that, like ancient dialectic, is a two-way street, a method of mutual learning through discourse.

A persuasive argument cannot be a logical demonstration, but that does not mean it is a "mere rationalization." As literary critic Wayne Booth has argued, to reduce reason to logical calculation and proof about matters that do not matter enough to engage commitment is to create a torn picture of the world, with all our values on one side and all our rational capacities on the other. In this view controversy about values is essentially nonrational, and persuasion is simply a method of manipulating people rather than mutual learning through discourse.[23]

To say anything of importance in public policy requires value judgments, and these must always be explained and justified. This is one reason why persuasion is so pervasive in politics. However whimsically policy makers come to their conclusions, plausible reasons for their choices must always by given if they are to be taken seriously in the forums of public deliberation.[24] These reasons may be quite different from those that led to the adoption of the policy in the first place. Hence persuasive arguments of this sort are often dismissed as attempts to justify a posteriori one's actions by means of rational reasons rather than the "real" motives.

But it is not necessarily dishonest or merely "rationalizing" to explain a decision and persuade other people to accept it by giving reasons different from those that actually led to the decision. Policy arguments, we have repeatedly pointed out, are not formal proofs. A logical or mathematical proof is either true or false; if it is true, then it automatically wins the assent of any person able to understand it. Arguments are only more or less plausible, more or less convincing to a particular audience. Moreover, there is no unique way to construct an argument: data and evidence can be selected in a wide variety of ways from available information, and there are several alternative methods of analysis and ways of ordering values. Hence there is nothing intrinsically reprehensible in selecting the particular combination of data, facts, values, and analytic methods that seems most appropriate to convince a given audience.

A legal analogy may help to clarify this point. A judge may decide a case on the basis of his or her subjective notion of fairness, but that opinion must be framed in the objective categories of legal argument. Any subsequent developments in the case (for example, an appeal) will be based on the published opinion, not on the actual process the judge followed in coming to the conclusion. Most legal systems allow the opinion stating the reasons for a judicial decision to follow rather than precede that decision. Also, different judges may agree on a decision, but disagree about the best way to justify it; in the American system they have an opportunity to present their positions in separate arguments.

Such procedural rules seem absurd to somebody who assumes that a judicial opinion must be an accurate description of the judge's decision process. If, however, the opinion is viewed as a report of justificatory procedures employed by the judge, then the appeal to legal and logical considerations that may have played no role in the actual decision process becomes quite understandable.[25]

In politics as in the law, decisions must always be justified, and this is one reason why persuasion is so pervasive in public life. A second reason is the difficulty of introducing new policy ideas. As suggested above, the analyst's job is not only to find optimal solutions within given constraints but also to push out the boundaries of the possible in public policy. Major policy breakthroughs (like the Keynesian "revolution" in fiscal policy) become possible only after public opinion has been persuaded to accept new ideas. But new ideas face powerful intellectual and institutional obstacles. Economic, bureaucratic, and professional interests combine to restrict the range of options that are submitted to public deliberation or seriously considered by the experts. At the same time new ideas, precisely because they are new, usually lack conclusive empirical and theoretical support. Time is needed until favorable evidence accumulates and auxiliary theories come to the rescue. For this reason objective analysis, unassisted by advocacy and persuasion, is seldom sufficient to achieve a major policy breakthrough.

To be effective, then, an analyst must often be an advocate. But most analysts are firm believers in the virtues of the scientific method, and this belief is generally associated with a distaste for advocacy and persuasion. One way to defuse the conflict between practical effectiveness and scientific integrity is to note that many outstanding scientists have not hesitated to use persuasion when the situation seemed to require it. The work of Galileo, for example, has been likened to propaganda by historians of science, one of whom observed, "But propaganda of this kind is not a marginal affair that may or may not be added to allegedly more substantial means of defense, and that should perhaps be avoided by the 'professionally honest scientist.' In the circumstances we are considering now, *propaganda is of the essence*. It is of the essence because interest must be created at a time when the usual methodological prescriptions have no point of attack; and because this interest must be maintained, perhaps for centuries, until new reasons arrive."[26]

As one would expect, persuasion plays an even more significant role in the social sciences. For example, it is generally recognized today that Adam Smith did not give a rigorous proof of the consequences of a system of free exchange. The logically correct demonstration was provided by another economist, Robert Torrens, some forty years after the idea had been sold. Had Smith tried to give a logically airtight demonstration, instead of a masterfully persuasive statement of the benefits of free exchange, he might never have made his point popular.[27] Many other examples could be given. According to economist George Stigler, persuasive arguments "have preceded and accompanied the adoption on a large scale of almost any idea in economic theory."[28]

If advocacy and persuasion play such an important role in the development of scientific ideas, can policy analysts afford to slight them in the name of a historically mistaken view of scientific method? In policy analysis, as in science and in everyday reasoning, few arguments are purely rational or purely persuasive. The practical question, therefore, is not whether to use persuasion, but which form of persuasion to use and when. In some situations the use of persuasion, far from violating the analyst's code of professional behavior, is not only effective, but also rationally and ethically justifiable.

Sometimes persuasion is a necessary preliminary to get the policy maker's or the public's attention, to make them "listen to reasons" when they are blinded by wishful thinking or stereotypes. For example, Walter Heller, a former chairman of the Council of Economic Advisors, writes, "In 1961, with over five million unemployed and a production gap of nearly $50 billion, the problem of the economic adviser was not what to say, but how to get people to listen. Even the President could not adopt modern economic advice, however golden, as long as the Congress and the public "knew" that it was only fool's gold. . . [M]en's minds had to be conditioned to accept new thinking, new symbols, and new and broader concepts of the public interest."[29]

Many policy analysts and advisers have found that policy makers often think in traditional categories or in terms of alternatives that are unduly restricted in relation to their own objectives. Persuasion is needed to induce the policy maker to consider different formulations or approaches to the issue under discussion, since purely factual arguments may not be psychologically strong enough to overcome the inertia of long-established patterns of thought.

In some situations the motivation to attack a persistent problem comes well in advance of the means to solve it. For example, policy instruments for an adequate treatment of the problem may not be available, or good evidence on causal factors may be hard to get. In such cases, public education and persuasion (bolstered by whatever empirical and theoretical knowledge is available) may keep the issue alive until adequate methods of solution have been developed.

In all these cases, it may be argued that persuasion is justifiable on ethical and professional grounds. Pragmatically, we should also point out that since the conclusions of a policy argument can seldom be rigorously proved, persuasion can play a useful role in increasing both the acceptability of the advice and the willingness to act on less than complete evidence. To explain and defend a reasonable course of action when the theoretical optimum is unknown or practically unattainable is an essential part of the adviser's job. To draw a sharp line between explanation and advocacy in such cases is next to impossible.

However, the main justification for the use of advocacy and persuasion in democratic policy making is their function in the process of mutual learning through discourse. Keynes's contributions to the public debate on the problems of wartime finance in the late 1930s are an excellent example of this process. In addition to producing a stream of memoranda, articles, broadcasts, and letters to the press, Keynes held numerous meetings with officials, politicians, students, and trade union leaders. As a result of these discussions, he introduced several modifications into his original scheme for deferred payment on compulsory savings, such as family allowances to protect large low-income families, stabilization of the prices of the basic items of consumption, and a postwar capital levy to repay the compulsory savings and redistribute wealth. Thus modified in a process of debate and persuasion, his proposals gained wide acceptance. The 1941 budget, which set the pattern for all subsequent wartime financial policy, was truly Keynesian in inspiration and presentation.[30]

This chapter began by asking what policy analysis can contribute to the process of public deliberation. The answer, I argued, depends on the idea of rationality one accepts. Instrumental rationality reduces policy analysis to a set of techniques of optimization or data analysis. Arguments about values and beliefs are considered to be outside the pale of rational discourse—"mere rhetoric," propaganda, or rationalization. This artificial separation between our values and our rational capacities is a threat to all notions of public deliberation and defensible policy choices. To overcome this separation and the threat it poses to the democratic system of government by discussion, it is helpful to revert to the Greek notion of rationality: an action is rational if it can be explained and defended by arguments acceptable to a reasonable audience. Analysis-as-argument holds that any topic relevant to public discussion is an appropriate subject for serious inquiry. Analysts of this school do not reject means-ends calculations, where they are appropriate, but maintain that good arguments and open communication are not merely means to the end of efficiency, but ends in themselves.

CHAPTER 8

Political Leadership:
Managing The Public's Problem Solving

Ronald A. Heifetz and Riley M. Sinder

Prevailing ideas about what is good for society often determine how problems are posed, which actions are taken, and by whom. Public ideas have the power to lead and mislead. What then are the responsibilities of those who make and implement policy in regard to such ideas? In Chapter Six, Robert Reich argues that, at least on occasion, public managers have an obligation to instigate public deliberation rather than simply make policy decisions, that in directing public attention toward these ideas, public managers broaden the range of possibilities for public action and deepen society's self-understanding. In Chapter Seven, Giandomenico Majone suggests that policy analysts as well as office holders have responsibility for improving the quality of public discourse by probing assumptions, raising issues, and thereby helping the public consider different formulations of problems and a wider set of possible solutions.

In this chapter, we examine political leadership. We suggest that the idea of leadership itself shapes the processes by which a society does its work, and further that the current view restricts and diminishes the public's capacity to address the complex problem situations of public policy. We examine this prevailing view and some of its shortcomings, and we introduce a different account of political leadership and its role in public problem solving.

The Idea of Leadership

Perhaps better than any theorist, Richard Nixon summarized the conventional wisdom on leadership. In his "Silent Majority" speech of 1969, he described the task as he saw it:

A leader must be willing to take unpopular stands when they are necessary. . . .
And when he does find it necessary to take an unpopular stand, he has an
obligation to explain it to the people, solicit their support, and win their
approval.[1]

Nixon articulated the task of leadership as it is generally understood in the public sector. First, a leader identifies himself* by taking
stands, even unpopular stands. The assumption is that a leader must
have an agenda, even if it is controversial. Second, to implement his
agenda, a leader is expected to reach out to the people, explain his
position, solicit the support of the people, and gain their acceptance.
The mark of leadership is to succeed in carrying out one's stand; the
means of succeeding involve skillfully interacting with the people.

Many scholars have also attempted to define leadership.[2] Kellerman's recent study describes the task of presidential leadership in
terms similar to Nixon's:

Since directive presidential leadership is an interactive process heavily
dependent on the informal use of sources of power. . .a president must have (1)
the vision and motivation to define and articulate his agenda so as to broaden
his base of support; and (2) some considerable ability to perform effectively in
those interpersonal transactions necessary for bringing about his most
important goals.[3]

Although Kellerman makes the important tactical point that presidential leadership requires the skillful use of informal sources of power,
leadership is again defined as having a vision or agenda of one's own,
coupled with the ability to articulate one's message, gain support
through transactional means, and bring one's own goals to fruition.

The same idea of leadership appears to prevail in the private sector.
In a recent study of ninety leaders, Bennis and Nanus summarized the
conventional wisdom in this way:

Leadership is what gives an organization its vision and its ability to translate
that vision into reality.

The leader, as social architect, must be part artist, part designer, part master
craftsman, facing the challenge of aligning the elements of the social
architecture so that, like an ideal building, it becomes a creative synthesis
uniquely suited to realizing the guiding vision of the leader. . . . The effective
leader needs to articulate new values and norms, offer new visions, and use a
variety of tools in order to transform, support, and institutionalize new
meanings and directions.[4]

Throughout this chapter, masculine pronouns denote a person of either sex.

Here again, the task of leadership consists of providing a vision and taking action to realize that vision through the medium of an organization. Leaders in corporations, like leaders in the public sector, are often expected to "offer new visions" and bring in "new values and norms." They must project their idea of the future, their vision, their values and norms in a way that institutionalizes what they see. The mark of leadership, once more, is the leader's success in realizing his guiding vision; the means of implementation are interactive. In a similar vein, organization and group theorists typically describe a leader as "an individual who has the authority to decide, direct, and represent the objectives and functions of an organization."[5]

Most notions of leadership share certain basic assumptions. The preceding descriptions are illustrative in that they emphasize (1) providing vision or taking stands, and (2) interacting effectively when managing power and authority in order to generate sufficient organizational and political alignment to realize the leader's intentions. These common assumptions form a prevailing underlying theory or idea of leadership.

The Demand for Leadership

Governments, corporations, and individuals spend a great deal of time and money training people in "leadership." Programs in leadership are sprouting up in cities, consulting firms, and schools all over the country.[6] The frequently expressed concern that the United States is undergoing a "crisis in leadership" and the emphasis placed on judging President Reagan's leadership qualities (as opposed to President Carter's) suggest that people are looking to leadership for answers. It is as if many of us are swept up in a groundswell of excitement, even a clamoring, for effective leadership.

The prevailing idea of leadership, then, may be important to investigate, not only for its intrinsic interest but because the kind of leadership we praise, teach, and operate with may shape the futures of many people. The idea itself may affect the realities we live with and make.

But it would be a mistake to suggest that our interest in leadership is something new. We can certainly see a clamoring for leadership as far back as the days of the prophet Samuel, who pondered with God how to answer the people's curious longing and demand for a king. Neither Samuel nor God could see the reason for it. God, having just saved the Hebrew tribes from attack by the Philistines, interpreted the yearning for a king as a rejection of His authority and guidance, according to Samuel. The prophet tried to dissuade the people.

But the people refused to hearken unto the voice of Samuel; and they said: "Nay; but there shall be a king over us; that we may be like all the nations; and that our king may judge us, and go out before us, and fight out battles."[7]

The inclination of people to look to leaders for answers may well go back as far as the first agricultural societies with complex economies.[8] The yearning for leadership is an ancient phenomenon. And like any demand that finds its way into the marketplace, this yearning has been met with a supply. Leaders have appeared, or were chosen.

The supply of leadership seems to have been shaped by the character of the demand for it. People facing complex and frustrating situations wanted answers, protection, and order. Those who came forward to supply those demands were called leaders. Different styles of leadership were called forth depending on the particular situation and the norms of society, yet these styles were variations on a common theme. The basic idea of leadership remained fairly constant.

The Character of the Demand and How It Has Shaped the Conventional Wisdom

"What do your constituents expect or demand of you as a leader?" We posed this question to hundreds of executive and midcareer students at the Kennedy School of Government at Harvard University. The group included elected, appointed, and career officials from federal, state, and local governments; civil servants from many foreign lands; and corporate executives responsible for business-government relations. There were mayors, top- and middle-level managers in government agencies and private corporations, entry-level public servants, members of Congress, congressional staff, diplomats, all levels of military officers, foreign ministers, and heads of banks. Their responses were remarkably consistent.

Constituents expect them to provide solutions, security, and meaning. Constituents also demand many variations on these themes: answers, vision, inspiration, hope, consistency, order, direction, and "just tell me what to do." The officials in turn believe that these expectations are the norm and that their task as leaders is to fulfill them.

The prevailing conception of leadership seems to conform to the laws of supply and demand, in that leaders and theorists of the subject have adopted an idea of leadership that follows from what "followers" are asking for. Constituents appear to want answers to their questions, solutions to their problems, security in their surroundings, and a sense that their individual activities are connected to larger purposes and thus are meaningful. And leaders have viewed leadership accordingly: taking stands, providing solutions, having a vision, and interacting with constituents by explaining, supporting, and ordering so that they feel part of the vision and secure in knowing what to do.

The Traps Inherent in the Conventional Wisdom

Of course, no leader can consistently provide constituents with solutions, security, or meaning. Perhaps all that a leader can reliably provide, given such expectations, is failed expectations. Although individuals are generally more sensible than to expect leaders to provide all those things, cultural norms and public ideas are not formed simply by individuals. They are formed by group systems of political, organizational, and social interaction. (*Group* is used generically in this chapter to include each of these systems.) Public ideas arise when individuals repeatedly base decisions on their perceptions of what most other people think the norms and public procedures are. For example, if people think that nearly everybody around them understands an issue in a certain way, they will be inclined to act in agreement with that prevailing understanding. Even authority figures, although they may not agree with the prevailing understanding, will have to base their actions on how they think their public will view events, if they are to achieve practical results. Public ideas and conventional wisdom take on a life of their own, quite apart from anyone's private sensibilities.

The conventional wisdom on leadership does not dictate that a leader fulfill all the specific expectations of the constituents. As Nixon suggested, a leader's solution may run contrary to the trends in the group. Still, the conventional view requires that a leader design and implement some solution. He must have some agenda to call his own. Although a leader may have the leeway to innovate by coming up with new solutions, it would be quite unleaderlike, according to conventional wisdom, not to come up with any solution at all.

Theorists have invested great effort in discovering and assessing the means by which a leader can provide and implement solutions, as well as the special personal qualities needed to implement his solutions.[9] Many recent writers have attempted to transcend making value judgments of a leader's particular solution or vision, focusing instead on the strategic and tactical means by which a leader can accomplish his aims—whether through a better understanding of political interchange and the mechanisms for managing power and influence, practical insights into the design and behavior of organizations, or effective communication, the development of trust, and efforts to empower others.[10] In effect, scholars and theorists have based their work on the popular understanding of leadership, which is left unquestioned.

There are dangers in using the expectations of the group to define the idea of leadership. The group insists that the leader provide solutions. Yet only a very limited number of problematic situations can be resolved by a leader providing solutions; and therein lies the trap. Even in situations where solutions can be given, the very act of providing them will reinforce the group's presumption that leaders can be relied upon to find solutions and should be expected to do so.

The trap has two victims: the leader and the group. When the leader is successful in providing solutions, the group will probably expect more of him in the future. Conventional success in leadership will prompt the group to "up the ante." Although this response may flatter a leader's vanity, it is full of peril. It is possible that success will establish a track record that buys the leader some latitude and time to have failures, perhaps even enough time for him to die a natural death while remaining a hero to his people. But if the problems are great, the group's rising expectations may eventually surpass the leader's magical powers, causing his downfall. The twentieth century is full of such leaders (Ferdinand Marcos, Lyndon Johnson, Indira Gandhi, Benito Mussolini) whose early successes fostered unrealistic expectations, both within themselves and in their constituents.

The trap is equally dangerous for the group. First, conventional success in leadership may decrease the group's own adaptive capacity. Repeated success, just as it increases dependency on the leader, may weaken the constituents' ability to face, define, and solve problems. The danger for the group could be reduced if the leader took steps, during and after success, to discourage the predilection to look to him for more answers in the future. Of course, leaders, operating by the conventional wisdom, usually do just the opposite when they meet with success; they bolster the group's inflated expectations.

Second, and perhaps more telling, conventional leadership operates with a basic misconception regarding how a society succeeds in addressing complex public problems. Difficult public policy situations are hard to define and resolve precisely because they demand the work and responsibility of the constituents. Thus many complex problems are not amenable to solutions provided by leaders; their solutions require that constituents address the problematic situations that face them.

A Typology of Situations

By way of analogy, consider the job of a physician. Patients and their families routinely come to physicians expecting solutions, and physicians, like leaders, try to provide them. The role of the physician and the conventional wisdom that reinforces it have been shaped by the group's demand. Physicians define their job in terms of providing solutions; they diagnose, treat, and try to cure illness.

This characterization of the doctor's job is perfectly adequate in some situations. To a patient with an infection, for example, the physician can sometimes say, "I have an antibiotic medication that will almost definitely cure you without any effort or life adjustment needed on your part. The medication is virtually harmless. I can give you one shot, or a week of pills, whichever you prefer." We can call this a Type I situation—one in which the patient's expectations that the doctor can provide a solution are realistic and the problem situation can be defined, treated, and cured using the doctor's expertise and requiring very little work on the part of the patient. These are the straightforward mechanical situations in which one can go to somebody and "get it fixed." And from the doctor's point of view, these are those gratifying moments when he can actually solve a patient's problem. Although the patient's cooperation will be crucial in Type I situations, the weight of problem defining and problem solving falls on the physician.

Type II situations are far more common. Here the problem is definable but no clear-cut technical solution is available; the doctor can offer some remedies but no cures. Heart disease sometimes presents a Type II situation. The patient can be restored to more or less full operating capacity, but only if he takes responsibility for his health by making appropriate life adjustments; in particular, he may have to consider the doctor's prescriptions regarding long-term medication, exercise, diet program, stress reduction, and so forth. Type II situations can be managed only partially by the physician in a mechanical way. He diagnoses and prescribes, but his recommendations will have side effects requiring the patient's evaluation of the tradeoffs.

In Type III situations, the problem definition is not clear-cut, and no technical fixes are available. Chronic disability or impending death from any cause fits this category. In these situations, the doctor can continue to operate in a mechanical mode by diagnosing and prescribing remedies (and a remedy of some sort can usually be found). But if he does so, the problem-defining and -solving work of both doctor and patient will be avoided. In these situations, treating the illness is too narrow a way to define the physician's task. The problem, and consequently the required work, have to be understood more broadly than the particular diagnosis. When critical aspects of the situation are probably unchangeable, the problem must be distinguished from the medical condition—the diagnosis. For example, if the patient's diagnosis is an advanced stage of cancer in which the likelihood of cure is remote, it may be useless—indeed, a denial of reality—to define the primary problem as cancer. Cancer, in this case, is a condition. To the limited extent it can be treated at all, it is only part of the problem. To define cancer as the primary problem leads everyone involved to concentrate on finding solutions to the cancer, thus diverting their attention from the work at hand. The patient's work consists of facing and making adjustments to harsh realities that go beyond his health condition and that include several possible problems: making the most out of life; considering what the children may need after he is gone; preparing a spouse, parents, loved ones, and friends; completing important tasks, and so forth.

Table 8.1 summarizes the characteristics of the three types of situations.

Table 8.1 Situational Types

	Problem Definition	*Treatment*	*Primary Locus of Work*
Type I	clear	clear	physician
Type II	clear	unclear	physician and patient
Type III	unclear	unclear	patient

In Type III situations, and often in Type II, the physician can help the patient face the situation, define problems, and develop solutions, but he cannot "fix it." Therefore it is counterproductive for the doctor to define his task within a framework based on patients' expectations (i.e., to provide solutions, to diagnose and treat illness).

An alternative definition of the physician's job—"helping the patient do his work"—would serve well in each of these situations. If the problem definition and treatment are clear-cut (Type I), then helping the patient face and adjust to his problematic reality will consist of telling him he has a certain problem and recommending the appropriate treatment. If the problem definition is clear-cut but the treatment is not purely technical (Type II), so that the patient must evaluate and make life adjustments, then education and persuasion may be needed to mobilize the patient's resources to do that work. And if the problem situation is complex and the treatment unclear (Type III), then the treatment will require the patient's participation in defining the specific problems within the overall situation and devising solutions for each. The doctor cannot do this work, only the patient and his family can determine how the problems should be defined in the first place, let alone treated. Although the particular style of the physician will have to change depending on the type of situation, the basic stance of the physician—to help the patient do his work—will remain constant.

The Realm of Public Policy

Many important problems in any realm are of Type II and Type III. Public policy is no exception. The problems are messy. Many people are involved, and many of them disagree on the definition as well as the treatment of the problem. With poverty, crime, international disputes, pollution, education policy, and so forth, much of the work consists of defining the problem, not just solving it. Furthermore, in public policy situations of types II and III, the defining and solving comprise significant political and social learning processes as the various constituencies involved sort out their orientation, values, and potential tradeoffs. No "leader" can magically do this work.

Only the group—the relevant community of interests—can do this work. It must do the sorting and learning necessary to define what constitutes a problem. It must make the adaptations and adjustments to the problem situation that most solutions require. Solutions in public policy generally consist of adjustments in the community's attitudes and actions. Who else but those with stakes in the situation can make the necessary adjustments? For example, for a nation to successfully go to war, the constituents will have to join the effort and make adjustments in their lives accordingly. In Churchill's first major statement as prime minister—"I have nothing to offer but blood, toil, tears, and sweat"—he referred to the group's work, not merely his own. For a community to improve public education, constituents will have to make schools a high priority and then evaluate and choose among numerous alternatives, such as setting higher performance standards, upgrading curricula, spending more money on teachers, addressing local poverty, and increasing parent involvement.

To illustrate further, consider the situation of drug abuse. If the supply of drugs is driven primarily by the demand, and if the demand is a product of economic, social, and psychological forces, then defining the problem as drug supply, as is often done, avoids the reality of demand. Unrealistic definitions may mislead the public by directing its attention to an unrealistic set of solutions. More accurate definitions of the problem include drug-related crime and the self-destructive demand for drugs.

Parts of these problems appear to have technical solutions. Many people suggest that drug-related crime would be solved in large part by making drugs legal—that the motives for crime would disappear by making access to drugs cheap. Others argue, however, that this way of defining the problem is too narrow because it fails to address costly tradeoffs regarding social values and responsibility.

In either case, the problem of crime is only one aspect of the drug situation. The problem of people wanting drugs and using them in ways that are personally harmful will not be solved by legalizing drugs or by any other technical remedy. Any solution to this problem will have to consist of adjustments on the part of the community. The elimination of self-destructive drug use may require public education, altering family structures, diminishing unemployment, and changing the ways in which people derive meaning from life.

Upon entering into a problem-solving process, a public official cannot be sure which type of situation he and his constituents face. If he begins with the common assumption of constituents—that problematic situations are of Type I and that the public official can and should "fix them"—he is likely to accept unwittingly a problem definition and a routine of action that neglects important parts of the situation. In the case of drug abuse, he may view the problem as drug supply. On the other hand, if he starts with the assumption that most situations are of Type II or Type III, then he will be ready when necessary to help constituents confront those aspects of the situation that are not clearly defined or solved, and that require their work.

As work on issues advances, Type III situations can be broken down partially into Type II and Type I components. As with the drug abuse situation, when conditions are distinguished from problems, and alternative problem definitions are created and sorted through, policy makers and constituents will generate a series of discrete frames for the problem. The point for the policy maker is not to lock any situation into a particular category, but to establish an approach that routinely steers the community toward addressing the essential but frequently most difficult and ignored aspects of a problematic reality—for example, that the demand for drugs may originate within the community itself.

Because constituents may cling rigidly to one way of viewing the situation, the work of defining and solving problems must provoke learning. The act of sorting out their values and points of view on a complex issue, of debating the merits of various competing frames for the problem, is itself part of the adjustment process by which constituents achieve solutions.

Inventive people have sometimes been able to turn Type II and Type III situations into Type I; they find a cure. With advances in natural or social scientific understanding, we occasionally convert messy situations into clear-cut ones. The discovery of penicillin transformed most cases of pneumonia into situations of Type I. Many of us no longer have to live with the uncontrollable flooding of rivers because thousands of years ago some people invented the dam.

Few if any public policy problems are clear-cut, however. Even the building of a dam has problematic side effects. Dams require resources that might be applied to other efforts; they change the demography, ecology, and social structure of an area, with mixed consequences for social values, norms, and behavior. They can burst open with catastrophic results downstream. Though flooding may appear to be a Type I situation, a problem that can be solved by a dam, evidently it is not. Policy makers will be faced with questions like: who is to know how broadly or narrowly to define the problem for which building a dam then becomes the solution? Who is to determine which technical solution to choose among several alternatives, each with a different set of side effects?

Since most situations are of types II and III, the expert in public policy has to become expert, not in providing answers, but in managing the dynamics of the group struggling with its work. In the case of the president, this entails managing Congress, the press, his own agencies, interested parties, and anyone else whose involvement is required for progress in a particular problematic situation. In the case of the middle manager, this involves managing his superiors, subordinates, lateral colleagues, outside parties, and anyone else whose participation is needed to frame and resolve a problematic situation. In the case of the general citizen, this demands engaging organizations, interested parties, the press, political representatives, other citizens—whoever has to be involved in the process by which a group learns its way from a current state of affairs to one that is better.

This job challenges even the most courageous. There is enormous pressure on public officials, like doctors, to maintain the narrow, answer-giving conception of their jobs. Constituents want solutions, particularly when they confront harsh realities. The task of helping them take responsibility for their work becomes daunting. First, it means going against their expectation that the leader can fix things for them—frustrating them in their initial desires. Second, it means holding steady as constituents, over time, begin to face their situation—maintaining one's poise, resolve, and capacity to listen when under attack. Third, it means helping constituents carve out of their messy situations discrete problems needing their attention and work—challenging their assumptions regarding the situation and provoking the discovery of alternative problem definitions. Finally, it necessitates managing the iterative process of devising solutions, making adjustments, and redefining problems as the situation changes and as constituents reorder their priorities along the way.

In all of this, the task of pacing the work is crucial. It takes time for any group to face, assess, and change or adapt to tough situations. Leadership, in this sense, requires expertise. In addition to solving well-defined problems, the public official has to manage the deliberative process by which constituents accomplish work. Beyond technical know-how, he needs the improvisational flexibility and insight to manage others in doing work on frustrating situations where the definition of the problem, let alone the solution, is not clear.

Rather than posing as a wizard who can always pull the right rabbit out of the hat at the right time, a leader must be wary of ever pulling out rabbits. Such feats tend to create solutions with unintended and unforeseen side effects; worse, they reinforce the conventional wisdom that tough problems require wizards. And everyone knows what happens to wizards when they run into situations for which they have no rabbit.

The Conventional Wisdom as a Paradigm of Authority

As we have seen, the conventional wisdom regarding leadership has been shaped by people's demands that someone come up with solutions to their problems. If the problem is malaise, then people will demand something to believe in. He who provides something to believe in—regardless, too often, of what that something is—will be chosen as leader.

The demand for solutions in group settings leads to a shift in the locus of work from those facing the problem situation to someone else, usually someone in authority. This does not mean that every organization or social system is structured to pass the buck. It suggests that every social system finds ways to distribute and sometimes avoid work by establishing systems of authorization.

Perhaps no social system can remain viable without some system of authorization by which labor is distributed and oriented to a task, channels of communication and command are established, and structures of empowerment are set in place.[11] Systems of authorization are not only formalized arrangements with set positions; they are, in large part, informal arrangements. The office, the formal authorization, is rarely a sufficient source of leverage by itself to provide power.[12] A high office holder has to gain informal authorization (i.e., respect, trust, fear, bargaining advantages, admiration) if he is to increase his authority, his power to influence. He does so by fulfilling the expectations for which the group informally confers authority.

The conventional idea of leadership describes which expectations an office holder has to promise to fulfill in order to obtain the group's formal and informal authorization. The group authorizes a leader to provide solutions, meaning, and security—in the words of the Bible, to "go out before us, and fight our battles." To gain authority, that is what he must do, promise to do, or appear to do. But in doing so, thus fulfilling his authorization, is he exercising leadership or authority? The two may be very different matters. Because the expectations associated with authority impose sharp limits on behavior, having authority constrains leadership. Stepping across the line jeopardizes one's authority. Furthermore, since groups will tend to pressure authority figures for simple remedies as a way to avoid harsh and complex problems, shouldn't we expect them to collude routinely and even unwittingly in the avoidance of work?

The person with authority in a given setting and situation may not even be in the appropriate role to exercise leadership. Rather than lead people to come to terms with difficult realities, authority figures have often been expected to give, and have given, tranquilizing but fake remedies. Adolf Hilter's use of scapegoating and delusions of grandeur provides an extreme example.

The conventional wisdom blurs this distinction. The tendency is both to equate authority and leadership, and to use the expectations of the group as the frame of reference for defining leadership. When someone gains high office (formal authority), or trust, admiration, and a following (informal authority)—that is what traditionally passes for leadership. But if leadership and authority are distinguished, one sees that the demands of the group provide a frame of reference only for authority. From this perspective, "doing what is expected" outlines the exercise of formal and informal authority, but not leadership.

Proper management of the functions of authority—providing an orienting vision, hope, security, "doing battle for," and so forth—is crucial. Indeed, to go back to the medical analogy, the physician's capacity to lead (i.e., to help the patient do his work) virtually depends upon meeting enough of the patient's expectations to gain his attention and trust. Authority, both formal and informal, is a primary tool for exercising leadership. By fulfilling the functions of authority, one establishes a secure relationship with constituents, making it possible to contain and pace their conflicts and stress in doing problem-defining and problem-solving work. Like the walls and valve of a pressure-cooker, authority can provide the instruments, the power, to hold together and harness the conflictive process of doing work.

If we release the idea of leadership from its mooring as a product of group expectations, what shall we use as a reference point in its stead? Authority and leadership can be seen as two sets of functions that sometimes overlap. Authority protects and maintains the expectations of which it is a product—the group's norms, problem definitions, and current set of solutions. The exercise of authority revolves around the dynamic of power: how and why people confer power and how people gain and make use of power. A more useful framework for an idea of leadership, however, may be found elsewhere.

The exercise of leadership revolves around the dynamic of work: how work is both accomplished and avoided by social systems. Leadership mobilizes groups to do work. Often this demands innovation in defining problems, generating solutions, and, perhaps foremost, locating responsibility for defining and solving problems. Power and work provide the axes that orient authority and leadership. They often go hand in hand, but they function distinctly.

The functions of authority are associated with specific formal and informal positions in a social system. The functions of leadership, in contrast, are never defined by a position. For example, the position of assistant secretary in the Department of Transportation will be defined by a series of authorizations—to oversee specific departmental activities, direct particular projects, manage certain people's access to the secretary, and so forth. Similarly the informal position of "devil's advocate" will often be defined by a series of informal authorizations—to question current assumptions, provide deviant ideas, but yet remain a congenial member of the group by knowing when to stop being troublesome. The authorization simultaneously creates a discrete position and enables a set of functions.

Yet one might exercise leadership from any position. Indeed, as soon as one's leadership actions became associated with a specific position, they would merge with the general system of expectations, becoming authority as well as leadership. Thereafter a leader would have to consider carefully both the power and constraints inherent in his authorization. He would be exercising the functions of leadership with both the resources and the extra baggage of an authority position, which carries a host of expectations and its own set of functions. In other words, whereas authority can be described in the domains of both function and position, leadership can be described only within the domain of function. To equate leadership with a position is once again to equate leadership with authority.

A Concept of Leadership

The common thread between authority and leadership appears to lie in the concept of work. People authorize other people, by and large, because they think they will do some piece of work. And in certain clear-cut situations where technical expertise can provide solutions, authorizing others to do one's work will succeed. But in situations where the group's values are unclear, the shapes of problems are indistinct, and solutions have yet to be fashioned, success requires shifting the primary locus of work back to the group. To do this demands leadership that goes beyond or against the expectations inherent in one's authority. In other words, a person is rarely, if ever, authorized to exercise leadership.

The idea that leadership is a function distinct from authority, and therefore that it lacks positionality, has numerous implications. First, leadership can be exercised at once by several people from varying positions of authority. One organization may exercise leadership vis-à-vis other organizations. Second, there may be no such thing as "seizing leadership," since leadership is not a position but an activity. How can one seize an activity? Third, although some will gain high position and enormous informal authority, they may never exercise leadership. Those whom we call leaders may not be leaders at all, simply figures of authority. From a functional point of view, a leader is anybody who serves the functions of leadership, however he may be perceived by others.

If leadership is the mobilization of a group's resources to do work, and if many situations in the realm of public policy are of types II and III, then the exercise of leadership will require devising policies or taking actions that serve as catalysts of work, rather than solutions to problems. For example, when Mohandas Gandhi set out on a hunger fast, he did so not to solve the problems of his day, but to engage people in the problems of his day. Fasting was no solution. Fasting aimed to provoke questions, involvement, and responsibility.

Similarly, if the task of the middle manager as leader is to mobilize the resources of the group (superiors, subordinates, lateral colleagues, the press, outside parties) to do work (come to terms with problematic situations), then the task will generally consist of capturing and directing attention to the problem situation, containing the stress and frustration that inevitably come from facing tough situations, corralling the various constituents into working relationships with one another, and managing that work process (defining, refining, and resolving problems) over time. A leader becomes a guide, interpreter, and stimulus of engagement, rather than a source of answers.

This kind of leadership isn't easy. Particularly in group settings, people develop ingenious patterns for avoiding work. These patterns are often accepted as normal and go unnoticed. People in positions of authority, like doctors, are quite vulnerable to being drawn into those work-avoidance patterns. For example, physicians are often tempted to provide false information and to cooperate in the denial of seriously ill patients. People who are overweight easily find physicians who prescribe diet pills rather than help their patients do work (gain self-acceptance, change their self-image, control their diet, exercise routinely). Similarly, a nation facing a perilous situation may generate a demagogue, complete with "evil" scapegoats, to provide the illusion of a Type I situation and thus a false sense of security. It is extremely difficult (and risky) for an authority figure to present constituents with the reality they face and the work that is theirs. Taking pride in the authorized and conventional view of oneself as a problem solver may compound the difficulty.

In the realm of public policy, citizens, interest groups, executive agencies, the press, and Congress turn to those they have authorized as problem solvers to take care of problem situations on their behalf. Each level seeks out an authority figure in the next echelon up, until often the president becomes the physician of last resort. And, as we have discussed, as long as those situations are easily defined and technically remediable (Type I), work does indeed get done. But when the situation calls for leadership and not simply the fulfilling of one's authority—that is, when the situation calls for mobilizing the group's resources to face, define and resolve its problems—then a leader, a person trying to get work done, will come up against the group's natural inclination to avoid taking the work back onto its own shoulders. In these situations leadership often requires going against the patterns of constituents, beyond their expectations, and thus outside of one's authority, to get work done. But unlike Richard Nixon's idea of leadership—which assumes that a stand is a policy answer, and answers are to be explained so that the people are won over—this view of leadership sees a stand as a tool for engaging the people in doing work, and sees popular approval as a possible indication of work avoidance within the group.

Of course, it isn't that the person exercising leadership knows what the work is. It isn't that he knows "what to do." The need for leadership arises precisely because there are many highly problematic situations in which no one knows what to do. If the direction were clear, the solution available through technical expertise, then an authority in that field would suffice; one could presumably bring him in, or elect him.[13]

In the conventional wisdom, effective political leadership is defined as the capacity to achieve one's declared goals, to get one's program enacted. The emphasis is not only on having a program one can call one's own, but on being able to manage one's influence to achieve it.[14] This perspective, even in what appear to be Type I situations, may be a trap for those in authority who want to exercise leadership. As a simple example, consider the authority figure who thinks he has a solution and whose primary stake is to enact a specific policy—say a president who passionately believes in a particular energy policy. As Kellerman describes in *The Political Presidency*, the primary requirement for success, even here, will be the president's capacity to engage the relevant community of interests (Congress, press, interest groups, public, cabinet) in the work of facing, assessing, and creating terms for resolving the problematic situation. This leadership process demands continuous engagement and intent listening so that the president can include in his definition of the problem and its policy solutions as much of the political landscape as he can. Getting a program enacted will require incorporating the various points of view represented in the community of interests—a process of learning and compromise that will tend to produce a program no longer one's own. Clinging to a specific policy as "one's own" will often lead to failure because it is essentially an apolitical policy formulation and implementation strategy. That is, the work has been conceived as the individual's rather than the group's. The fundamental error lies in dealing with Type II and Type III situations as if they were Type I.

Many leadership theorists and practitioners have fallen into the same trap as have "followers." They identify the primary locus of work with the individual authority rather than with the community of interests that has the problem. Societies that operate according to the conventional wisdom tend to produce "leaders" who perpetuate the mistake of misidentifying the primary locus of work and thus fail to engage the problem-defining and problem-solving resources of the group. Individual efforts remain unintegrated with a systemic solution. John Stuart Mill describes this dynamic.

The mischief begins when, instead of calling forth the activity and powers of individuals and bodies, [a government] substitutes its own activity for theirs; when instead of informing, advising, and upon occasion, denouncing, it makes them work in fetters, or bids them stand aside and does their work instead of them. The worth of a state, in the long run, is the worth of the individuals composing it ... a State which dwarfs its men, in order that they may be more docile instruments in its hands even for beneficial purposes—will find that with small men no great thing can really be accomplished.[15]

Leadership and Public Problem Solving as Group Phenomena

No situation can be described, a priori, as a problem. Situations seem problematic because people value one state of affairs over another. People would rather not be poor, for example, so joblessness is deemed a problem. In the public realm, the kinds of situations we define as problematic often change. For example, inequality of opportunity is defined as a problem today, but at times in the past it was simply a generally accepted condition sustained by a set of prevailing understandings.

Work on any large-scale problem situation may be impossible without first shifting the prevailing understanding so that the situation is seen as problematic. Advocates of various public concerns and causes often serve this function by bringing what they think is a problem or opportunity to general attention. In this way, a vision of the future acts as a stimulus, rather than an answer. It is the grain of sand in the oyster, not the pearl.

The work process moves forward as competing frames for the problem are carved out from the overall problematic landscape. This process will require that the various components of the relevant community, each representing a different perspective on the problem situation, engage one another. Ways to test the parameters of the situation must be developed and implemented. Problems have to be distinguished from conditions. As suggested before, problems are those aspects of a situation that potentially can be resolved, while conditions are those aspects that are probably unchangeable. To fail in this distinction is usually to mistake illusion for reality. For example, in U.S.-Soviet relations, each nation's vulnerability to the other's weapons (nuclear, chemical, biological) is a condition central to a problematic situation. Although many might like to view this condition as the crux of the problem and then imagine a technical Type I cure for it—a perfect "Star Wars" defense, for example—such a vision denies essential aspects of reality. Few people actually suppose that we can make ourselves invulnerable, not only to nuclear weapons, but to biological and chemical weapons as well. Defining "mutual vulnerability" as a problem rather than a condition is thus inaccurate. Alternative problem definitions are: improving security within the condition of mutual vulnerability by improving U.S.-Soviet relations, crisis prevention and management, strengthening deterrence through arms control, diminishing the displacement of Third World tensions into the U.S.-Soviet relationship, and so forth. To produce work, a vision needs to be rooted in reality; it has to have accuracy, and not simply imagination and appeal.

Most situations policy makers face involve a multitude of related problems at varying stages of definition and development. Some facets of the situation are just beginning to be perceived by the community as problematic, others have long been seen as problems but remain unsolved and appear unremitting, while perhaps a few problems are near resolution. A policy to address one problem will often affect not only the way other problems are defined but also the resources available to address them. As time passes, work in one problem area may stimulate insights that lead to problem redefinition in other areas, and in turn to changes in policy and resource allocation. Indeed, since situations and resources are overlapping, many such insights may be possible. For example, our investigation of the 1986 explosion of the space shuttle *Challenger* should yield insight into the mismanagement of organizations in general, not just the National Aeronautics and Space Administration. Furthermore, we may discover something about the impact of rapid privatization on the management systems of public agencies and the danger of seeing such a policy as a mechanical cure-all for the ills of government, society, and other nations. Although the privatization of public bus systems may constitute good policy in some cities, pushing NASA to act like a profit-making business with rigid production deadlines evidently was not.

In this complex and somewhat fluid environment, the public official is faced with the challenge of managing the discovery, shaping, and rediscovery of each step in the problem-defining and -solving process over time. He must be able to lead the relevant community of interests in facing unwanted situations, investigating what can be changed and what cannot, discovering what it is willing to define as a problem, applying insights from other areas, and fashioning the life adjustments that will constitute the material of any solution.

This expertise operates on a razor's edge. An expert at leadership has to manage the means, pace, authority structures, and other devices for containing and focusing the usually turbulent process of putting people's problems back in their own laps without abandoning them. A leader is likely to encounter plenty of frustration, conflict, and anger as he challenges the community to tolerate the confusion and discomfort of learning. Success will depend on (1) identifying the problem situations that the community indicates are ripe for its attention, (2) determining the composition of the relevant community of interests, (3) designing positions and policies to address the ripe situations so that the relevant community learns its way to a solution, and (4) implementing and assessing actions according to their effects on the community's work process.

Franklin Roosevelt's management of leadership illustrates this expertise quite well. Especially before the 1937 court-packing fiasco, Roosevelt routinely left the various communities of interest in confusion until policy directions emerged from their struggle with their uncertainty, values, and doubt.

Situations had to be permitted to develop, to crystallize, to clarify; the competing forces had to vindicate themselves in the actual pull and tug of conflict; public opinion had to face the question, consider it, pronounce upon it—only then, at the long frazzled end, would the President's intuitions consolidate and precipitate a result.[16]

For example, during the depth of the Depression, rather than establish an official economic policy, Roosevelt avoided becoming attached to any particular strategy, economic theory, or solution. Of course, he had his own preferences. The point, however, was not primarily to implement his preferences. The point was to track the trends in the group for clues to the issues that were ripe for its attention and for which he could use his formal authority and personal power to provoke its work. Roosevelt's expertise did not lie in inventing solutions and implementing them, but in improvising temporary catalysts of work in the form of policies and positions, depending on the way the work was progressing, or being avoided, in the group at the time.

Yet Roosevelt saw himself in a favorite simile as a quarterback in a football game. He could not say what the play after next was going to be until the next play was completed. "If the play makes ten yards," he told a press conference in April 1933, "the succeeding play will be different from what it would have been if they had been thrown for a loss. I think that's the easiest way to explain it." And, from his point of view, the Frankfurters and the Tugwells, the

Johnsons and the Hulls represented alternative plays, not alternative strategies. Each ideological system, as he must have felt it, described certain aspects of American reality, each missed out on certain vital features, and effectiveness might therefore most probably lie not in taking one or the other but in combining and applying both to meet the needs of a particular situation.[17]

Sometimes, for purely tactical reasons, a leader will indeed take clear stands or put his full weight behind a specific policy. Taking such a position, even if it does not conform to his personal values and program, may serve as a heuristic device to stimulate and guide the conflictive and deliberative work of problem defining and problem solving. Stands and policies are thus designed both to generate work and to test the waters (i.e., gather more information). Based upon his analysis of how and which issues are ripening in the relevant community, a leader may well shift his weight or change his stance over time. For example, to prevent premature closure on an argument when the point of view represented by the weakening side is not being faced by the larger community of interests, a leader might find ways to reinforce the weaker side, even if he himself is ideologically opposed to it, so as to keep the process sufficiently fluid for the work to continue. In this regard, a leader is like a midwife trying to keep the mother from pushing the baby out too soon.

A leader may have to gauge, interpret, and manage not only which situations or issues are ripe for attention, but also the vicissitudes any hard work is bound to encounter. As suggested earlier, when the work itself requires that the community wrestle with its conflicting points of view, there are bound to be many diversions and other mechanisms of work avoidance.

Chief among these mechanisms is the penchant for looking to the person in authority for answers. Thus to exercise leadership, the authority figure may have to pace the rate at which he fails the demand for answers, perhaps very slowly. He may have a "honeymoon period," but if he does not act carefully in giving the work back to the group at a rate it can manage, the community in its frustration may well scapegoat its authority figure by pulling him down and replacing him—all in the belief that "if only we had the right leader our problems would be solved."

Alternatively, the community may avoid taking responsibility for a difficult situation by defining the problem so narrowly that it appears amenable to a technical solution. Or the community and its authorities may create a diversion by producing a new situation—for example, a war. Rather than telling the people what they want to hear, leadership involves telling the people over time what they need to hear to get them to face and solve their problems.

In managing the identification and resolution of difficult issues, a leader will be managing community processes of learning: assessing current situations, questioning previous assumptions, learning the different points of view embodied by opposing interests, inventing frames for defining problems that take in a sufficient breadth of those interests, implementing solutions by adjusting actions and attitudes as a community, and redefining problems and solutions as the situation changes and as various points of view change. Each of these tasks consists of learning.

Learning processes may be more successful in the long run than seductively narrow problem definitions and easily administered technical solutions. But learning is difficult, conflictive, and takes time. "Learning its way there" may also be the only way a society progresses from one level of success to another. Schlesinger describes Roosevelt's presidency this way: "If politics was essentially an educational process, deeds, of course, were the most important teacher. The New Deal itself became a great schoolhouse, compelling Americans to a greater knowledge of their country and its problems."[18]

Learning processes are difficult to gauge. The bottom line may be long in coming. Perhaps the best index a leader may have to gauge his success in the short run is simply the extent to which the community is thinking in the direction of its work. As Roosevelt wrote to H.G. Wells in 1935, "I believe our biggest success is making people think during these past two years. They may not think straight but they are thinking in the right direction."[19]

Democracy

Democracy is often seen as a means to protect individual and inalienable rights and freedom. From the perspective outlined in this chapter, however, democracy appears to be a system for turning the work of the community back over to the community. As suggested by others in this volume, these two ideas of democracy may be complementary.

Thus democracy is not primarily a political structure, but a shared set of attitudes by which the community itself takes responsibility for work rather than pushing the work onto the shoulders of its authorities. Democracy might flourish within many kinds of political structures (such as monarchy or socialism) as long as the community effectively takes responsibility for work. Conversely, efforts to institute a democratic political structure in a community that does not take responsibility for its own work will not necessarily produce democracy. Eugene Debs went to the heart of this distinction: "Too long have the workers of the world waited for some Moses to lead them out of bondage. He has not come; he will never come. I would not lead you out if I could; for *if you could be led out, you could be led back again.*"[20]

Perhaps democracy as a political structure owes its success as a problem-defining and problem-solving apparatus not simply to the morality of protecting and distributing "rights and privileges," but to its capacity, within a group structure and as a community set of attitudes, to distribute the responsibility for work in the only place where the work can be done.

Further Inquiry

The alternative conception of leadership and public policy suggested in this chapter and by this volume will require more analysis and testing. Readers will undoubtedly find they have many important and unresolved questions. In the spirit of the ideas presented here, we have intended to stimulate thinking on such questions, not to answer them definitively. These questions might include:

- How can one analyze the trends in a society to gauge when an issue is ripe for the group's attention?

- Is the current "crisis in leadership" a sign of growing frustration with complex situations, evidence of a work-avoidance mechanism, or an indication that work is getting done?

- What interpretive frameworks can be used to help communities define and solve the problems they face?

- How does one exercise leadership at times of crisis, when there is apparently little or no time to shift the locus of work back to the relevant community?

- What is the difference between policy designed as a heuristic device and policy designed as a solution?

- What are the implications of this concept of leadership for developing political strategy and tactics to get work done?

- Which political structures might be appropriate for promoting democracy as a value system and in which settings?

- What knowledge and training would a leader need?

CHAPTER 9

The Media and Public Deliberation

Martin Linsky

We have argued that prevailing ideas about what is good for society often tacitly define public problems, the range of possible solutions to them, and the proper allocation of responsibility for solving them. All of those engaged in making public policy have a role to play in helping the public confront these assumptions, thereby expanding the range of possibilities for public action and enhancing the public's understanding of its obligations.

Thus far, we have focused on the roles and responsibilities of actors in the policy-making process who are actually on the public payroll, such as public managers, policy analysts, and political leaders. In this chapter, I explore the role of the press. The media are not part of the government, but journalists' actions have an enormous direct impact on public policy making and a crucial influence on the nature and content of public deliberation.

Reporters and commentators from the press believe they have a duty to assess how well government officials are meeting their responsibilities for enhancing public deliberation. Writing early in 1986, James Reston of the *New York Times*, one of the country's most respected contemporary commentators on public affairs, expressed his concerns on this score:

. . . from Roosevelt to Reagan, the arts of public relations and political advertising have not only tended increasingly to dominate our politics, but also to diminish the influence of the printed word and distort the facts of national life. . .Managing the news, of course, is the oldest game in town. . .What is new, however, is that in the conduct of the public's business, the power of the unelected and largely uknown "specialists" or manipulators, who write the speeches for the executives downtown and frame the questions for the legislators on The Hill, has increased to such a point that while we know who is speaking, we don't know where the words come from. . . . Publicity is not merely an instrument of government here these days: it is government. . . . The Founding Fathers didn't imagine that the great conflicts between nations, let alone the mysteries of outer space, could be decided by public opinion, except at election time.[1]

Reston the journalist blames this problem on the policy makers, particularly the politicians and their hired hands. This chapter turns his telescope around and examines the responsibility of the press for the quality of the dialogue over public ideas.

The Centrality of the Media

The press is the vehicle for much of the discussion that now takes place around public issues. (The words *press* and *media* are used interchangeably in this chapter, to refer to all the public affairs media, both print and electronic, although my focus is on daily journalism and the reporting of news.) Officials communicate with the public through the media. When policy makers want to disseminate ideas about public issues, they hold press conferences, distribute press releases, leak information, and give speeches designed to receive press coverage. Even when they want to communicate only to other policy makers, they are very likely to do so through the press.[2]

Certainly communication about public affairs also proceeds through channels other than the press. Dialogue on public affairs is sometimes conducted face to face, as in formal and informal conversation among elected legislators, within private associations (including the family), and among interest groups. One-to-one, if not face-to-face, communication occurs when officials use direct mail and citizens write letters. The governed and the governors communicate directly through town meetings in small communities and in analogous gatherings in larger municipalities. Some communication about public issues occurs when elected and appointed officials meet outsiders in their offices or address the public. Public hearings and public meetings are vehicles for such communication. Yet press coverage of such events is often as significant an element of the communication as the direct conversation itself.

Even where there is no press coverage, as in private conversations, the views of the parties undoubtedly have been affected by the news they have consumed. Most of us, including policy professionals, get ideas about public issues from newspapers, magazines, and radio and television programs, as well as from our experiences and our conversations. They do not spring forth full-blown from our imaginations.

Beyond its inherent place in the dialogue around public ideas, the press has begun to take on a new, institutionalized and more essential role in recent years. This transformation has been dramatically illustrated during international crises. In reflecting on his experience as assistant secretary of state for public affairs, Hodding Carter has noted the importance of television in bringing information to government officials.[3] Previously the press came to the State Department daily to learn much of what it reported about events going on in the rest of the world. In the Iranian hostage crisis, government officials were glued to the television sets, relying on the journalists and their networks' cameras to tell them what was happening. In the hijacking of the TWA airplane in 1985, reporters interviewed both the hostages and hostage-takers, providing assurances to the families of the hostages' safety and relaying conditions and other messages (if not doing some actual negotiating) from the captors to the U.S. government and the American people.

Similarly, the press has begun to mediate the nominating process during elections, a function previously performed by the political parties. In the first hundred years of American history, the conversations, publications, and continuing ceremonies of political parties were a primary institution for whatever deliberation over public ideas took place between officials and citizens. Now, according to the 1985 Gallup public opinion poll, only 70 percent of the American people of voting age belong to one of the major parties. That is nearly a record low for that figure. The route to electoral office no longer requires, although it still may include, coming up through the ranks of the party. A century ago, for example, it was natural that even a young man as well connected as Theodore Roosevelt would have to spend a lot of time in his local Republican ward clubhouse in New York City before winning the party endorsement for State Assembly, as he did in 1881.[4]

Such apprenticeship seems anachronistic today. Consider the hot primary contest in 1986 for the Middlesex and Suffolk seat in the Massachusetts State Senate, for example. Five of the six candidates seeking the Democratic nomination were politically socialized somewhere other than the local Democratic party organization. With a single exception, they had not put in years of attending meetings, toadying to local party bigwigs, and demonstrating their loyalty and skill. A foundation in party affairs is no longer required, both because the parties have become less important and because candidates can win the party nomination by using the mass media to reach party voters.[5]

Even the dialogue within the parties has become less explicative, less like deliberation. The explosive growth in the use of paid advertising in major primary elections, particularly on television, has legitimized persuasive rather than deliberative communication as a vehicle for seeking party endorsement and for communicating about public issues inside the parties themselves.

Another aspect of the changing role of the press is the decline over the last hundred years in the number of communities with more than one newspaper. When most major cities had several newspapers, most people had access to alternative views of events and their meaning. In 1923, 795 communities in the United States had only a single newspaper or two newspapers with single ownership. There were 1,362 such communities in 1953 and over 1,500 by 1978.[6] Multiple perspectives undoubtedly enrich the conversation about public issues. In one-newspaper towns, there is a shared, often unchallenged and unchallengeable, view of events and their significance. A single authoritative version of reality necessarily limits the content and the vitality of the discussion.[7]

The new, more central role of the press is not simply attributable to changes in the media such as improvements in technology or decreases in the number of news outlets. Nor has the transition necessarily occurred through the conscious choice of journalists. Other institutions, such as the parties, have also changed. The United States' position in the world community is different from what it was a hundred or even fifty years ago. The press's current place in public affairs has been affected by changes taking place around it, and in turn the media have influenced the conduct of public business. Yet because so much of the conversation about public issues, particularly between officials and citizens, uses the mass media of communication, the press is necessarily central to the quality of public deliberation. At stake is the very nature of the conversation about public policy: what is discussed and how it is discussed. It is hard to imagine how that conversation could be pursued in a modern populous democratic society without a major role for the press.

The Implications of Press Centrality

What are the implications of the press's centrality in public dialogue? Marshall McLuhan may have gone too far, but the medium is certainly at least part of the message.[8] When we read, listen, or watch, the views of reality we absorb are determined both by the substance of the message and by the nature and qualities of the messenger. The form in which the information is presented has its own content. The way in which the message is delivered affects how we receive it and what we think of it. Some of this is conscious, and some less so.

For example, one of the filters we use in assessing information is the stake of the presenter. Particularly in delivering news, the press organization itself usually does not offer the information as an interested participant in the dialogue. The media see themselves as mere carriers of information and ideas, not as the creators. Editorials are understood to be the exception. There the news organization is explicitly offering its institutionalized view of a particular slice of the world. As consumers of those editorials, we are aware that the news organization is trying to influence our views and we take that into account. Perhaps we are less aware of the influence on us of a news organization's decision to put a story on the front page or at the beginning of a newscast. Does that placement reflect marketing considerations, importance, newsworthiness, completeness, or what? What stake does the organization have in those stories?

Even in editorials, news organizations present ideas about public issues piecemeal, day by day and article by article. We draw the ideas out from their journalistic context, whether it is the reporting of a news event, an opinion column, a story providing analysis and background, or investigative reporting of malfeasance. Each of these story forms is marked by distinctive qualities and constraints. For example, an opinion column is about an *opinion* and is seen as unauthoritative in that sense. It is "just an idea," as my son Sam used to say when he tentatively broached an alternative to my carefully laid out agenda. Similarly an exposé must present some wrongdoing, not just controversial conduct or a provocative idea, and certainly not an instance of rightdoing in an unexpected place.

More important, story forms are limited by the conventions and constraints of current practice, and of the particular news organization's culture. A column is shorter than most news stories, and it is not supposed to be on the front page or at the beginning of a news program. In some news organizations, to take another example, it is not acceptable to describe the subject of a story by race; in others it is. Clearly, ideas about what is at stake in the story depend to some extent on whether that information is included. The story form and the news organization's rules condition what information is presented and how. What we think about the ideas offered for our consumption is necessarily affected.

Because the media are so essential, both the content and the process of the dialogue on public issues are undoubtedly influenced by the nature and qualities of the medium itself, as well as by the story form. It would be a different dialogue if it took place primarily through the political parties or primarily through small community meetings. We would understand what we were reading differently if it appeared on the front page or on the editorial page. Each vehicle has its own peculiar characteristics. As McLuhan emphasized, those qualities have consequences for the content of the communication, not just the form.

Television, for example, provides a sense of immediacy and reality that print simply cannot deliver. The late John William Ward, a historian and president of Amherst College, once chaired a commission investigating corruption in state government. When the commission held a series of public hearings, Ward followed them nightly on the evening news. He reported an intense sense that if you saw it on the news, you knew what had happened as well as if you had been there yourself. This was true, he said, whether the television report captured the essence of the day accurately or distorted it.[9] Print, on the other hand, allows a consumer of news the luxury of reading the story later, or again, or clipping it and putting it away with other stories on similar subjects, or copying it and distributing it around the office.

If the press is central to public deliberation on public issues, then it is important to think hard about its effect. Is the press as it presently operates an asset or a liability in this regard? What are the essential constraints and practices? How do the media's special characteristics influence what is communicated and who does the communicating? How well constituted is the press to contribute to our vision of public deliberation?

The Role of the Media in Producing Public Ideas and Promoting Public Deliberation

The media are a highly problematical piece of the picture in any effort to promote public deliberation. Their role is too central to be avoided.

But at least as presently organized and under its current conventions, the press is a substantial barrier to overcome in attempting to move toward a richer, more participatory, broader, more explicative dialogue on public affairs. The resistance is both theoretical and a matter of practice.

Issues of Philosophy and Reality

Traditional journalistic notions about the press and its proper role in society inhibit the media from even addressing their relationship to public deliberation. Journalists and news organizations like to see themselves as observers of public affairs, not as participants in them. They feel accountable to their own individual readers and viewers or to their employers, not to the institutions of the community or to society at large. Thus the basic notion that news organizations could contribute to a different and better public dialogue is difficult for them to internalize. They want to believe that the nature and quality of the dialogue about public issues is none of their business, that they just report the news.

Furthermore, asking what the press *could* contribute to the dialogue hints that there might be something the press *should* contribute. That sounds like a duty, and the idea that journalists have a duty to society is an anathema to most of them. Most journalists interpret the First Amendment as freeing them from any such obligations in the ethical and community as well as legal and constitutional senses. They talk of the Constitution as giving them the right to be irresponsible. Their obligations, as they see them, are to their employers and then to their readers, viewers, and listeners. Thus there is a significant threshold problem in getting news organizations to think that the pursuit of a better conversation about public issues has anything to do with them beyond, perhaps, their interest in reporting on it.

It is obvious why journalists want to see themselves as observers and not as participants in public affairs and why they do not want to be accountable to anyone but their employers and their consumers. This stance frees them from restrictive obligations, particularly obligations to institutions of government and democratic processes that others engaged in public affairs cannot escape (in part because of the scrutiny of the press). The journalists' preferred perspective also frees them, as individuals and institutions, from accepting responsibility for the logical consequences of their performance. To assume that responsibility, journalists believe, would pose a weighty inhibition on their work.

It would force them to identify in advance the likely results of publishing significant stories, to make value judgments about the desirability of those results, and to act—that is, to publish or not to publish—on the basis of their conclusions. Such an exercise would produce near-paralysis, they argue, and would result in far less information being made available to the public.

This view does not square with either ethical conduct or real-life public affairs. An ethical person (or organization) takes responsibility for the logical consequences of conduct. When a journalist knows that publication will most likely lead to certain results, he or she is no less responsible for those results than the legislator who helps enact laws with certain predictable outcomes or the executive branch official who adopts policy. It is not always easy to predict consequences, and in many circumstances some unhappy known consequences ought to be endured for some higher purpose. The issue is whether journalists have a moral obligation to consider those questions when making reporting or publishing decisions. Under present practice, news organizations entertain such consideration only at the extremes, as when lives are at stake or national security is clearly endangered.[10]

Thus there is a real issue for journalists at the outset. The media have a central influence on the nature of public deliberation. If journalists are unwilling even to consider the consequences of their conduct for the public dialogue on the ground that doing so will undermine their primary responsibilities, they will resist changing their practices and conventions accordingly.

When journalists cast themselves as outsiders in public affairs to relieve themselves of the worry about consequences, they not only raise ethical questions about responsibility, but also fly in the face of reality. Journalists, news organizations, and officials all know that what is published and broadcast has a powerful influence in policy making. It affects how legislators vote, what policies are considered, and how decisions are made. Policy makers are very clear on the enormous impact of the press. The tasks of newspeople and government officials can be distinguished, to be sure, but both are very much a part of policy making. Both have stakes. Officials stand to gain or lose, professionally and sometimes personally as well, from the outcome of a policy debate. News organizations almost always have a stake in the story continuing. They are like stockbrokers, who do not care too much whether the market is moving up or down as long as it is moving. Journalists need news, and when nothing is happening there is no news. The

Iranian arms deal and all its related stories that became public in 1986 provide a good illustration. The press clearly pushed to keep the story going. Once the story broke, newspapers began to provide special treatment for the coverage and quickly introduced volatile language such as "scandal" and "Watergate" to help create a big story and keep it alive. Little tidbits, sometimes unverified, were published to keep it moving along. Among these were the president's alleged sharp response to Nancy Reagan and the idea that some of the money from the arms sale found its way into the fall congressional campaigns.

Officials are the primary players, to be sure. News organizations function a bit like the chorus in a Greek drama, commenting to the audience on the actors' performances, interpreting their conduct, sometimes interacting with them. Although not central characters in the plot, they are set apart from the audience and are just as integral to the events of the drama as are the actors themselves. What they publish changes the reality for the policy makers. They help to set the agendas and frame the issues, for both the officials and the public. Like it or not, news organizations ought to begin by acknowledging that they are now playing a new, enlarged, and robust role in public affairs. The media are a functional element of the world of public deliberation and decision making, a critical piece of the democratic process. There is no longer a serious question about whether the press is an active player; the issue now is the nature of its role and what responsibilities flow from that.

Issues of Practice and Convention

Difficult as it is to engage the press on the subject of its role in public deliberation and its obligations to the conduct of public affairs, it is even more challenging to effect changes in practice. The central foundations of the practice of contemporary journalism (to the extent that they can be determined inductively, since they are not written down) run counter to the vision of public deliberation over public ideas. This is best understood by exploring two fundamental tenets of American journalism: the definition of what constitutes news and the deference to the ideal of objectivity.

The Definition of News. Under the current conventions, newspaper and television news has the following characteristics: it is new, it is dramatic, and it is visible or audible. These are elements of both content and form that reflect a search for what consumers want to know and what will be commercially successful, rather than what consumers ought to know to be good democratic citizens. This explains, for example, why we read on the front page about big fires and last night's murders, rather than about the behind-the-scenes maneuvering over a bill in the legislature. For practical reasons, time and space are limited. News organizations have to make decisions about what is news. The issue is what standards should be used and whether some new considerations should infuse those decisions.

The current definition of news has important consequences. Once an idea has been in circulation it is no longer newsworthy; the more sensational the item, the more likely it is to be news; and the more it is an event or an utterance, the more likely it is to be covered. In addition, an item that squares with consumers' existing notions of how the world works is more likely to be news than if it runs counter to those expectations. The community's majoritarian values are reflected on the news pages. For example, communists are supposed to be the enemy, and their failures and deficiencies are highlighted more than their successes. We do not regularly see stories debunking religion. Minor party and fringe candidates are not covered seriously.

None of this bodes well for our purposes. Daily newspapers and television news programs are not well geared to furthering the dialogue we envision. News is specific, not general. It presents characters and plots that are familiar and do not cut against the grain. It drives toward the anecdotal, not the theoretical. A big fire is news; the continuing debate about the causes of fires is not.

The event-orientation of news is a particular problem, for it steers coverage away from ideas and context and does nothing to encourage the drawing of connections between stories. For example, the signifi-cance of a fire depends on whether it is one of a series or an isolated instance; whether it results from arson or some other cause; whether the loss is insured or not; and whether it fits within or outside of some current or needed dialogue about public purposes. Though fires do not exist out of context, they are reported that way. Consider the rash of stories about children who need organ transplants. Sophisticated parents have become adroit at generating "news" that may produce money and/or an organ. Yet it is hardly news that people need transplants. (In that sense the stories meet the second and third but not the first of the requirements cited above; the fact that they are not new has contributed to a gradual reduction in their frequency.) Moreover, it seems hardly appropriate, or in the public interest, to allocate financial support and available organs on the basis of a family's capacity for getting news coverage. News stories about individual cases of need have probably contributed to the policy debate now taking place among public officials and health care professionals. But among the broader public, as the Massachusetts Organ Transplantation Task Force Report pointed out, the dialogue centers on the individual case; the public purposes at issue in the general policy questions are largely ignored except by those (such as hospital administrators) with special and more particular interests.[11]

Journalists take to heart the old saying that yesterday's newspaper wraps today's fish, but they do not understand its implications. Newspapers and television stations assume that something printed or broadcast yesterday is old and should not be repeated today. But no one reads the paper thoroughly every day or watches the same television news every night. Readers and viewers need to be told over and over again what happened before. Good stories have to be repeated if they are to be understood and absorbed. Yet time and space pressures make that almost impossible, particularly for television. With only twenty-two minutes of actual network news time each night, it is unlikely that information will be repeated in order to provide viewers with some background for the latest development in a continuing story.

The cumulative story is different from each of the parts, and more than their sum. Background, context, and synthesis create the difference. The *Washington Post's* William Greider understood this, and David Stockman found it out.[12] Newly installed as director of the Office of Management and Budget, and planning to engineer the Reagan Revolution, Stockman agreed to meet with Greider for a series of breakfast conversations during the early days of the Reagan administration. Stockman would provide a running account of what was happening behind the scenes, with the understanding that Greider would not publish anything until it was all over. What was meant by "all over" became a subject of some disagreement between them, and Greider published a long article in *The Atlantic* at the end of 1981.[13] The story had an enormous impact, revealing the shallowness and hypocrisy of the administration's economic policies. In his defense, Stockman observed that everything in Greider's *Atlantic* story had already appeared in print. He was probably correct in a literal sense, but putting it all together made it a qualitatively different story.

Unfortunately Stockman's earlier revelations, as dribbled out in news stories during the course of that year, had had no impact.

Convention demanded that the budget and tax fight be covered as a political story of the new Reagan administration trying to work its will on the Democratic Congress. Far more important than a blow-by-blow account of the political battle, however, was an understanding of the true economic stakes. The kind of contextual, in-depth reporting that characterized Greider's *Atlantic* article did not fit the conventional definition of news. Had it found its way onto the news pages of the *Washington Post*, the *New York Times*, and the *Wall Street Journal* during the year in which the policies were decided, the results might have been different.

This is not a comment on the public's ability to synthesize. To understand the whole picture, a reader would have had to read and distill every day, and to bring external knowledge to bear on the task. Few readers can do that, nor should they have to. Reporters and editors know more than they publish. They synthesize as they go along for their own personal understanding, but under the rules of the news game they publish the next event rather than sharing those judgments with us.

Objectivity.   The definition of news that governs current practice is limited and confining. It is a major barrier to enriched political debate. But even if the concept of news could be broadened to include more context and reduce the orientation to events, coverage of public affairs would still be unnecessarily constrained by the conventional pursuit of objectivity.

Journalistic deference to the mythical god of objectivity would be the most significant barrier to overcome, were the media interested in furthering deliberation over public ideas. The notion of objectivity as an editorial guideline was created by the wire services in the late nineteenth century as a way to ply their trade. They realized that if they were to sell the same stories to outlets in different communities, their stories had to have an aura of neutrality, believability, and lack of controversy. The result was the birth of the wire service story form, typically longer than the average published news story and full of hard facts.

There is nothing objectionable about those qualities in themselves. They were well suited to the wire services' function of providing information the news organizations could not afford to obtain first hand. Over time, however, the values behind the wire service story form were employed to further other objectives. In the late nineteenth and early twentieth centuries newspaper publishers began to see great potential profits in advertising. Retailers were looking for the right environments in which to sell their goods. Newspapers that reached a lot of people and offended none were ideally suitable. Hard-hitting partisan publications would not do. Bland was beautiful, and the transfer of objectivity from a wire service principle to a broad-based editorial goal had begun. In a few decades objectivity became internalized by reporters as a fundamental editorial principle.[14] The important point here is that objectivity began as a way to sell newspapers to more people and make more money, certainly not to generate more or better dialogue.

Walter Lippmann, the closest equivalent to a press philosopher this country has ever had, made his own paradoxical contribution to the elevation of objectivity in his landmark work *Public Opinion*.[15] Lippmann argued compellingly that we all see events and absorb information through individualistic perspectives, and that given the complexity of events and human failings, objectivity is impossible. An elitist as well as a pessimist, Lippmann believed that only a handful of people were smart enough, knowledgeable enough, and well enough trained to sort out the facts and put them together as a truth on which policy making could somewhat confidently be based. His solution was to call for specialists to perform this function for officials and other interested people.

Though one might have thought Lippmann's insight would have put the notion of objectivity to rest, its actual effect was to reinforce objectivity as an ideal, however unreachable. The result was to accelerate the elevation of this publishers' commercial gimmick to an editorial aspiration and value. By making an editorial principle out of objectivity, newspapers were striving to be only observers, relieved of any responsibility to or for the public debate.

Objective Reporting and Objective Journalism. I believe there is a crucial distinction between objective reporting and objective journalism. Objective reporting is a valuable but limited principle. Objective journalism is an undesirable and unattainable goal. Objective reporting requires that a journalist who sees a red bird does not report that it is blue. Objective journalism requires that whether that bird if red or blue, that fact is published without interpretation, without the journalist's judgment about what it means, why it is being reported, and how it fits together with other facts.

Objective reporting establishes meaningful, but minimal, guidelines. If journalists were not required to report true facts, the quality of public discussion obviously would be much worse. Consumers of news need to be able to rely on the veracity of what might be called core facts. If the newspaper reports that someone is six feet tall, the public should at least be able to assume that the person is closer to six feet than to five or seven. Getting the fellow's height right is the least readers and viewers should be able to expect. But reporting the fact accurately is only a floor below which no news organization should fall; the problem is mistaking it for the ceiling as well. The significant questions are whether that information is important, and if so, why. As Lippmann brilliantly demonstrated, facts in isolation mean nothing. Everything depends on the decision as to what facts to report, in what order to place them, and what connective tissue to use to hold them together. Bland is not necessarily beautiful. And objective journalism, analysis-free reporting, has nothing inherently to do with truth.

For example, objective journalism dictates that whatever important people say is news, whether or not it is well founded or true. The classic and most obvious perversion of objectivity in this regard was the scope given to Senator Joseph McCarthy for his baseless accusations. More recent examples can be found in the ability of elected officials, particularly governors and presidents, to set the agenda by their utterances. After the failure of the Iranian hostage rescue attempt, President Jimmy Carter made a conscious decision to downplay the hostage crisis by not talking about it. Just as he had kept the crisis on the front pages, he was able to keep it off. The importance of the crisis had not changed in any tangible way except the extent to which the White House focused on it in public. In the fall of 1986, there was a big to-do about an alleged White House plan to use disinformation, or lies, to confuse and destabilize Libyan leader Moammar Khadafy. The debate was about the propriety of the Reagan administration's using the press in this way. The debate should also have been about how readily prestigious newspapers, initially in this case the *Wall Street Journal*, printed whatever the administration offered up without verification.

How can the newspapers or the network news programs help citizens think about public ideas when they feel obliged to print and broadcast everything the president says, no matter how valid it may be? If the president says that a trade bill will cost millions of jobs, or the White House says that Khadafy is preparing for another round of terrorism, must those statements be the lead of the news regardless of their accuracy? Objectivity here does not further truth, and it does not put events in a broader context that encourages an enlightened dialogue about what is at stake.

Khadafy coverage also illustrates another and different tension among objectivity, truth, and the quality of the dialogue. In a front-page news story in April 1986, the *Boston Globe* referred to Khadafy's "alleged" terrorist support. Then the newspaper published an interview with him in which he disavowed terrorism.[16] The significant issue here is whether or not Khadafy supports terrorists. "Objectively" covering the U.S. government's allegations and Khadafy's denials tells the reader what is happening at only the most banal level. It is hardly news that the U.S. government and the Libyan leader are yelling at each other. If the reporters and editors do not believe Khadafy is financing terrorists, they should tell us and tell us how they know; if they think he is supporting terrorists, they should not pretend they don't know. If they don't know, then that is what they ought to be writing about. A story that addressed the question of Khadafy's responsibility for terrorism and made reasoned and thoughtful, if tentative, conclusions would not meet the test of objectivity, or objective journalism, because it would require explicit exercise of judgment, sorting out the facts and putting them in order, as Lippmann understood, so that they would approach important reality and not hide it.

The silly pursuit of the false goal of objectivity leads to some absurd results. Consider the treatment of accusations. If I come into the newsroom and charge that you have discriminated against me, it will probably not be a story, unless both of us are pretty important people. If I hold a press conference and make the charge, there is a better chance of a story because I have created an event. If I file a complaint with a state agency, it will almost surely be news. Objectivity permits coverage of accusations when they are formal—that is, when they are filed in writing with some public body, whether or not they bear any relationship to the truth. Filing charges takes more effort, but does it signal more truth?

Making news depends in part on knowing how to pervert the objectivity ideal. When Oliver Sipple prevented Sara Jane Moore from shooting President Gerald Ford, two prominent San Francisco gay activists asked the newspapers to interpret this event as showing that gay people have courage. Sipple said that his sexual preference was not relevant, and besides he was not even going to say whether he was gay. Further, he asked the reporters not to write about his sexual preference at all. Nevertheless, the gay activists were able to make news because they presented their story so as to fit the conventional definition of objectivity. The published story did not say that Sipple was gay, but reported that on the evening of the assassination attempt there had been a celebration in a prominent gay bar because of the gay community's pride in what Sipple had done. The effect on Sipple and his privacy, of course, was the same as if the story had dealt directly about his sexual preference.[17]

News organizations sometimes turn themselves inside out in pursuit of objectivity. It was objectivity, presumably, that led the networks to use captions to tell viewers that Israeli censors had cleared the film they showed of the Israeli invasion of Beruit. And it is objectivity that requires that dispatches from South Africa under a state of emergency are published with a note saying that they were sent under emergency restrictions. If the information is not to be trusted, then why is it shown? If it can be trusted, then why superimpose the message? Was something deleted? If so, is the result incomplete? If not, why the warning? At first glance the point may appear petty, but American policy is significantly influenced by the attitude of the American public toward foreign governments and their activities. If the consumer warning is intended to affect public attitudes, the news organization would make a greater contribution by dealing with that issue head-on and directly enhancing the debate.

Objectivity is different from truth. It is a way of carrying on the business of reporting, a method that helps insulate the news organization from criticism because everything reported is so easily verifiable. Truth is something else altogether, much more elusive, and much more important to the deliberation over public affairs.

Many other aspects of the news business stand in the way of more public deliberation about public ideas. Some of the chief incentives that motivate journalists and news organizations do not necessarily help: prizes, profits, and competition. Quality and success are too often a function of ratings, circulation numbers, and dramatic impact. News is a business in America; there is nothing inherently wrong with that unless the business drives the news. News organizations and news professionals believe they deliver an important product to people. They feel an obligation to report what is happening or to write what *Washington Post* publisher Philip Graham once called "the first rough draft of history."[18] But they are under pressures that too often force them to forget the distinction between objective reporting and objective journalism.

Journalists also shy away from dealing with the inherent subjectivity of their work because the responsibility for their decisions is so awesome. Yet in the nature of their work, journalists and news organizations obviously make subjective judgments all day and every day. They cling to visions of themselves as being outside of public affairs, to narrow and confining definitions of news, and to an unrealistic and limited standard of objectivity as a way of cushioning and insulating themselves from the complexity and importance of the choices they inevitably make in order to do their jobs.

The idea of helping to generate an elevated, interactive, and explicative discussion runs counter to journalists' images of themselves, which emerged from the pressures to be linear, literal, and oriented to the short term. Reporting is driven by events and people, rather than issues, not because that approach is a better way of getting at the truth or informing the people, but because it conceals journalists' inherent subjectivity and bias. The news is literal, rather than interpretive, analytic, or probing because otherwise journalists and editors would be forced to make clear their judgments and would be held accountable for them. Public affairs journalism needs a new paradigm, new standards for decision making that acknowledge the power of the press and encourage its exercise in the public interest.

Realism and Small Steps

Because the media are so important in furthering public deliberation over public ideas, they deserve attention. Because they are so ill disposed and ill equipped to do so, they deserve constructive and realistic concern.

For the press, the first task is conceptual. News organizations should internalize Lippmann's central point: whether they like it or not, they are not neutral conveyor belts. They have great discretion about what is reported and how. They make judgments that, intentionally or not, reflect certain world views and assume certain norms. That is true even though those judgments may seem to be driven by current news media conventions and values and may actually be grounded in considerations of what is fashionable or what will sell.

When judgments are made implicitly or unconsciously, as they usually are, they hold back public learning because the dialogue is framed in a short-term, case-specific manner that is descriptive rather than normative, responsive rather than challenging. The coverage of Nicholas Daniloff's ordeal is a case in point. In the fall of 1986, Daniloff, a *U.S. News & World Report* correspondent, was arrested by the Soviet government and charged with spying. U.S. journalists understandably felt an enormous stake in his safe return, and their coverage reflected this bias. Newspapers managed to keep the story on the front page even though often there was no new news. Editorials emphasized the free press issues over the foreign policy considerations inherent in exchanging Daniloff for a Soviet diplomat held on similar charges by U.S. authorities. News organizations hammered away at the theme that the upcoming summit could not proceed until Daniloff was free. The strategy worked and Daniloff was released, apparently in exchange for release of the Soviet counterpart, and the president was hailed for his role. Newspapers ran value-laden headlines such as "Daniloff released, Soviet spy expelled."

The more important issues in the case—the activities of U.S. journalists in unfriendly countries, the activities of Soviet diplomats in the United States, and the connection of all of that to U.S.–Soviet relations—was lost. There was no continuing debate, in part because this was a story that was to end when Daniloff returned. With the summit just around the corner, officials did not want to explore further the activities of Soviet citizens in this country. For two reasons, journalists were more than willing to oblige. First, under the conventional definitions of news it is difficult to keep a policy story going when officials do not want to engage in the dialogue. Second, journalists themselves did not want to generate a debate about the performance of their colleagues abroad and its impact on international affairs. Such journalistic reticence does not contribute to the search for meaning, connectedness, context, causation, or history. The effect is a presumption in favor of the status quo and the conventional wisdom.

Occasionally a news organization is driven by the results of its reporting to raise the level of the public conversation because what is observed does not fit the current frame. That was the case with the reporting of the Vietnam War by CBS. When Walter Cronkite finally went to Vietnam to see for himself, he was expanding participation in the dialogue, broadening the questions that were to be addressed, and looking for truth and understanding rather than just joining the debate.[19] CBS understood that it had an opportunity, and perhaps an obligation, to contribute to the deliberation. Perhaps even more important, the organization knew that the truth lay somewhere beyond bare isolated facts and that outcomes would be affected by what the network chose to put on the air and how it presented the material. News organizations must begin to accept the selectivity in their work, the centrality of their role in public affairs, and the impact and influence they exercise.

We need to encourage news organizations more consciously to add more perspective in reporting and to examine and make clear their own assumptions about what is really going on. The effort is worthwhile despite its difficulty. It is integral to everything else about the functioning of public discussion in a democracy, and it could make a huge difference in the result. The enormous power of the press can serve any of a number of purposes, including the enhancement of democratic communication.

Beyond liberating news reporters from a comforting but unrealistic image of their job, we need new models for public affairs journalism that speak more honestly to the role the media play without asking them to be more than they can be. Substituting a criterion of "importanceworthiness" for newsworthiness might be a start. If editors and reporters thought about whether a subject was important and why, and reported it so as to make that clear, they would begin to move toward issues and ideas in their orientation rather than relying on people and events. The justification for story design and placement would require the kind of analysis and interpretation of events that under current conventions immediately take the item out of the category of news.

Finally, it is important for everyone interested in the quality of the public dialogue, but especially for journalists themselves, to generate specific ideas for practice that can be implemented and will help to enrich public deliberation. Outsiders should offer direction, if not detailed mechanics, that is palatable, concrete, and not hopelessly naive. Thoughtful newspeople are already concerned about the society at large and their own role in its progress. There is no need for a revolution here, just the challenge of identifying some existing tendencies and innovations that should be promoted because they will advance the dialogue about public ideas. In at least five areas—non-news-based coverage of public affairs, making news, planning coverage, nonlinear beats, and multiparty communication—we already see worthwhile exceptions to inadequate journalistic conventions.

Some of the closest current analogies to public deliberation are conducted through the mass media, although not typically under the rubric of daily news. Newspapers publish editorials to put public policy questions in a broader context. Radio talk shows, however banal, increase participation. Some magazines, such as *The Public Interest* and *The Nation*, try to present issues in terms of broader public values. *Public Opinion* magazine tells officials and elites what people are thinking, although that is certainly a very attenuated form of citizen-to-policy maker communication. Some publications, such as *Commentary* and the *New York Review of Books*, encourage continuing dialogue within their own pages. At their best, television documentaries enrich the discussion by packaging evidence and opinion so as to make them accessible and enlightening to millions of people.

When defending their efforts to keep themselves out of a story, journalists often assert that it is their job to report news, not to make it. Yet once news organizations begin to accept more comfortably the reality that they too are players on the field of public affairs and that their choice of what to report has an impact, they may be more inclined to take more responsibility for making news. There is already some movement in this direction. Many news organizations, both print and electronic, stage debates between candidates, which often themselves generate news. Local television stations have created minidebates by providing an electronic link between candidates in different locations. At press conferences, journalists often compete very aggressively with the officials in establishing the agenda for the day. Television networks have offered air time to foreign leaders who then use the networks to make important statements to U.S. officials, which are overheard, so to speak, by millions of Americans. In all these cases, the news organizations are doing more than reporting what is happening out there. If the press relaxes its resistance to making news deliberately, it can play a much more robust role in moving the dialogue about public affairs to more significant areas and to a more productive level.

News organizations routinely plan their coverage of special events well in advance. For everything from elections to the Super Bowl, news organizations think strategically about how to get the event under control. Decisions about how to cover an election—whom to assign, how much coverage to give, whether to do polling or to cover polls, and how much to concentrate on issues or on the horse races—are subjective and significant, and will affect the election itself. Yet news organizations increasingly recognize that if they have a plan and know what they are doing and why, they will do a better, more defensible job.

This notion could be extended to other kinds of coverage relatively easily. News organizations could plan coverage of issues in the same way, realizing that their planning carries with it some impact and some responsibility for outcomes. Such was the case with T.R. Reid's *Congressional Odyssey*, which traces the legislative history of a bill raising fees for use of inland waterways.[20] Previously defeated several times, the bill finally passed in the year during which it was the subject of Reid's continuing series in the *Washington Post*. Even its primary legislative sponsors acknowledged that without the *Post's* scrutiny, the bill would have died once again. Thus a story about how legislating really works became a story about the impact of the press as much as anything else.

Imaginative planning of coverage can be complemented by thoughtful self-auditing. News organizations often review their own coverage for accuracy; it might be revealing also to assess its implicit message and its impact. This would require going beyond the minimal conventional standards of objective reporting to think about the nature and quality of the truth that was being transmitted. News organizations ought to look back at their coverage—or lack of coverage—of important issues and try to do it better the next time around. If an important issue or idea does not get covered, it may be because the news organization did not take the initiative to seek it out.

The press might also consider the notion of covering issues and ideas as such. Beats, like news, are traditionally allocated according to the tangible and concrete. Journalists cover people, like a governor, or institutions, like the White House, Capitol Hill, or the Environmental Protection Agency. Some movement away from these narrow definitions has already begun. For years, Haynes Johnson of the *Washington Post* has taken time to travel around the country to report on the public mood.[21] A series of articles he wrote with David Broder in 1971 provided policy makers in Washington with a broad and compelling picture of reality in the hinterlands, which George McGovern was smart enough not to dismiss. McGovern has said that he used these reports to help him understand the electorate on the way to the presidential nomination in 1972. Similarly Adam Clymer covers public opinion for the *New York Times*.

There is no inherent reason why ideas, trends, or concepts could not be the regular focus of a journalist's beat. In the 1960s and 1970s, perhaps, reporters might have been assigned to cover automation or divorce. In the 1980s, they could follow nationalism, homophobia, or disarmament. Such assignments would result in coverage and therefore discussion that addressed issues at a broader level of abstraction, and might have other salutary side effects as well. Reporters and editors might be encouraged to take further training so that they would have a sounder foundation of knowledge on which to make connections, interpret events, and see trends. Publication of idea stories would also undoubtedly affect the definition of news. A trend could legitimately merit news treatment even if it "happened" over a period of months or even years, rather than in a day.

Finally, there is the question of two-way communication. News organizations do not see their role as involving interactive two-way communication. Often, however, for purposes of balance, a news story will include quotes from "both sides" (balance often means *both* sides, whether there are one, two, or twenty sides). This counterpoint creates a sort of dialogue since the parties whose comments are connected might never have spoken, particularly not "to" each other, had not the news organization asked them the right questions.

Newspapers already engage in some more explicit two-party communication. Many papers have a popular letters exchange feature through which readers can write to each other, although the subjects pursued are usually personal rather than public affairs. Letters to the editor, which sometimes produce responses upon responses, are another form of two-way communication. News organizations use editorials and op-ed pages to generate a dialogue among officials and interested elites. Regular columns by officials are rare in metropolitan daily newspapers, but it is easy to envision a regular column by, say, the area congressman answered just as regularly by a column from a spokesperson for another point of view or an interested citizen.

In several ways news organizations already wittingly or unwittingly allow the public to talk with officials. Policy makers often say they learn what the people are thinking by reading the newspapers or watching the nightly news. Their reasoning is that the media set the frame for what people know, so an official can discover what people are thinking at roughly the same moment the people are first learning about it themselves. Radio talk shows, especially with guests taking telephone calls from listeners, are an even more direct example of this form of exchange. Polling enables large numbers of people to speak, in very general and anonymous ways, with their leaders. News organizations know how to keep a story alive by going from one interested party to another and asking questions that move the conversation along. This kind of technique could also be applied to a broader dialogue between officials and the public. The *Washington Post* idea of sending reporters around the country could be a regular part of local and regional coverage as well, presumably with similar effects. If news organizations realized the extent to which officials read the people by reading the news, they might take their responsibilities in this area more seriously. Once freed from conceptions that limit their focus, news organizations will have many opportunities to broaden participation in the dialogue.

These thoughts are far from comprehensive. They are, as my son said, just ideas. But they are evidence that news organizations can be vehicles for moving public deliberation toward broader purposes and norms, thereby expanding the dialogue and increasing public learning, and that journalists can think about ways to move toward this goal without slipping into either heresy or fantasy.

Notes

Introduction

1. This stylized version does not, of course, do justice to the subtleties of diagnosis and artfulness of analysis that characterize and differentiate these arguments as they appear in the writings of such political economists and political scientists as Gordon Tullock, James Buchanan, Mancur Olson, George Stigler, William Niskanen, Anthony Downs, Morris Fiorina, Milton Friedman, and our colleague Richard Zeckhauser. But for the purposes of this discussion, my sketch should be adequate.

2. Most obviously, this view offers no way of deciding on the proper distribution of wealth in a society (although it suggests that the best way of redistributing wealth is to take advantage of market forces and give poor people cash, to use as they please, rather than things). And it provides no guide to comparing, or trading off, one person's preferences against another's.

3. For a critique of conventional economics' failure to differentiate between an individual's strict self-interest and what he wants for his society, see Amartya Sen, "Rational Fools: A Critique of the Behavioral Foundations of Economic Theory," *Philosophy and Public Affairs* 6 (Summer 1977): 5. For a philosopher's attempt to find the difference, see Brian Barry, "The Public Interest," in Anthony Quinton, ed., *Political Philosophy* (Oxford: Oxford University Press 1967), pp. 112–27.

4. In my recent *Tales of a New America* (New York: Times Books, 1987), I discuss why the core questions that have shaped American debate in recent years offer only partial, and in some ways dangerously incomplete, guides to the real choices the nation confronts in an altered world, and why, therefore, the public is ready for leaders who will give new and pertinent voice to the challenges before us.

5. One commentator has even argued that such interactive technologies should replace representative assemblies. See James C. Miller III, "A Program for Direct and Proxy Voting in the Legislative Process," *Public Choice* 7 (Fall 1969): 107.

6. For two insightful discussions of this richer notion of democracy, see

Arthur Maass, *Congress and the Common Good* (New York: Basic Books, 1983), and Benjamin Barber, *Strong Democracy* (Berkeley: University of California Press, 1984). The philosopher J.A. Passmore has suggested that in examining social institutions we should not ask "what end or purpose does it serve?" but rather "of what conflicts is it the scene?" It is often only through conflict that societies learn what their ends and purposes are. See Passmore's introduction to John Anderson, *Studies in Empirical Philosophy* (Sydney: Angus and Robertson, 1962), p. xxii.

7. For a more detailed discussion, see Samuel H. Beer, "The Strengths of Liberal Democracy," in William S. Livingston, ed., *A Prospect of Liberal Democracy* (Austin: University of Texas Press, 1979), pp. 215–29.

8. Max Weber, *The Theory of Social and Economic Organization*, trans. A.M. Henderson and Talcott Parsons (New York: Oxford University Press, 1947), p. 337.

9. Niccolo Machiavelli, *The Prince*, (Modern Library ed., New York: Random House, 1950), p. 61.

10. Edmund Burke, "Address to the Electors of Bristol," November 3, 1774, in *Collected Works* (Boston: Little, Brown, 1865–1867), vol. 2, pp. 89–98.

11. Edmund Burke, *Reflections on the Revolution in France*, ed. Connor Cruise O'Brien (1790; reprint, New York: Penguin, 1968).

12. John Stuart Mill, "Representative Government," in *Utilitarianism, On Liberty, and Representative Government* (London: Everyman's Library, 1910), p. 243.

13. See Gordon S. Wood, *The Creation of the American Republic, 1776–1787* (New York: Norton, 1972), pp. 65–70; Herbert Storing, *What the Federalists Were For* (Chicago: University of Chicago Press, 1981).

14. Alexis de Tocqueville, *Democracy in America* (reprint, New York: Vintage, 1945), vol. 1, p. 252.

15. Walter Bagehot, in his introduction to the second edition of *The English Constitution* (1872; reprint, London: Oxford University Press, 1928), p. 311.

16. For an insightful analysis of these ideas, see Albert O. Hirschman, *The Passions and the Interests* (Princeton: Princeton University Press, 1977), pp. 66–113.

17. Sir James Steuart, *Inquiry into the Principles of Political Economy*, ed. A.S. Skinner (1767; reprint, Chicago: University of Chicago Press, 1966), vol. 1, pp. 143–44.

18. F.Y. Edgeworth, *Mathematical Physics: An Essay on the Application of Mathematics to Moral Sciences* (London: Keyworth, 1881), p. 16.

19. For an illuminating discussion of the differences between democracy and "guardianship" see Robert Dahl, *Controlling Nuclear Weapons: Democracy versus Guardianship* (Syracuse, NY: Syracuse University Press, 1985).

20. On the relationship between America's wartime experience of totalitarianism and subsequent shifts in public philosophy, see Edward Purcell, Jr., *The Crisis in Democratic Theory: Scientific Naturalism and the Problem of Value* (Lexington: University of Kentucky Press, 1973).

Chapter One: Beyond Self-Interest

I am grateful to Philip Guentert for his able research assistance and to Robert Klitgaard and Richard Zeckhauser for their insightful comments on an earlier draft.

1. Thomas C. Schelling, *Micromotives and Macrobehavior* (New York: W.W. Norton, 1978).
2. See Daniel P. Moynihan, *The Politics of a Guaranteed Income: The Nixon Administration and the Family Assistance Plan* (New York: Random House, 1973), pp. 375–97; Otto A. Davis and John E. Jackson, "Representative Assemblies and Demands for Redistribution: The Case of Senate Voting on the Family Assistance Plan," in Harold M. Hochman and George E. Peterson, eds., *Redistribution through Public Choice* (New York: Columbia University Press, 1974), pp. 261–88.
3. F.Y. Edgeworth, *Mathematical Psychics: An Essay on the Application of Mathematics to the Moral Sciences* (London: C. Kegan Paul and Co., 1881), p. 16.
4. For an introductory and widely read exposition of the microeconomic model, see Paul A. Samuelson and William Nordhaus, *Economics*, 12th ed. (New York: McGraw Hill, 1985).
5. The literature criticizing neoclassical economics is voluminous. One recent book, written for a nontechnical audience, is Lester Thurow's *Dangerous Currents: The State of Economics* (New York: Random House, 1983). Despite recent efforts to introduce more accurate conceptions of human nature into the microeconomic model (some of which are noted below), economic reasoning for the most part remains anchored in the original assumptions of neoclassical theory. Since the simplest version of the microeconomic model is widely acknowledged as the accepted version, it is scrutinized here.
6. The postulate of given and fixed preferences has stood for centuries as a pivotal contention of economics; for just as long, economists have disclaimed any interest in where preferences come from. According to Albert O. Hirschman, "Any number of quotations from economists and economics textbooks could be supplied to the effect that economics had no business delving into the reasons why preferences are what they are, and it is implicit in such denials that it is even less appropriate for economists to inquire how and why preferences might change." *Shifting Involvements* (Princeton: Princeton University Press, 1982), p. 9.

   Economists have begun to incorporate changes of tastes into their market models. See, for example, Carl Christian von Weizsacher, "Notes on Endogenous Changes of Tastes," *Journal of Economic Theory* 3 (December 1971): 345–72; Robert A. Pollak, "Endogenous Tastes in Demand and Welfare Analysis," *American Economic Review* 68 (May 1978): 374–91; Tibor Scitovsky, *The Joyless Economy* (New York: Oxford University Press, 1976).

Also see Hirschman's *Shifting Involvements* on how consumer preferences shift as a result of people's consumption experiences and John Kenneth Galbraith's discussion of how consumer tastes are shaped by production decisions and corporate advertising, in *The New Industrial State* (New York: New American Library, 1967), chaps. 18 and 19.

The doctrine of rational utility maximization is another central tenet of economic orthodoxy. As Richard Zeckhauser notes, "Should behavior in certain salient areas be found to violate rationality, it will be treated as beyond economics . . . , classified in the same category as the source of preferences or values, something about which we have little to add as economists." "Comments: Behavioral versus Rational Economics: What You See Is What You Conquer," *Journal of Business* 59 (October, 1986): S436. Recently, the doctrine of rationality has been challenged by some economists. One of the most comprehensive critiques appears in Daniel Kahneman, Paul Slovic, and Amos Tversky, eds., *Judgment Under Uncertainty: Heuristics and Biases* (New York: Cambridge University Press, 1982). Herbert Simon has argued persuasively that consumers are usually content with modest success, "satisficing" rather than maximizing. See his *Models of Man* (New York: Wiley, 1957) and *Administrative Behavior* (New York: Free Press, 1957). In "Rational Fools: A Critique of the Behavioral Foundations of Economic Theory," *Philosophy and Public Affairs* 6 (Summer 1977): 317–44, Amartya Sen cites a large number of studies that cast doubt on the utility-maximizing theory of economics and suggests an alternative theory based on commitment.

7. Milton Friedman, *Capitalism and Freedom* (Chicago: University of Chicago Press, 1962), p. 110.
8. Thurow, *Dangerous Currents*, p. 217.
9. Thomas Babington Macaulay, "Mill's Essay on Government," in *Critical and Historical Essays*, vol. 1 (Boston: Houghton-Mifflin and Co., 1900), pp. 416-17.
10. The first fully developed statement of welfare economics is A.C. Pigou's *The Economics of Welfare* (London: Macmillan and Co., 1924). Also see Francis M. Bator, "The Simple Analytics of Welfare Economics," *American Economic Review* 47 (March, 1957): 22–49; Abram Bergson, "A Reformation of Certain Aspects of Welfare Economics," *Quarterly Journal of Economics* 52 (February 1938): 310–34. For a useful introductory summary of welfare economics, see Edith Stokey and Richard Zeckhauser, *A Primer for Policy Analysis* (New York: W.W. Norton, 1978), chap. 13.
11. Francis M. Bator, "The Anatomy of Market Failure," *Quarterly Journal of Economics* 72 (August 1958): 351–79 and *The Question of Government Spending: Public Needs and Private Wants* (New York: Harper and Row, 1960); Stokey and Zeckhauser, *A Primer for Policy Analysis*, chap. 14.
12. Kenneth J. Arrow, *Social Choice and Individual Values* (New York: John Wiley and Sons, 1963).
13. I.M.D. Little, *A Critique of Welfare Economics*, 2d ed. (Oxford: Oxford University Press, 1960), pp. 79–80.

14. See Mark H. Moore, "Realms of Obligation and Virtue," in Joel L. Fleishman, Lance Liebman, and Mark H. Moore, eds., *Public Duties: The Moral Obligations of Government Officials* (Cambridge: Harvard University Press, 1981), pp. 3–31, especially pp. 17–21. Also, Charles Wolf, Jr., "A Theory of Non-market Failures," *The Public Interest* (Spring 1979), pp. 114–33, and Richard Zeckhauser, "The Muddled Responsibilities of Public and Private America," in Winthrop Knowlton and Richard Zeckhauser, eds., *American Society: Public and Private Responsibilities* (Cambridge, MA: Ballinger, 1986), pp. 45–77.

15. The most celebrated and influential pluralist thinker in modern political science is Robert Dahl. See *A Preface to Democratic Theory* (Chicago: University of Chicago Press, 1956), *Who Governs?* (New Haven: Yale University Press, 1961), and *Pluralist Democracy in the United States* (Chicago: Rand McNally, 1967). Nelson Polsby's *Community Power and Political Theory*, 2d ed. (New Haven: Yale University Press, 1980) is an incisive analysis of the arguments for and against pluralist theory. Other important expressions of pluralist thought include David Truman, *The Governmental Process* (New York: Knopf, 1951) and Charles E. Lindblom, *The Intelligence of Democracy* (New York: Macmillan, 1965).

   Like neoclassical economics, pluralism has spawned an enormous body of criticism. See Theodore J. Lowi, *The End of Liberalism* (New York: W.W. Norton, 1969); Jack L. Walker, "A Critique of the Elitist Theory of Democracy," *American Political Science Review* 60 (June 1966): 285–95; and E.E. Schattschneider, *The Semisovereign People* (New York: Holt, Rinehart and Winston, 1960).

16. Pluralism is sufficiently diffuse to comprise much of contemporary political science, even if nobody adopts it in its entirety. Furthermore, just as some economists have tried to amend the microeconomic model, so some political scientists have reformulated their original views about pluralism. The principal revision has been a heightened appreciation of the power of private corporations in America. See, for example, Robert A. Dahl, *After the Revolution? Authority in a Good Society* (New Haven: Yale University Press, 1970) and "Pluralism Revisited," *Comparative Politics* 10 (January 1978): 191–203; and Charles E. Lindblom, *Politics and Markets* (New York: Basic Books, 1977). These revisions have not fundamentally altered the central tenets of pluralist theory discussed in this chapter.

17. Kenneth Prewitt and Sidney Verba, *An Introduction to American Government* (New York: Harper and Row, 1983), p. 254. But just as in economics, the eventual distribution of prizes depends on the initial allocation of resources.

18. Karl Marx and Frederick Engels, *The German Ideology* (New York: International Publishers, 1974), p. 39.

19. Joseph Schumpeter, *Capitalism, Socialism and Democracy* (New York: Harper and Row, 1950), pp. 131–41.

20. Thomas J. Peters and Robert H. Waterman, *In Search of Excellence: Lessons from America's Best Run Companies* (New York: Warner Books, 1984), and

Terrence E. Deal and Allan A. Kennedy, *Corporate Cultures: The Rise and Ritual of Corporate Life* (Reading, MA: Addison-Wesley, 1982).

21. Dahl, *Who Governs?*, pp. 89–103.

22. The most visible dissenter from pluralism along these lines was C. Wright Mills. See *The Power Elite* (New York: Oxford University Press, 1956).

23. James Q. Wilson, *Political Organizations* (New York: Basic Books, 1973); Robert H. Salisbury, "An Exchange Theory of Interest Groups," *Midwest Journal of Political Science* 13 (February 1969): 1–32.

24. V.I. Lenin, *What Is to be Done?* (New York: International Publishers, 1969).

25. Wilson, *Political Organizations*, chap. 3.

26. The following discussion draws on the more extensive treatment of this point in Sidney Verba and Gary Orren, *Equality in America* (Cambridge, MA: Harvard University Press, 1985), chap. 11.

27. David O. Sears, Carl P. Hensler, and Leslie K. Speer, "Whites' Opposition to 'Busing': Self-Interest or Symbolic Racism?" *American Political Science Review* 73 (June 1979): 369–84; David O. Sears, Richard R. Lau, Tom R. Tyler, and Harrison M. Allen, Jr., "Self-Interest Versus Symbolic Politics in Policy Attitudes and Presidential Voting," *American Political Science Review* 74 (September 1980): 670–84; David O. Sears, Tom R. Tyler, Jack Citrin, and Donald R. Kinder, "Political System Support and Public Response to the Energy Crisis," *American Journal of Political Science* 22 (February 1978): 56–82; Bruce M. Russett and Elizabeth C. Hanson, *Interest and Ideology: The Foreign Policy Beliefs of American Businessmen* (San Francisco: W.H. Freeman, 1975); Richard R. Lau, T.A. Brown, and David O. Sears, "Self-Interest and Civilians' Attitudes Toward the Vietnam War," *Public Opinion Quarterly* 42 (Winter 1978): 464–83; John E. Mueller, *War, Presidents and Public Opinion* (New York: John Wiley, 1973).

28. W.M. Denney, J.S. Hendricks, and Donald R. Kinder, "Personal Stakes Versus Symbolic Politics," paper delivered to the annual meeting of the American Association for Public Opinion Research, Cincinnati, Ohio, May 29 to June 3, 1980; D. Roderick Kiewiet, *Macroeconomics and Micropolitics: The Electoral Effects of Economic Issues* (Chicago: University of Chicago Press, 1983); Donald R. Kinder, "Presidents, Prosperity, and Public Opinion," *Public Opinion Quarterly* 45 (Spring 1981): 1–21; Donald R. Kinder and D. Roderick Kiewiet, "Economic Discontent and Political Behavior: The Role of Personal Grievances and Collective Economic Judgments in Congressional Voting," *American Journal of Political Science* 23 (August 1979): 495–527; David Lowery and Lee Sigelman, "Understanding the Tax Revolt: Eight Explanations," *American Political Science Review* 75 (December 1981): 963–74; Kay Schlozman and Sidney Verba, *Injury to Insult* (Cambridge, MA: Harvard University Press, 1979).

29. Verba and Orren, *Equality in America*. ·

30. Although early theories of voting behavior were based on the socioeconomic characteristics of voters, later thinking has focused on group allegiance and, most recently, the role of policy issues. See Peter B. Natchez, *Images of Voting/Visions of Democracy* (New York: Basic Books, 1985).

31. As Mancur Olson explains, a single individual is unlikely to have much impact on the outcome of large-scale collective activities. In any case that person will be able to enjoy the results whether he or she contributes or not. In fact, however, people spurn these "free rides" far more than the deductive logic predicts, participating in political activities ranging from voting to demonstrations and riots. In most cases they are not motivated by material self-interest but by the solidary attachments and purposive goals emphasized in this chapter. Mancur Olson, Jr., *The Logic of Collective Action* (New York: Schocken Books, 1968); Sidney Verba and Norman Nie, *Participation in America* (New York: Harper and Row, 1972); and Wilson, *Political Organizations*, chaps. 2 and 3.

32. Donald R. Kinder and David O. Sears, "Public Opinion and Political Action," in Gardner Lindzey and Elliot Aronson, eds., *The Handbook of Social Psychology*, 3d ed. (New York: Random House, 1985), p. 699.

33. Macpherson argues that the unifying idea behind English political thought from the seventeenth to the nineteenth centuries was a new belief in the possessive rights of the individual. Similarly, Hirschman traces the growing respectability and eventual supremacy of the idea of self-interest in the seventeenth and eighteenth centuries. C.B. Macpherson, *The Political Theory of Possessive Individualism* (Oxford: Oxford University Press, 1964) and Albert O. Hirschman, *The Passions and the Interests: Political Arguments for Capitalism Before Its Triumph* (Princeton: Princeton University Press, 1977). In *Shifting Involvements*, especially chapter 8, Hirschman discusses how the ideology of self-interest encourages privatization. Alexis de Tocqueville placed the self-sufficiency of individuals and their preoccupation with their own needs and appetites at the core of his analysis of America in the 1830s. *Democracy in America*, ed. Phillips Bradley (New York: Alfred A. Knopf, 1945), especially vol. 2, bk. 2, pp. 99–171.

Recent books that lament the individualism of modern society include: Christopher Lasch, *The Culture of Narcissism* (New York: W.W. Norton, 1978); Richard Sennet, *The Fall of Public Man* (New York: Vintage Books, 1978); and Robert M. Bellah, Richard Madsen, William M. Sullivan, Ann Swidler, and Steven M. Tipton, *Habits of the Heart: Individualism and Commitment in American Life* (Berkeley: University of California Press, 1985).

34. Kinder and Sears, "Public Opinion and Political Action," p. 672.

35. Philip E. Converse, "The Nature of Belief Systems in Mass Publics," in David Apter, ed., *Ideology and Discontent* (New York: Free Press), pp. 206–61.

36. Harry G. Frankfurt, "Freedom of the Will and the Concept of a Person," *Journal of Philosophy* 68 (January 14, 1971): 5–20; Amartya Sen, "Rational Fools," pp. 317–44, especially pp. 335–41.

37. Don K. Price, *America's Unwritten Constitution: Science, Religion, and Political Responsibility* (Baton Rouge: Louisiana State University Press, 1985).

38. Quoted in Fred Barnes, "Bradley's Triumph," *The New Republic*, June 2, 1986, p. 12.

39. John Maynard Keynes, *The General Theory of Employment, Interest, and Money* (New York: Harcourt Brace, 1936), p. 383.
40. Robert Klitgaard, "From Insight to Ideology," unpublished manuscript, April 1986.
41. V.O. Key, Jr., *Public Opinion and American Democracy* (New York: Knopf, 1961), p. 8.
42. Quoted in George P. Brockway, "The Psychology of Economists," *New Leader*, February 7, 1983, p. 15.

Chapter Two: Why Public Ideas Matter

1. Alexander Hamilton et al., *The Federalist* (New York: Modern Library, 1937), p. 337.
2. The material in this chapter is adapted from the author's forthcoming *Making Public Policy: A Hopeful View of American Government* (New York: Basic Books, 1987).
3. Anthony Downs, *An Economic Theory of Democracy* (New York: Harper and Brothers, 1957), pp. 27–28.
4. James Buchanan and Gordon Tullock, *The Calculus of Consent* (Ann Arbor: University of Michigan Press, 1962), p. 20.
5. Gordon Tullock, *The Vote Motive* (London: Institute for Economic Affairs, 1976), p. 5.
6. Mancur Olson, *The Logic of Collective Action* (Cambridge, MA: Harvard University Press, 1965).
7. George J. Stigler, "The Theory of Economic Regulation," *Bell Journal of Economics and Management Science* 2 (1971): 3–21.
8. William A. Niskanen, Jr., *Bureaucracy and Representative Government* (Chicago: Aldine Publishing Company, 1971), pp. 38–39.
9. Gordon Tullock, "What Is to Be Done?" in Thomas E. Borcherding, ed., *Budgets and Bureaucrats: The Sources of Government Growth* (Durham: Duke University Press, 1977), p. 285. See also Winston C. Bush and Arthur T. Denzau, "The Behavior of Bureaucrats and Public Sector Growth," in the same volume, and James M. Buchanan, *The Limits of Liberty: Between Anarchy and Leviathan* (Chicago: University of Chicago Press, 1975), p. 160.
10. David R. Mayhew, *Congress: The Electoral Connection (New Haven: Yale University Press, 1974)*, p. 5.
11. Ibid., pp. 52–53, 61.
12. Ibid., pp. 124–125.
13. Morris P. Fiorina, *Congress: Keystone of the Washington Establishment* (New Haven: Yale University Press, 1977).
14. Buchanan and Tullock, *The Calculus of Consent*, p. 20.
15. Gordon Tullock, "Public Choice in Practice," in Clifford S. Russell, ed., *Collective Decision Making* (Baltimore: Johns Hopkins University Press, 1979), pp. 31, 33.
16. See Jane Allyn Piliavin et al., *Emergency Intervention* (New York: Academic Press, 1981), p. 47 and chap. 3 generally.
17. Martin L. Hoffman, "The Development of Empathy," in J. Philippe

Rushton and Richard M. Sorrentino, eds., *Altruism and Helping Behavior* (Hillsdale, NJ: Lawrence Erlbaum Associates, 1981), p. 44.

18. See Piliavin et al., *Emergency Intervention*, p. 164 and chap. 7 generally.
19. Ibid., p. 45.
20. See Edward O. Wilson, *Sociobiology* (Cambridge: Harvard University Press, abr. ed., 1980), chap. 5, and Donald T. Campbell, "On the Genetics of Altruism and the Counter-Hedonic Components in Human Culture," *Journal of Social Issues* 27 (1972): 27.
21. Wilson, *Sociobiology*, chap. 5.
22. Hoffman, "The Development of Empathy," p. 55.
23. Joseph A. Carens, *Equality, Moral Incentives and the Market* (Chicago: University of Chicago Press, 1981), p. 123.
24. William A. Kelso, *American Democratic Theory* (Westport, CT: Greenwood Press, 1978), p. 183.
25. Emile Durkheim, *The Elementary Forms of Religious Life* (New York: Macmillan, 1915).
26. James M. Buchanan, "Politics, Policy, and the Pigovian Margins," in James M. Buchanan and Robert D. Tollison, eds., *Theory of Public Choice* (Ann Arbor: University of Michigan Press, 1972), p. 177.
27. Richard A. Musgrave, "Leviathan Cometh—or Does He?" in Helen F. Ladd and T. Nicholaus Tideman, eds., *Tax and Expenditure Limitations* (Washington: Urban Institute Press, 1981), pp. 97–98. The argument is similar to the one economists make against the notion that oligopoly pricing or large corporate profits explain inflation: unless one can demonstrate that oligopolization has increased during the period of inflation, any effect of oligopolies on the price level (inflation) will have already occurred previously.
28. See R. Douglas Arnold, "The Local Roots of Domestic Policy," in Thomas E. Mann and Norman Ornstein, eds., *The New Congress* (Washington: American Enterprise Institute, 1981), pp. 281–83.
29. See Martha Derthick and Paul J. Quirk, *The Politics of Deregulation* (Washington: Brookings Institution, 1985).
30. This is more true in other democratic countries than in the United States.
31. See Downs, *An Economic Theory of Democracy*, pp. 265–73.
32. William H. Riker and Peter C. Ordeshook, "A Theory of the Calculus of Voting," *American Political Science Review* 62 (March 1968): 25 –41.
33. Brian Barry, *Sociologists, Economists, and Democracy* (Chicago: University of Chicago Press, 1978), pp. 17–18.
34. See, for example, Bernard Ashball, *The Senate Nobody Knows* (New York: Doubleday, 1978) and Elizabeth Drew, *Senator* (New York: Simon and Schuster, 1979).
35. Mayhew, *Congress*, pp. 124–25.
36. Economists often posit theories that do not require conscious awareness in order to guide an actor's behavior. Even if businessmen are not familiar with the theory of marginal productivity, for example, it can still explain wage determination. This is because market pressures bearing on individuals require behavior corresponding to the theory, even without

conscious understanding. But there are no impersonal pressures to produce the behavior Fiorina hypothesizes.

37. Gerald H. Kramer, "Short-Term Fluctuations in U.S. Voting Behavior, 1896–1964," *American Political Science Review* 65 (March 1971): 131–43; Samuel I. Popkin et al., "What Have You Done for Me Lately? Toward an Investment Theory of Voting," *American Political Science Review* 70 (September 1976): 779–805.

38. A prescient early discussion of this issue, emphasizing ethnic variations in voting behavior driven by public spirit, is James Q. Wilson, "Public-Regardingness as a Value Premise in Voting Behavior," *American Political Science Review* 58 (December 1964): 876–87.

39. Donald R. Kinder and D. Roderick Kiewiet, "Economic Discontent and Political Behavior: The Role of Personal Grievances and Collective Economic Judgments in Congressional Voting," *American Journal of Political Science* 23 (August 1979): 495–527. See also Donald R. Kinder, "Presidents, Prosperity and Public Opinion," *Public Opinion Quarterly* 45 (Spring 1981): 1–21.

40. David O. Sears et al., "Whites' Opposition to 'Busing': Self-Interest or Symbolic Racism?" *American Political Science Review* 73 (June 1979): 369–84; Richard R. Lau et al., "Self-Interest and Civilians' Attitudes Toward the Vietnam War," *Public Opinion Quarterly* 42 (Winter 1978): 464–83; and David O. Sears et al., "Self-Interest vs. Symbolic Politics in Policy Attitudes and Presidential Voting," *American Political Science Review* 74 (September 1980): 670–84.

41. Bruce M. Russett and Elizabeth C. Hanson, *Interest and Ideology: The Foreign Policy Beliefs of American Business* (San Francisco: W.H. Freeman, 1975), pp. 123–24.

42. These phenomena have been accounted for in the political science literature. Sears, reflecting his own background in social psychological research on socialization, suggests that respondents' views may be largely noncognitive affective responses based on early childhood socialization, rather than driven by ideas about what kinds of policies are right. He presents this view as speculation, neither supported nor disconfirmed by available data.

Several observations should be made. First, the childhood socialization view cannot account for the findings of Kinder and his colleagues on views of the performance of the economy and voting behavior, since views of economic performance clearly change over time, in response to actual performance, and have a minor symbolic component. Furthermore, Sears's data show that "sophisticated" respondents (those with high degrees of political knowledge and interest) are more influenced than others in their attitudes by non-self-interest factors. If childhood socialization were the determining factor, one would expect the opposite effect, since less sophisticated people are more likely to stick atavistically with childhood indoctrination.

Finally, the political socialization literature suggests that attitudes change considerably in the late adolescent and early adult years, when people are clearly capable of independent thought. When young people were interviewed, with their parents, at the ages of seventeen and twenty-four, political party identification changed more significantly among the young people than among their parents during that interval. There was even greater difference between parents and children in the stability of their views on particular issues.

The political science literature also explores the possible influence of self-reliant ideologies in weakening the connection between self-interest and political attitudes. The unemployed may not be particularly likely to favor government jobs programs because they believe that they, not the government, are responsible for coping with their own problems. This suggestion is backed by a fair amount of empirical data. It should be pointed out that such self-reliance is an example of a general idea (and not a selfish one) about what policies government should follow. Moreover, one still needs to account for the behavior of those citizens, unemployed or not, who *do* favor government intervention.

43. Russett and Hanson, *Interest and Ideology*, p. 117.
44. Harold D. Lasswell, *Psychopathology and Politics* (Chicago: University of Chicago Press, 1977).
45. See James David Barber, *The Lawmakers: Recruitment and Adaptation of Legislative Life* (New Haven: Yale University Press, 1965) and Richard Fenno, *Congressmen in Committees* (Boston: Little, Brown, 1973).
46. For a study emphasizing this finding, see Robert H. Salisbury, "The Urban Party Organization Member," *Public Opinion Quarterly* 29 (Winter 1965–66): 550–64. See also Barber, *The Lawmakers*.
47. Robert E. Lane, *Political Man: Why and How People Get Involved in Politics* (New York: Free Press, 1959), p. 127.
48. Barber, *The Lawmakers*.
49. See W. Lloyd Warner et al., *The American Federal Executive* (New Haven: Yale University Press, 1963), chap. 13.
50. U.S. Merit Systems Protection Board, *The 1984 Report on the Senior Executive Service* (Washington: Merit Systems Protection Board, 1984), p. 15.
51. Edward E. Lawler III, *Pay and Organizational Effectiveness: A Psychological View* (New York: McGraw Hill, 1971), pp. 55–56. Lawler notes that this pattern may be partly due to a reduction of cognitive dissonance that occurs after coming to the job, rather than to motivations that lead a manager to the job in the first place.
52. Dean E. Mann and James W. Doig, *The Assistant Secretaries* (Washington: Brookings Institution, 1965), pp. 162–64.
53. See David P. Campbell, *Handbook for the Strong Vocational Interest Blank* (Stanford: Stanford University Press, 1971). To determine what answers incline a student toward given occupations, the test is first administered to a "sample of successful, satisfied men performing [an] occupation in a

typical manner" (p. 25). The more a student's answers resemble those of people already in the jobs, the better the indicated match between individual and occupation.

54. Hamilton, *The Federalist*, p. 337.
55. See Robert A. Dahl, *A Preface to Democratic Theory* (Chicago: University of Chicago Press, 1956).
56. Ibid., p. 104.
57. Buchanan and Tullock, *The Calculus of Consent*, p. 138.
58. Cited in Robert N. Bellah et al., *Habits of the Heart* (Berkeley: University of California Press, 1985), pp. 253–54.
59. Alexis de Tocqueville, *Democracy in America* (New York: Vintage Books, 1945), vol. 1, p. 334.
60. See, for example, Dennis H. Robertson, *Economic Commentaries* (London: Stamples Press, 1956). A good discussion of these issues appears in Albert O. Hirschman, "Against Parsimony," *Economics and Philosophy* 1 (April 1985): 16–19.
61. Jacqueline R. Macaulay, "A Shill for Charity," in J. Macaulay and L. Berkowitz, eds., *Altruism and Helping Behavior* (New York: Academic Press, 1970), p. 43. See also Ervin Staub, *Positive Social Behavior and Morality* (New York: Academic Press, 1979), vol. 1, pp. 198–220.
62. See Dennis L. Krebs, "Altruism—An Examination of the Concepts and a Review of the Literature," *Psychological Bulletin* 73 (1970): 268, 272.
63. Morris P. Fiorina and Charles R. Plott, "Committee Decisions Under Majority Rule; an Experimental Study," *American Political Science Review* 72 (June 1978).
64. Ibid., p. 578.

Chapter Three: What Makes Public Ideas Powerful

1. For a more complete discussion of the alcohol example, see Mark H. Moore and Dean Gerstein, *Alcohol and Public Policy: Beyond the Shadow of Prohibition* (Washington, DC: National Academy Press, 1981).
2. Center for Biochemical and Biophysical Sciences and Medicine, Harvard Medical School, *Toward a Biological Understanding of Alcoholism* (Cambridge, MA: Endowment for Research in Human Biology, 1984), pp. 24–27.
3. Ibid.
4. Norman H. Clark, *Deliver Us from Evil: An Interpretation of American Prohibition* (New York: W.W. Norton and Co., 1976).
5. Moore and Gerstein, *Alcohol and Public Policy*, pp. 17–20.
6. Ibid., pp. 29–34.
7. Ibid., pp. 58–59.
8. Philip J. Cook, "The Effect of Liquor Taxes on Drinking, Cirrhosis, and Auto Accidents," in Moore and Gerstein, *Alcohol and Public Policy*, pp. 255–85.
9. Moore and Gerstein, chaps. 5 and 6.
10. Two publications by the Rand Corporation revived these ideas. See Jan Chaiken and Marcia Chaiken, *Varieties of Criminal Behavior* (Santa Monica,

CA: Rand Corporation, 1982) and Peter W. Greenwood and Alan Abrahamse, *Selective Incapacitation* (Santa Monica, CA: Rand Corporation, 1982).

11. For a more complete discussion of this example, see Mark H. Moore, Susan Estrich, Daniel McGillis, and William Spelman, *Dangerous Offenders: Elusive Targets of Justice* (Cambridge: Harvard University Press, 1984).

12. Greenwood estimated that selective imprisonment policies could reduce robbery rates by 20 percent, or imprisonment rates by 15 percent. See Greenwood and Abrahamse, *Selective Incapacitation*, p. 79.

13. Michael Sherman and Gordon Hawkins, *Imprisonment in America* (Chicago: University of Chicago Press, 1981).

14. Robert Martinson, "What Works: Questions and Answers About Prison Reform," *Public Interest* 35 (1974): 22–54; Twentieth Century Fund Task Force on Criminal Sentencing, *Fair And Certain Punishment* (New York: McGraw-Hill, 1976).

15. Chaiken and Chaiken, *Varieties of Criminal Behavior*.

16. Greenwood and Abrahamse, *Selective Incapacitation*. See also Moore et al., *Dangerous Offenders*, pp. 76–78.

17. Greenwood and Abrahamse, *Selective Incapacitation*.

18. Andrew von Hirsch, "The Ethics of Selective Incapacitation: Observations on the Contemporary Debate," *Crime and Delinquency* 30 (1984): 175–94; Daniel J. Freed and Patricia M. Wald, *Bail in the United States, 1964* (Washington, DC: U.S. Dept. of Justice and Vera Institute, 1964); Andrew von Hirsch, *Doing Justice: The Choice of Punishments* (New York: Hill and Wang, 1976), pp. 212–13; William Spelman, *The Depth of a Dangerous Temptation: Another Look at Selective Incapacitation* (Washington, DC: Police Executive Research Forum, 1986).

19. Moore et al., *Dangerous Offenders*, pp. 87–89.

20. Ibid., pp. 65–66.

21. Donald M. Gottfredson, Leslie T. Wilkins, and Peter B. Hoffman, *Guidelines for Parole and Sentencing* (Lexington, MA: D.C. Heath and Co., 1978).

22. Moore et al., *Dangerous Offenders*, pp. 66–68.

23. For an account of this movement in one state, see "Jerome Miller and the Massachusetts Department of Youth Services," Kennedy School of Government Case #C94-76-101 (Cambridge, MA: Kennedy School of Government, Harvard University, 1976).

24. Edwin H. Sutherland and Donald Cressey, *Principles of Criminology*, 7th ed. (Philadelphia: Lippincott and Co., 1966), pp. 74–81.

25. Erving Goffmann, *Asylums* (New York: Doubleday, 1961).

26. Edwin Schur, *Radical Non-Intervention* (Englewood Cliffs, NJ: Prentice-Hall, 1973).

27. Gordon Chase, "Contracting for Human Services," Kennedy School of Government Case #C14-79-268 (Cambridge, MA: Kennedy School of Government, Harvard University, 1979).

28. Peter Greenwood, *One Last Hope: The Rehabilitation of Juvenile Offenders* (Santa Monica, CA: Rand Corporation, 1985)

29. Mark H. Moore et al., *From Children to Citizens: Vol. I: The Mandate for Juvenile Justice* (New York: Springer-Verlag, forthcoming).

30. For a more detailed discussion of this example, see Mark H. Moore, "Re-Organization Plan #2 Reviewed," *Public Policy* 26 (Spring 1978): 229–262.

31. The Domestic Council Drug Abuse Task Force, *White Paper on Drug Abuse* (Washington, D.C.: Government Printing Office, 1974), pp. 29–34.

32. Mark H. Moore, "Limiting Supplies of Drugs to Illicit Markets," *Journal of Drug Issues* (Spring 1979), pp. 291–308.

33. Ibid. For a more recent discussion, see Mark H. Moore, "Drugs and Organized Crime" in President's Commission on Organized Crime, *America's Habit: Drug Abuse, Drug Trafficking, and Organized Crime* (Washington, DC: Government Printing Office, 1986).

34. Personal experience. From 1974 to 1975, I was the chief planning officer of the Drug Enforcement Administration.

35. For a history of ATF, see Mark H. Moore, "Gun Control (B): The Bureau of Alcohol, Tobacco, and Firearms," Kennedy School of Government Case #C95-81-404 (Cambridge, MA: Kennedy School of Government, Harvard University, 1981).

36. Ibid., p. 6.

37. Ibid., p. 7.

38. Ibid., p. 15.

39. Joseph L. Bower, "William Ruckelshaus and the Environmental Protection Agency," Kennedy School of Government Case #C16-74-027 (Cambridge, MA: Kennedy School of Government, Harvard University, 1974).

40. Ibid., pp. 12–14.

41. Ibid., pp. 2, 8.

42. Ibid., pp. 2, 9.

43. Ibid., p. 6.

44. Ibid., pp. 5–6.

45. Ibid., p. 7.

46. Ibid., pp. 15–16.

47. Joseph R. Gusfield, *The Culture of Public Problems: Drinking-Driving and the Symbolic Order* (Chicago: University of Chicago Press, 1981).

48. James B. Jacobs, "Putting Drunk Driving in Perspective" (New York University: unpublished mimeo, July 1986).

49. For a discussion of the concept of "issue networks," see Hugh Heclo, "Issue Networks and the Executive Establishment," in *The New American Political System* (American Enterprise Institute, 1978).

50. Thomas J. Kuhn, *The Structure of Scientific Revolutions* (Chicago: University of Chicago Press, 1962).

51. Moore et al., *Dangerous Offenders*, pp. 89, 192–94.

52. For a discussion of the tax compliance issue, see Mark H. Moore, "On the Office of the Taxpayer and the Social Process of Taxpaying," in *Income Tax Compliance: A Report of the ABA Section of Taxation; Invitational Conference on Income Tax Compliance* (New York: American Bar Association, 1983).

53. See Charles E. Lindblom, *The Policy-Making Process* (Englewood Cliffs, NJ: Prentice-Hall, 1968). For a more particular discussion of the role of ideas,

see Laurence E. Lynn, *Knowledge and Policy: The Uncertain Connection* (Washington, DC: National Academy Press, 1978).

54. See Thomas J. Peters and Robert H. Waterman, *In Search of Excellence*, (New York: Harper and Row, 1982), chap. 9.

55. For a theory, see Neil J. Smilser, *A Theory of Collective Behavior* (New York: Free Press, 1963). For an illustrative example, see Gusfield, *The Culture of Public Problems*.

56. I am indebted to Nino Majone for observing and emphasizing this point.

57. For the nature of this challenge, see Mark H. Moore, "Social Science and Policy Analysis: Some Fundamental Differences," in Daniel Callahan and Bruce Jennings, eds., *Ethics, The Social Sciences, and Policy Analysis* (New York: Plenum, 1983).

58. John D. Steinbruner, *The Cybernetic Theory of Decision* (Princeton: Princeton University Press, 1974), pp. 88–139.

59. For a provocative discussion of how America learned these lessons, see Norman H. Clark, *Deliver Us from Evil: An Interpretation of American Prohibition* (New York: W.W. Norton, 1976).

60. Richard E. Neustadt and Ernest R. May, *Thinking in Time: The Uses of History for Decision-Makers* (New York: Free Press, 1986).

61. For a juxtaposition of a simple gestalt with a more complicated but more accurate view of a problem, see Moore and Gerstein, *Alcohol and Public Policy*, pp. 6–47.

62. The tradition is not a very old one. For a pillar of this tradition, see Edith Stokey and Richard Zeckhauser, *A Primer for Policy Analysis* (New York: W.W. Norton, 1978).

Chapter Four: How Government Expresses Public Ideas

1. There is no better description of the entire process than that given by John W. Kingdon in *Agendas, Alternatives, and Public Policies* (Boston: Little, Brown, 1984).

2. Robert B. Reich, *Tales of a New America* (New York: Times Books, 1987).

Chapter Five: The Political Theory of the Procedural Republic

An earlier version of this essay appears in Allan C. Huthinson and Patrick Monahan, eds., *The Rule of Law* (Toronto: Carswell, 1987).

1. Robert Reich, chap. 6 in this volume.

2. Richard B. Stewart, "Regulation in a Liberal State: The Role of Non-Commodity Values," *Yale Law Journal* 92 (July 1983): 1539.

3. Reich, chap. 6 in this volume, and Stewart, "Regulation," pp. 1547–56, 1560–66.

4. Stewart, "Regulation," pp. 1556–59.

5. In this and the following section, I draw on the introduction to Michael Sandel, ed., *Liberalism and Its Critics* (Oxford: Basil Blackwell, 1984).

6. John Stuart Mill, *On Liberty* (Indianapolis: Hackett Publishing Co., 1978), chap. 1.

7. See Immanuel Kant, *Groundwork of the Metaphysics of Morals* (1785; trans. H.J. Paton, New York: Harper and Row, 1956), and "On the Common Saying: 'This May Be True in Theory, But It Does Not Apply in Practice'" (1793), in Hans Reiss, ed., *Kant's Political Writings* (Cambridge: Cambridge University Press, 1970).

8. John Rawls, *A Theory of Justice* (Oxford: Oxford University Press, 1971), pp. 3–4.

9. H.L.A. Hart, "Between Utility and Rights," in Alan Ryan, ed., *The Idea of Freedom* (Oxford: Oxford University Press, 1979), p. 77.

10. Rawls, *A Theory of Justice*, p. 560.

11. Alasdair MacIntyre, *After Virtue* (Notre Dame: University of Notre Dame Press, 1981), p. 205.

12. Hannah Arendt, *The Human Condition* (Chicago: University of Chicago Press, 1958), pp. 52–53.

13. For examples of the liberal view, see Louis Hartz, *The Liberal Tradition in America* (New York: Harcourt Brace, 1955), and more recently, Isaac Kramnick, "Republican Revisionism Revisited," *American Historical Review* 87 (1982), and John Diggins, *The Lost Soul of American Politics* (New York: Basic Books, 1984). For examples of the republican view, see Bernard Bailyn, *The Ideological Origins of the American Revolution* (Cambridge, MA: Harvard University Press, 1967); Gordon Wood, *The Creation of the American Republic* (New York: Norton, 1969); and J.G.A. Pocock, *The Machiavellian Moment* (Princeton: Princeton University Press, 1975).

14. Gordon Wood, *The Creation of the American Republic* (Chapel Hill: University of North Carolina Press, 1969), pp. 24, 61.

15. Laurence Tribe, *American Constitutional Law* (Mineola, N.Y.: Foundation Press, 1978), pp. 2–3.

16. See, for example, James Madison, *The Federalist*, No. 51, Jacob E. Cooke, ed. (Middletown, CT: Wesleyan University Press, 1961) and Herbert Sotring, *What the Anti-Federalists Were For* (Chicago: University of Chicago Press, 1981), chap. 3.

17. Alexis de Tocqueville, *Democracy in America* (New York: Alfred Knopf, 1945), vol. 1, chap. 5.

18. In this and the following section, I draw from Michael Sandel, "The Procedural Republic and the Unencumbered Self," *Political Theory* 12 (1984): 81–96.

19. Herbert Croly, *The Promise of American Life* (Indianapolis: Bobbs-Merrill, 1965), pp. 270–73.

20. Samuel Beer, "Liberalism and the National Idea," *Public Interest*, Fall (1966): 70–82.

21. See Ronald Dworkin, "Liberalism," in Stuart Hampshire, ed., *Public and Private Morality* (Cambridge: Cambridge University Press, 1978), p. 136.

Chapter Six: Policy Making in a Democracy

1. Alexander Hamilton et al., *The Federalist*, No. 78, B. Wright, ed. (Cambridge, MA: Harvard University Press, 1961), pp. 103-10.

2. Jurisprudential schools have risen and fallen with some regularity. Some

have confined their concerns to constitutional norms, while others have taken on the whole corpus of judicial activity, including statutory construction and common law adjudication. But regardless of their precise field of vision, most have somehow addressed themselves to the fundamental question of how judicial discretion can be reconciled with democratic values.

3. Woodrow Wilson, "The Study of Administration," *Political Science Quarterly* 2 (June 1887): 197–217.

4. Progressives were no less confident about the capacity of managers in the private sector to discover the "single best way" of making and delivering goods and services. See, for example, Frederick Winslow Taylor, *The Principles of Scientific Management* (New York: Harper and Brothers, 1911), pp. 20–28. For a general discussion, see Robert B. Reich, *The Next American Frontier* (New York: Times Books, 1983), chap. 4.

5. See, for example, Ernst Freund, *Legislative Regulation* (New York: Commonwealth Fund, 1932).

6. See, for example, *Panama Refining Co. v. Ryan*, 293 U.S. 388 (1935); *Schechter Poultry v. United States*, 295 U.S. 495 (1935).

7. These arguments were advanced by Felix Frankfurter in *The Public and Its Government* (New Haven: Yale University Press, 1930), and James Landis, in *The Administrative Process* (New Haven: Yale University Press, 1938). See also James W. Fesler et al., *The Elements of Public Administration* (New York: Prentice-Hall, 1946), pp. 7–9.

8. For a thoughtful treatment of this issue, see Edward Purcell, Jr., *The Crisis of Democratic Theory: Scientific Naturalism and the Problem of Value* (Lexington: University of Kentucky Press, 1973).

9. See, for example, Robert A. Dahl, *A Preface to Democratic Theory* (Chicago: University of Chicago Press, 1956); David Truman, *The Governmental Process: Political Interests and Public Opinion* (New York: Knopf, 1951).

10. Joseph Schumpeter, *Capitalism, Socialism, and Democracy* (New York: Harper, 1942); Anthony Downs, *An Economic Theory of Democracy* (New York: Harper, 1957).

11. See Fesler et al., *The Elements of Public Administration*, pp. 37–41; *The John F. Kennedy School of Government: The First Fifty Years* (Cambridge, MA: Ballinger, 1986), pp. 25–48.

12. *Office of Communication of the United Church of Christ v. Federal Communications Commission*, 359 F. 2d 994, 1000-06 (C.A. D.C. 1966).

13. See, for example, *Scenic Hudson Preservation Conf. v. Federal Power Commission*, 354 F. 2d 608 (C.A. 2, 1965), cert. denied, 384 U.S. 941 (1966); *Friends of the Earth v. Atomic Energy Commission*, 485 F. 2d 1031, 1033 (C.A. D.C. 1973); and other cases cited in Richard Stewart, "The Reformation of American Administrative Law," *Harvard Law Review* 88 (1975): 1667.

14. 15 U.S.C. 57a(h) (1976).

15. For a summary of these and related reforms, see generally Stewart, "Reformation," and Colin Diver, "Policymaking Paradigms in Administrative Law," *Harvard Law Review* 95 (1981): 393.

16. 5 U.S.C. 552b (1976).

17. In *Sierra Club v. Morton*, 405 U.S. 727 (1972), the Supreme Court denied

standing to the Sierra Club to contest an Interior Department ruling, on the ground that the club's asserted interest in the broad principle that wilderness areas should be preserved did not place the club or any of its members in jeopardy of a material injury by the department's proposed actions. The club's assertion in a subsequent proceeding that the rule would deny certain of its members the enjoyment of the wilderness area in question was deemed by the court to be sufficient to confer standing. Some commentators have criticized these seemingly inconsistent decisions as examples of legal legerdemain; they argue that almost any ideological group can contrive some material injury to one of its members sufficient to gain standing. But this critique misses the important difference between the two instances in these cases. A view about what constitutes a good society does not readily lend itself to hard bargaining; by contrast, a specific and identifiable injury, as to particular individuals' enjoyment of particular wilderness areas, lends itself to negotiation and perhaps compensation. In the latter case, the public manager-as-intermediator can do his job.

18. For example, the Consumer Product Safety Commission's product safety rules must "express in the rule itself the risk of injury which the standard is designed to eliminate or reduce" (15 U.S.C. 2058(b), 1976).

19. The Reagan order forbad any regulatory action, whether major or minor, by executive agencies unless "the potential benefits to society . . . outweigh the potential costs to society" and the alternative chosen to achieve the goal maximizes the aggregate net benefit to society. Executive Order No. 12,291, 46 Fed. Reg. at 13,193 (1981).

20. *Pilai v. CAB*, 485 F. 2d 1018 (C.A. D.C. 1973); *Portland Cement v. Ruckelshaus*, 486 F. 2d 375 (C.A. D.C. 1973), cert. denied 417 U.S. 921 (1974); *Aqua Slide N' Dive v. Consumer Products Safety Commission*, 569 F. 2d 831 (C.A. 5, 1978).

21. See Edith Stokey and Richard Zeckhauser, *A Primer for Policy Analysis* (New York: W.W. Norton, 1978), p. 281.

22. In one real-world example, the Civil Aeronautics Board (CAB) was presented with two conflicting estimates of the changes in air traffic that would result from a fare increase then under consideration. The CAB staff offered estimates based on an analysis of air traffic and prices over the previous twenty years. The industry, using an analysis that omitted certain years considered to be unrepresentative, offered a very different estimate. The CAB ultimately accepted neither estimate completely, but found it could "form the basis for a reasonable judgment on the issue." Its "reasonable judgment," not surprisingly, fell between the two estimates. See *Domestic Passenger Fare Investigation, Phase 7*, Part 9, 1971.

23. It has been suggested that certain of these devices are applicable even in absence of formal democratic institutions. See, for example, Stokey and Zeckhauser, *Primer*: "Most of the materials in this book [concerning the techniques of policy analysis] are equally applicable to a socialist, capitalist, or mixed-enterprise society, to a democracy or a dictatorship, indeed wherever hard policy choices must be made" (p. 4).

24. See Steven Kelman, *What Price Incentives?* (Cambridge, MA: Arbor House,

1981). It should also be noted that market prices and expressions of willingness to pay depend on the current distribution of wealth and income. If the current distribution is deemed to be unfair, then a different set of prices and expressions of willingness to pay might be more appropriate.

25. See M. Landy, "Policy Analysis as a Vocation," *World Politics* (April 1981): 469; Steven Kelman, "A Case for In-Kind Transfers," *Economics and Philosophy* 2 (1986): 55–73.
26. This illustration is based primarily on Henry Lee, "Managing Environmental Risk: The Case of Asarco," John F. Kennedy School of Government Case Program, Harvard University, 1985.
27. *Seattle Times*, June 30, 1984, A10, col. 3.
28. William Ruckelshaus, interview with author, February 27, 1985.
29. This illustration is based primarily on Arthur Applbaum, "Mike Pertschuk and the Federal Trade Commission," John F. Kennedy School of Government Case Program, Harvard University, 1981.
30. Michael Pertschuk, interview with author, March 7, 1986.
31. This illustration is based primarily on Glenn Tobin, "Creating Discussion in Modern America," unpub. ms. Kennedy School of Government, Harvard University, 1986.
32. Interview with author, June 4, 1986. The assistant's name is withheld at his request.
33. *Los Angeles Times*, August 13, 1983, 20, col. 3.

Chapter Seven: Policy Analysis and Public Deliberation

1. A.D. Lindsay, *The Modern Democratic State* (New York: Oxford University Press, 1962), p. 281.
2. Ernest Barker, *Reflections on Government* (New York: Oxford University Press, 1958), p. 36.
3. Ibid., pp. 56–60.
4. Karl W. Deutsch, *Politics and Government* (Boston: Houghton Mifflin Company, 1970), pp. 168–72.
5. Gertrude Himmelfarb, *The Idea of Poverty* (New York: Vintage Books, 1985), p. 12.
6. Charles W. Anderson, "The Place of Principles in Policy Analysis," *American Political Science Review* 73 (September 1979): 711–23.
7. Geoffrey Vickers, *The Art of Judgment* (London: Chapman and Hall, 1965).
8. Marver Bernstein, *Regulating Business by Independent Commission* (Princeton, NJ: Princeton University Press, 1955); Theodore Lowi, *The End of Liberalism* (New York: W.W. Norton, 1969); Alfred Marcus, "The Environmental Protection Agency," in James Q. Wilson, ed., *The Politics of Regulation* (New York: Basic Books, 1980), pp. 267–303.
9. Anderson, "Place of Principles," p. 714.
10. The following example is based on the case study by Brendan Gillespie, Dave Eva, and Ron Johnston, "Carcinogenic Risk Assessment in the United States and Great Britain: The Case of Aldrin/Dieldrin," *Social Studies of Science* 9 (1979): 265–302.

11. Carol Weiss, "Research for Policy's Sake: The Enlightenment Function of Social Research," *Policy Analysis* 3 (Fall 1977): 533.
12. Edmund Whittaker, *From Euclid to Eddington: A Study of Conceptions of the External World* (New York: Dover Publications, 1958), p. 69.
13. Anthony Downs, *Inside Bureaucracy* (Boston: Little, Brown and Company, 1966).
14. Albert O. Hirschman, "Obstacles to Development: A Classification and a Quasi-Vanishing Act," in Albert O. Hirschman, ed., *A Bias for Hope* (New Haven: Yale University Press, 1971), pp. 312–27.
15. Thomas N. Gladwin, Judith L. Bigelow, and Ingo Walter, "A Global View of CFC Sources and Policies to Reduce Emissions," in John H. Cumberland, James R. Hibbs, and Irving Hoch, ed., *The Economics of Managing Chlorofluorocarbons* (Washington, DC: Resources for the Future, 1982), pp. 64–113.
16. Talcott Parsons, *Societies—Evolutionary and Comparative Perspectives* (Englewood Cliffs, NJ: Prentice-Hall, 1966).
17. Peter Blau, *The Dynamics of Bureaucracy* (Chicago: University of Chicago Press, 1955), p. 38.
18. Ibid., p. 46.
19. Walsh McDermott, "Evaluating the Physician and His Technology," in John H. Knowles, ed., *Doing Better and Feeling Worse* (New York: W.W. Norton and Company, 1977), pp. 135–57.
20. David K. Cohen and Richard J. Murnane, "Merit Pay and the Evaluation Problem; Why Some Merit Pay Plans Fail and a Few Survive," *Harvard Educational Review* 56 (February 1986): 1–17.
21. William G. Ouchi, "The Relationship Between Organizational Structure and Organizational Control," *Administrative Science Quarterly* 22 (March 1977): 95–113.
22. Paul A. Sabatier, "What Can We Learn from Implementation Research?" in F.X. Kaufmann, G. Majone, and V. Ostrom, eds.., *Guidance, Control, and Evaluation in the Public Sector* (Berlin and New York: Walter de Gruyter, 1986), pp. 313–26.
23. Wayne C. Booth, *Modern Dogma and the Rhetoric of Assent* (Chicago: University of Chicago Press, 1974), p. xi.
24. Anderson, "Place of Principles," p. 714.
25. Richard A. Wasserstrom, *The Judicial Decision* (Stanford, CA: Stanford University Press, 1961).
26. Paul Feyerabend, *Against Method* (London: NLB, 1975), p. 52 (Feyerabend's italics).
27. Armen A. Alchian and W.R. Allen, *University Economics* (London: Prentice-Hall International, 1974), p. 211.
28. George Stigler, *Essays in the History of Economics* (Chicago: University of Chicago Press, 1965), p. 5.
29. Walter W. Heller, *New Dimensions of Political Economy* (New York: W.W. Norton, 1967), p. 27.
30. D.E. Moggridge, *Keynes* (London: Fontana Books, 1976), p. 120.

Chapter Eight: Political Leadership: Managing the Public's Problem Solving

The authors are deeply grateful to Sousan Abadian, Robert Andersen, Laurence Heifetz, Milton Heifetz, Philip Heymann, Alice Jones, Judith Keeler, Jack Montgomery, Mark Moore, Larry Navon, Elizabeth Neustadt, Alice Olson, Robert Reich, Marguerite Rigoglioso, Robert Ronnow, Ute Sacksofsky, Thomas Schelling, Edith Stokey, William Ury, and Richard Zeckhauser for their encouragement and feedback. In addition, the authors greatly appreciate the support of James Lester, Marvin Moss, and Philip Selwyn at the Office of Naval Research, Arlington, Virginia.

1. Quoted in William Safire, *Before the Fall: An Inside View of the Pre-Watergate White House* (New York: Doubleday and Company, 1975), pp. 178–79.
2. In his forthcoming *Leadership: A Seventh View*, Robert Terry of the University of Minnesota classifies the various views of leadership into six categories: (1) the trait approach, in which leaders are thought to be born with innate qualities; (2) the situational approach, in which leaders with different characteristics are thought to arise out of different situations depending on the needs of the moment; (3) organizational theory, in which leadership consists of serving specific functions that differ depending on one's position in an organization; (4) power theory, in which leadership consists of the successful management of power and authority to achieve one's aims; (5) vision theory, in which leadership consists of defining vision and effectively communicating vision to achieve political or organizational alignment; and (6) assessed vision theory, in which leadership consists of defining and communicating vision, and the ends themselves are assessed according to a framework of ethics or values. Though the differences among these approaches are of major import, so are the similarities. All these theories share certain basic assumptions, forming a paradigm of leadership that (1) equates leadership with formal or informal authority and (2) gives the leader the role of providing a vision or agenda.
3. Barbara Kellerman, *The Political Presidency: Practice of Leadership from Kennedy to Reagan* (Oxford: Oxford University Press, 1984), p. xi.
4. Warren Bennis and Burt Nanus, *Leaders: The Strategies for Taking Charge* (New York: Harper and Row, 1985), pp. 20, 139.
5. Robert A. Portnoy, *Leadership, What Every Leader Should Know About People* (Englewood Cliffs, NJ: Prentice-Hall, 1986), p. 4.
6. For example, many civic groups, such as local chambers of commerce, are now producing programs to train up-and-coming community members in leadership. These programs include Leadership Minneapolis, Leadership Dallas, Leadership Cleveland, Leadership Chattanooga, Leadership Atlanta, and Leadership Philadelphia.
7. I Samuel 8:19-20.
8. See Marshall Sahlins, *Stone Age Economics* (New York: Aldine, 1972); or Richard Leakey and Roger Lewin, *Origins* (New York: Dutton, 1977).

9. See Plato, *The Republic,* or, for modern efforts along these lines, Bernard Bass, *Stogdill's Handbook of Leadership* (New York: Free Press, 1981).

10. See Richard E. Neustadt, *Presidential Power* (New York: Wiley and Sons, 1980); Kellerman, *Political Presidency;* Edwin Hollander, *Leadership Dynamics: A Practical Guide to Effective Relationships* (New York: Free Press, 1978); Bennis and Nanus, *Leaders;* Associates, The Department of Behavioral Sciences and Leadership, *Leadership in Organizations* (West Point: United States Military Academy, 1981); or Paul Hershey, *The Situational Leader* (New York: Warner, 1984).

11. See A. Kenneth Rice, *Learning for Leadership* (London: Tavistock, 1965), or Arthur D. Colman and W. Harold Bexton, eds., *Group Relations Reader* (Washington, DC: A.K. Rice Institute, 1975).

12. Neustadt, *Presidential Power.*

13. This argument departs from Plato's notion that the expertise required of the leader is a vision of the absolute good. Plato's use of the physician analogy is well taken as an argument in favor of the need for expertise, but he apparently misunderstands the kind of expertise required. He fails to appreciate the medical difference between Type I situations and types II and III. Consequently he suggests that the expertise required is essentially of the answer-giving variety. See Plato's *Protagoras, Giorgias,* or *The Republic* for his extensive use of helmsman and physician analogies; also Renford Bambrough, "Plato's Political Analogies," in Peter Laslett, ed., *Philosophy, Politics, and Society,* 1st ser. (Oxford: Blackwell/Oxford University Press, 1956).

14. See Kellerman, *The Political Presidency.*

15. John Stuart Mill, *On Liberty* (1859; reprint, Indianapolis: Bobbs-Merrill, 1956), pp. 140–41.

16. Arthur Schlesinger, *The Coming of the New Deal* (Boston: Houghton Mifflin, 1958), p. 528.

17. Ibid., p. 193.

18. Ibid., p. 558.

19. Quoted in ibid., p. 558.

20. Cited by Mark E. Kann, "Challenging Lockean Liberalism in America: The Case of Debs and Hillquit," *Political Theory* 8 (May 1980): 214.

Chapter Nine: The Media and Public Deliberation

1. James Reston, *New York Times,* April 9, 1986, p. A27.

2. A three-year study of how the press affects federal policy making, which I directed, found that successful high-level policy makers often use the press to communicate with the rest of government; moreover, most senior officials use the media to find out what is going on in the government generally and in their own policy area. The findings of this study are included in Martin Linsky, *Impact: How the Press Affects Federal Policymaking* (New York: W.W. Norton and Company, 1986).

3. Conversation with the author.

4. Edmund Morris, *The Rise of Theodore Roosevelt* (New York: Coward, McCann and Geoghegan, Inc. 1979), chap. 5.

5. Jim Varanese, "Case Study of Candidates in the Democratic Primary Race for the Massachusetts State Senate Seat in the Belmont-Watertown-Cambridge-Allston-Brighton District," April 1986. This paper was written as an independent study project at the Kennedy School of Government, Harvard University.

6. Benjamin M. Compaine, *Who Owns the Media?* (New York: Harmony Books, 1979), p. 18.

7. For a rich discussion of the decline of multiple-newspaper towns and the consolidation of ownership, see Ben Badgikian, *The Media Monopoly* (Boston: Beacon Press, 1983).

8. Marshall McLuhan, "The Medium Is the Message," chap. 1 in *Understanding Media* (New York: McGraw-Hill Book Company, 1964).

9. Martin Linsky, *Television and the Presidential Elections* (Lexington, MA: Lexington Books, 1938), p. 14.

10. In certain other situations short of these extremes, news organizations seem to have assessed the consequences of publication and decided against publishing. However, such situations, are hard to distinguish on the basis of journalistic principle from many cases where such considerations are ignored. For instance, news organizations have recently decided overwhelmingly to protect the privacy of complainants in rape prosecutions by not publishing their names. This practice seems to reflect the recent increased sensitivity to sexual discrimination and women's rights, and the intimate nature of the crime. However, victims of other violent crimes, who may also feel deeply humiliated and exposed, are not generally accorded the same consideration.

11. Report of the Massachusetts Task Force on Organ Transplantation (October 1984). See also George Annis, "Regulating Heart and Liver Transplantation," and Marc Roberts, "The Economics of Organ Transplants," both in *Jurimetrics* 25 (Spring 1985).

12. William Greider, *The Education of David Stockman and Other Americans* (New York: E.P. Dutton, Inc., 1981).

13. William Greider, "The Education of David Stockman," *Atlantic Monthly*, December 1981.

14. For more on the history of objectivity in the press, see Michael Schudson, *Discovering the News* (New York: Basic Books, 1978).

15. Walter Lippmann, *Public Opinion* (New York: Macmillan Company, 1922).

16. *Boston Globe*, April 27, 1986, p. 14.

17. Martin Linsky and Deni Elliott, "The Oliver Sipple Story," *Bulletin of the American Society of Newspaper Editors*, September 1982.

18. For the origins of this quotation, see Chalmers Roberts, *The Washington Post: The First Hundred Years* (Boston: Houghton Mifflin and Co., 1977).

19. The best account of this episode is in David Halberstam's *The Best and the Brightest* (Greenwich, CT: Fawcett Publications, 1973).

20. T.R. Reid, *Congressional Odyssey: The Saga of a Senate Bill* (San Francisco: W.H. Freeman and Company, 1980).

21. Conversation with Haynes Johnson, June 16, 1986.

Index

Contributors

Ronald A. Heifetz teaches leadership at Harvard's John F. Kennedy School of Government. His research aims to provide public managers and politicians with better tools for political and organizational intervention. As a member of the school's Avoiding Nuclear War Project, his work concerns the management of conflict and crisis. He is a graduate of Columbia University, Harvard Medical School, and the John F. Kennedy School of Government.

Philip B. Heymann is professor of law at Harvard Law School and a member of the faculty of the John F. Kennedy School of Government. He was assistant attorney general in charge of the criminal division of the Department of Justice from 1978 to 1981 and worked with the Watergate special prosecutor. During the 1960s, after clerking for Supreme Court Justice John Harlan, he held various positions in the State Department and Justice Department. He is the author of a forthcoming book, *The Politics of Public Management*. Professor Heymann received his B.A. from Yale University and law degree from Harvard.

Steven Kelman is a professor of public policy at the John F. Kennedy School of Government, where he teaches public management and ethical theory. He is the author of *Regulating America, Regulating Sweden: A Comparative Study of Occupational Safety and Health Policy* (1981), *What Price Incentives: Economists and the Environment* (1981), and many articles in scholarly and general journals. He received both his A.B. and Ph.D. from Harvard University.

Martin Linsky teaches courses on the media, legislatures, political leadership, and politics at the John F. Kennedy School of Government, having come to the school in 1979 as assistant director of the Institute of Politics. Earlier he worked in journalism and government, as editor of the *Real Paper*, editorial writer for the *Boston Globe*, member of the Massachusetts House of Representatives, and assistant attorney general for the Commonwealth of Massachusetts. His publications include *Television and the Presidential Elections* (1983) and *Impact: How the Press Affects Federal Policymaking* (1986). He is a graduate of Williams College and Harvard Law School.

Giandomenico Majone is professor of statistics and policy analysis at the University of Calabria, Italy, and at the National School of Public Administration in Rome. He holds degrees from the University of Padua, Carnegie-Mellon University, and the University of California, Berkeley, and has taught at Yale, Harvard, and other universities in Europe and North America. His publications include *Pitfalls of Analysis* (1980) and *Guidance, Control, and Evaluation in the Public Sector* (1986).

Mark Moore is the Guggenheim Professor of Criminal Justice Policy and Management at the John F. Kennedy School of Government, with which he has been associated in various capacities since 1971. While on leave from the school he served as special assistant to the administrator and chief planning officer for the Drug Enforcement Administration of the U.S. Department of Justice in 1974–75. In addition to scholarly articles, his publications include *Dangerous Offenders: The Elusive Target of Justice* (1984). He was educated at Yale and the John F. Kennedy School of Government.

Gary Orren is associate professor of public policy at the John F. Kennedy School of Government. He has served as a political adviser in a number of election campaigns and has been a consultant for public opinion polling to the *New York Times* (where he played a leading role in the creation of the *New York Times*/CBS poll), the *Washington Post*, and the *Boston Globe*. Orren has written widely on aspects of this country's political system and is co-author with Sidney Verba of *Equality in America: The View from the Top* (1985). He was educated at Oberlin College and received his Ph.D. at Harvard University.

Robert B. Reich teaches political economy, law, and management at the John F. Kennedy School of Government. He is the author of *Minding America's Business* (with Ira Magaziner) (1982); *The Next American Frontier* (1983); *New Deals: The Chrysler Revival and the American System* (with John

Donahue) (1985); and, most recently, *Tales of a New America* (1987). His articles have appeared in *Harvard Business Review, Foreign Affairs, The New Republic* (for which he is a contributing editor), *Commentary*, and scholarly journals. Reich served as director of policy planning for the Federal Trade Commission in the Carter administration and assistant to the U.S. solicitor general in the Ford administration. He was educated at Dartmouth College, Yale Law School, and Oxford University, where he was a Rhodes Scholar.

Michael J. Sandel is associate professor of government at Harvard University (Faculty of Arts and Sciences), where he teaches political philosophy. He is the author of *Liberalism and the Limits of Justice* (1983) and the editor of *Liberalism and Its Critics* (1985). His current project is a book on liberal democracy in America. He received his B.A. and M.A. from Brandeis University and a D.Phil. from Oxford University.

Riley Sinder is a business systems analyst with the Electronic Marketing Group of Avnet, Inc. He holds degrees from the Massachusetts Institute of Technology and the University of California, Los Angeles. From 1975 to 1985 he was a consultant to the Department of Energy, Department of Labor, and Department of the Navy where he was co-author of numerous internal strategies for implementing business and management policies in the public and private sectors.